Immigrant Women

Immigrant Women

Rita James Simon
editor

Routledge
Taylor & Francis Group
LONDON AND NEW YORK

Chapter 1–4 originally published as the journal *Gender Issues*, Fall 1998, Volume 16, number 4, copyright © 1998. Chapters 5–8 originally published as the journal *Gender Issues,* Winter 1999, volume 17, number 1, copyright © 1999.

Published 2001 by Transaction Publishers

Published 2017 by Routledge
2 Park Square, Milton Park, Abingdon, Oxon OX14 4RN
711 Third Avenue, New York, NY 10017

First issued in hardback 2018

Routledge is an imprint of the Taylor and Francis Group, an informa business

Introduction copyright © 2001 by Taylor & Francis.

All rights reserved. No part of this book may be reprinted or reproduced or utilised in any form or by any electronic, mechanical, or other means, now known or hereafter invented, including photocopying and recording, or in any information storage or retrieval system, without permission in writing from the publishers.

Notice:
Product or corporate names may be trademarks or registered trademarks, and are used only for identification and explanation without intent to infringe.

Library of Congress Catalog Number: 00-059932

Library of Congress Cataloging-in-Publication Data

Immigrant women / Rita James Simon, editor.
  p. cm.
 Includes bibliographical references and index.
 ISBN 0-7658-0648-7 (pbk. : alk. paper)
  1. Women immigrants—United States. 2. Women immigrants—Australia. 3. Women immigrants—Canada. I. Simon, Rita James

HQ1421.I48 2000
305.48'9691—dc21   00-059932

ISBN 13: 978-1-138-52576-4 (hbk)
ISBN 13: 978-0-7658-0648-2 (pbk)

Table of Contents

	Introduction *Rita J. Simon*	vii
1	Benefits and Burdens: Immigrant Women and Work in New York City *Nancy Foner*	1
2	Gender and Citizenship in the Restructuring of Janitorial Work in Los Angeles *Cynthia Cranford*	21
3	The Impact of Resources and Family-Level Cultural Practices on Immigrant Women's Workforce Participation *M.D.R. Evans and Tatjana Lukic*	49
4	The Family Investment Model: A Formalization and Review of Evidence from Across Immigrant Groups *Harriet Orcutt Duleep*	81
5	Gender, Refugee Status, and Permanent Settlement *Monica Boyd*	103
6	Gender in Language and Life: A Dutch American Example *Suzanne M. Sinke*	125
7	A Dynamic View of Mexican Migration to the United States *Katharine Donato*	151
8	Women and Immigrants: Strangers in a Strange Land *Nina Toren*	175
	About the Contributors	197

Introduction

Rita Simon

Thirty-five years ago the topics of immigration and women would not have aroused much interest in the scholarly and professional marketplaces. But from different sources and for different reasons, both have become important research and public-policy issues. In 1986, Nancy Foner commented: "Migrant women have emerged from academic invisibility... Female migrants... have become a recognized presence."[1]

Immigration as a topic for research and debate emerged largely because Congress, after a long hiatus, began to debate immigration issues and enacted new standards and policies. On October 27, 1990, the U.S. Congress passed the first major immigration bill since 1965. The bill represented the first comprehensive revision of immigration law in sixty-six years. It increased the number of immigrants admitted per year from 540,000 to 700,000 for at least the first three years and it more than doubled the number of immigrants allowed entry because of their job skills. In addition, more than half of the visas were to be set aside for families of U.S. citizens and permanent residents.

Social scientists and public-policy analysts began focusing on immigration some thirty years ago when the first group of Cuban refugees was admitted to the United States following the Castro takeover in Cuba. The Cubans were the first in a series of refugees to be admitted to the United States in the post-World War II era. Shortly before the Cubans were admitted, 21,000 Hungarians came in under refugee auspices following the 1956 revolt, and prior to that 280,000 displaced persons were admitted in 1948. Subsequent to the entry of the first group of Cuban immigrants, Vietnamese, Soviet Jews, more Cubans, and other Hispanics from Central American countries were admitted as refugees in the 1970s and 1980s. In addition, growing numbers of immigrants have come across the border from Central American countries and Mexico, as well as from the Philippines, Korea, and other Asian countries.

The establishment of a Presidential Commission on Immigration in 1981 to study the social, economic, and cultural impact of immigrants on American society and to make recommendations about numbers and conditions of admission contributed to an intellectual reawakening of interest in the importance of immigrants to American society. Over the past two decades, this has resulted in numerous monographs and articles on immigrant entrepreneurs, the adjustment and absorption of refugees, the social mobility of various immigrant groups, language facility, and immigrant children's academic success.

Tracing the development of interest and work on women migrants involves recognition of the importance of the appearance of a women's movement in the late 1960s. In part as a function of that movement's visibility, interest in topics about women and funding for research on women's lives skyrocketed. Any topic concerning women was considered intellectually interesting, important, and highly marketable. The spate of recent work by social scientists on women migrants can be easily explained by the enormous attention that any topic on women receives. But coupled with the renewed interest in immigration, it is all the more obvious why social scientists have been paying so much attention to patterns of female migration.

With these explanations as background, it is important to note that the current studies of immigrants tend to have a somewhat different focus and to employ different methods than the work done during the earlier periods of immigrant research in the 1920s and 1930s. Many of the studies emanating from that period were done by the so-called Chicago School of Sociology, which focused on patterns of adaptation, acculturation, and assimilation by different immigrant communities into the larger American society. The methods for studying the communities were often observational and biographical. Scholars examined life histories in the form of letters, diaries, and other direct first-person accounts that explained transitions and passages in individual lives, in families, and in larger units. Studies reported on conflicts between immigrant parents and their first-generation American-born offspring. Accounts dealt with how quickly and in what form different immigrant communities became Americanized through loss of accent, change of names, style of dress, choice of foods, and movement into "nonethnic" neighborhoods. The unit of analysis was often the family or an entire immigrant community that had recently established itself in an urban neighborhood. Thomas and Znaniecki's *The Polish Peasant in Europe and America* is one of the classics to emerge from that era. [2]

The revival of interest in immigrants in the 1970s, 1980s, and 1990s did not restore the earlier research agenda either substantively or methodologically. The issues today tend to be different than they were seventy and eighty years ago, and

Introduction

the methods have changed as well. Today, economic issues are more likely to be the dependent variables. Thus, data on labor-force participation, educational background, job skills, work ethic, income, and mobility are collected through surveys or from archival sources such as the U.S. Census. The focus is more on individual behavior, which is then aggregated, than on families or whole communities. There are fewer observational studies, and researchers are less dependent on subjective accounts.

When women are the focus, economic variables, as shown in the collection included in this volume, still play an important role. In her history of *Immigrant Women*, Maxine Sellers argued that:

> Women came... to escape the economic, political, and religious oppression that all immigrants faced in their native lands, but many also come to escape forms of oppression unique to them as women... some fled sexual harassment, other unequal wages and working conditions that were more difficult than those endured by their male counterparts.[3]

Fertility patterns and changing roles within the family and vis-à-vis the host country are special topics included in the analysis of female migrants. But the methods employed are usually the same whether the target population is male or female, and the unit of analysis also tends to be the individual, irrespective of gender.

One fact that often goes unnoticed or unreported is that more women than men have immigrated to the United States since 1930. The predominance ranges from 51.4 percent to 74.9 percent. The latter occurred in 1947 and is attributable largely to the migration of "war brides," that is, wives of U.S. servicemen stationed overseas following World War II. In 1995, women accounted for 54 percent of all legal immigrants to the United States. Like their male counterparts, most female immigrants are under the age of thirty-five. The 1990 U.S. Census reported that the median age of the foreign born who entered the United States between 1980 and 1990 was twenty-eight years compared to the native population for which the median was 32.5 years.

In their 1997 publication, *The New Americans*, the National Research Council summarized the employment status of immigrant women as follows: "The picture for immigrant women is similar to that for immigrant men. They are disproportionately employed in some high-education occupations such as foreign language teachers and physicians, but they also make up a large share of employment in many more occupations that require little schooling: tailors, graders and sorters of agricultural products and private household service workers."[4]

Although at the time of entry immigrant women are more likely to have higher fertility rates than native women, 2.3 for immigrant women versus 1.9 for native women, within one generation the fertility rates of immigrant women generally converge to that of the native-born women.

The articles included in this volume appeared in print originally in the Fall 1998 and Winter 1999 issues of *Gender Issues*.

The first set of papers focused on the labor force experiences of women who immigrated to the United States and Australia from Mexico and Latin America, Eastern Europe, Korea, the Philippines, India, and other parts of Asia. The papers that appeared in the Winter 1999 issue were more heterogeneous. They dealt with social class and English language acquisition, the obstacles women have had to overcome in gaining refugee status in the United States and Canada, and a comparison of the motivations and patterns of movement between different communities in Mexico and the United States on the part of Mexican male and female immigrants.

"Immigrant Women and Work in New York City" by Nancy Foner assesses "the complex and often contradictory ways that migration changes women's status, both for better and for worse." Using 1990 census data, Foner reports that 60 percent of the foreign-born women are in the labor force compared to 54 percent of New York City women generally. But, there are big differences in the labor-force participation of women from different ethnic backgrounds with Filipino women at the top of the list with over 85 percent labor-force participation, especially in health-care jobs. At the other extreme, with their lower levels of education and more limited English language skills, are Dominican women whose participation in the work force is about 50 percent. Foner's article describes the various types of work and the pay scales of different groups of immigrant women, as well as the changes in family roles and statuses between husbands and wives that are a function of the migration and the labor force participation.

The piece by Cynthia Cranford focuses on Mexican and Salvadoran women who have relatively recently moved into janitorial work in Los Angeles. Cranford first describes the restructuring of janitorial work within the broader industrial shifts in Los Angeles, and then analyzes the changing demographics the restructuring brought about, focusing finally on the entry of Salvadoran and Mexican women into the industry in the 1980s. Today, these women are central players in the movement to reunionize the janitorial workforce.

With the article by Evans and Lukic, the scene shifts from the United States to Australia and an analysis of the labor-force participation and family strategies of women migrants from the former Yugoslavia against the experiences and strategies of woman migrants from the Mediterranean world and other parts of the Slavic

Introduction

world. Evans and Lukic argue that cultural differences on a country by country level may be all important in explaining differences in the length and type of labor for participation, child-rearing practices, and intergenerational wealth flows among female migrants. Their data show that Yugoslavian women migrants differ significantly on these matters from neighboring women in Mediterranean countries and in Slavic societies.

Economist Harriet Duleep describes and reviews evidence from what is known as the "family investment model," which hypothesizes that financing investment in host country skills of immigrant husbands is a factor that affects labor force decisions, human capital investment, and wages of married immigrant women. The higher the return to investment in the U.S. skills by the husbands, the more likely married immigrant women will work to support that investment. Duleep also reports studies that have compared immigrant women versus native-born women and examines whether the family investment model affects the behavior among the latter group.

The four articles in the Winter 1999 issue focused on different aspects of the immigrants' experiences. Monica Boyd's piece, "Gender, Refugee Status and Permanent Settlement" tackles the important and controversial issue of the unwillingness of the leading immigrant receiving nations (United States, Canada, and Australia) to declare gender as an explicit ground for persecution and thus for gaining refugee status. Boyd's piece provides data on Canada that show that women are less likely than men to be admitted for humanitarian reasons. While, like the United States, Canadian guidelines were revised in 1996 in ways that made them more "gender sensitive" they stopped short of declaring gender a social group, and thus they continue to produce a sex selective resettlement process whereby men are more likely to be resettled as refugees than women.

In "Gender in Language and Life" historian Suzanne M. Sinke illustrates how one immigrant community, Dutch Protestants who arrived in the United States in the early years of the twentieth century, made the linguistic shift from Dutch to English. Sinke analyzes how the language transition was intertwined with the changing roles and aspirations that the younger Dutch women immigrants experienced as they began to model their behavior after their American-born counterparts. Social class and religious beliefs were important variables in how quickly this transition from spoken and written Dutch to English was made.

A comparison of the migration patterns of Mexican men and women is the focus of Katharine Donato's article "A Dynamic View of Mexican Migration to the United States." Tracing migration from the 1940s to the 1990s, Donato compares the motivations, circumstances, frequency, and legal status of Mexican men and women immigrants from thirty-nine communities surrounding the city of Guadalajara. The data reveal that in the 1990s the major differences in the migration pattern of men and women is that for women there is greater likelihood of first migration only if the women have legal documents, whereas for men, the likelihood of first migration in the 1990s has increased both legally and illegally.

Using immigrant as a metaphor, Israeli sociologist Nina Toren compares the work experience of women academics at Israeli universities and two cohorts of Soviet Jewish immigrant scientists who came to Israel in the 1970s and in the early 1990s. Toren finds it useful to consider women in traditionally male occupations as strangers in a country that is not their homeland. She then examines the social processes that affect both the immigrant scientists and the women academics. Specifically the stereotypes that surround these two groups and the mechanisms of exclusion, segregation, and assimilation are examined and compared.

Notes

1. Nancy Foner, "Sex Roles and Sensibilities: Jamaican Women in New York and London," in *International Migration*, edited by R. J. Simon and C. Bretttell. (Totowa, NJ: Rowman and Allanheld, 1986), p. 133.

2. W. L. Thomas and F. Znaniecki, *The Polish Peasant in Europe and America*, edited and abridged by Eli Zertsky (Chicago: University of Illinois Press, 1984).

3. Maxine Sellers (ed.), *Immigrant Women*, (Philadelphia: Temple University Press, 1981) 6.

4. James P. Smith and Barry Edmonston (eds.), *The New Americans*, (National Academy Press, Washington, DC,1997) 218-19.

1

Benefits and Burdens: Immigrant Women and Work in New York City

Nancy Foner

Abstract: This article analyzes the complex and contradictory ways that migration changes women's status in New York City—both for better and for worse. The focus is on the impact of women's incorporation into the labor force. On the positive side, migrant women's regular access to wages—and to higher wages—frequently improves their position in the household, broadens their social horizons, and enhances their sense of independence. Less happily, many migrant women work in dead-end positions that pay less than men's jobs. Immigrant working wives also experience a heavy double burden since the household division of labor remains far from equal.

There is an underlying tension in much of the work on immigrant women. On the one hand, a growing number of studies show that women experience marked improvements in their status as women as a result of migration. These range from increased control over decision making in the household to greater personal autonomy and access to resources in the community at large (e.g., Foner, 1986; Grasmuck and Pessar, 1991; Hondagneu-Sotelo, 1994; Lamphere, 1987; Pedraza, 1991; Pessar, 1998; Simon, 1992; Brettell and Simon, 1986). On the other hand, the literature also emphasizes migrant women's continued oppression—what some call a triple burden or oppression, as gender inequalities are compounded by discrimination on the basis of class and race or ethnicity. Increasingly, recent research seeks to reconcile these two perspectives. As Patricia Pessar (1998) notes in a recent review of the literature, to ask whether migration is emancipating or subjugating for women is to couch their experiences in stark—and misleading—either/or terms. Feminist scholars now caution that migration often leads to losses as well as gains for women, and that, despite improvements, patriarchal codes and practices may continue to have an impact (see, for example, Espiritu, 1997; Morakvasic, 1984; Pessar, 1998).

In the spirit of the new feminist scholarship, this article offers an analysis of the complex and often contradictory ways that migration changes women's status—both for better and for worse. The focus is on the impact of women's incorporation into the labor force. This issue has been in the forefront of research on migrant women since it is wage work that so often empowers migrant women at the same time as it places severe burdens and constraints on them. The article is based on my larger comparative project on immigrants in New York City.[1] It draws on my own first-hand research on Jamaican women (see Foner, 1983, 1986, 1994)[2] as well as on available sociological and anthropological accounts for other immigrant populations. New York City continues to be a preeminent destination for the nation's immigrants: in 1996, about a third of its population was foreign born (Moss, Townsend, and Tobier, 1997). The city's immigrants include a wide variety of Asian, Latin American, and Caribbean groups; in 1990, the top five were Dominicans, Chinese, Jamaicans, Russians, and Guyanese, in that order. While the analysis presented here is sensitive to different patterns of labor-market incorporation and cultural background among the various groups, the emphasis is on common themes, experiences, and processes that emerge.

Female Immigrants: The Background

To set the stage for the analysis of the impact of wage work on New York City's migrant women, some basic background information is necessary on their numbers, migration patterns, and labor force and occupational profile.

Women migrants now outnumber men in virtually all of the major groups coming to New York. In large part, this is because United States immigration law favors the admission of spouses and children as a way to reunite families and has made it possible for certain kinds of workers, like nurses, to get immigrant visas (Donato, 1992; Houston, Kramer, and Barrett, 1984). In the early 1990s, there were ninety-two male immigrants for every one hundred female immigrants entering New York City, up from ninety-eight males per one hundred females in the 1980s (Lobo, Salvo, and Virgin, 1996).

It is not just that women predominate. Many women come on their own rather than follow in men's footsteps. The structure of U.S. immigration law, changing gender roles, and economic opportunities for women are all responsible for this trend. Immigrant women's concentration in specific high-demand occupations—like private household work and nursing—has also enabled many to play a pivotal role as pioneer immigrants, establishing beachheads for further immigration (Salvo and Ortiz, 1992). This has been especially true for certain groups like Filipinos, with large numbers of nurses, and West Indians, with substantial numbers of private household workers.

Once in New York, the majority of immigrant women go out to work. At the time of the 1990 census, 60 percent of foreign-born female New Yorkers of working age were in the labor force. The percentages are much higher for certain groups. Filipino women, who often came specifically to work in health-care jobs, stand out as having the highest labor force participation rate at over 85 percent. West Indian women are not far behind, with labor force participation rates in the 70–80 percent range. Dominicans come out near the bottom, with 52 percent in the work force, and they have a relatively large proportion unemployed as well (Kasinitz and Vickerman, 1995). In trying to explain these different rates, Sherri Grasmuck and Ramon Grosfoguel (1997) argue that Dominican women's lower levels of education and limited English language skills have made it more difficult for them to find jobs, especially jobs that pay enough to cover the costs of child care. Because Jamaican women arrive with English and, on average, higher educational levels, they have better employment prospects. They are also more disposed to go out to work because they come from a society with a strong tradition of female employment: almost 70 percent of women in Jamaica were in the work force in 1990 compared to only 15 percent in the Dominican Republic.[3]

In New York, there is an enormous variety in the kinds of jobs occupied by female immigrants; a good many have professional and managerial positions while others end up in low-level service and factory work. Census data for 1990 on immigrant women in the labor force who arrived in the 1980s show this variation. Twenty-seven percent of Asian women, 13 percent from the Caribbean, and 10 percent from Central and South America were classified as professionals and manager; at the same time, 21 percent of Asian women, 14 percent from the Caribbean, and 23 percent from South and Central America were operators (Mollenkopf, Kasinitz, and Lindholm, 1995).

That many immigrant women are able to obtain professional and managerial jobs is not surprising given the human capital they bring with them. Immigration and Naturalization Service (INS) data, although limited, show that a fifth of the working age women intending to live in New York City who reported an occupation to the INS when admitted for permanent residence between 1982 and 1989 were in professional/technical and administrative/managerial positions; in the early 1990s, the share in these categories went up to 36 percent. In both the 1980s and early 1990s, about one in every six immigrant women were in administrative support occupations such as secretaries, typists, and general office clerks (Lobo, Salvo, and Virgin, 1996).[4]

Of course, many immigrant women who had professional or white-collar jobs in their home society experience downward occupational mobility when they arrive in New York. Without American-recognized training, English proficiency, or green cards, highly qualified women are often consigned, at least temporarily, to relatively low-level positions when they arrive. Many Jamaican private household workers I interviewed in my research, for example, had been teachers and clerical workers back home, some experiencing what Maxine Margolis has called the transition from "mistress to servant" (Margolis, 1994; see also Colen, 1990). A number of Haitian and Hispanic aides in the New York nursing home I studied in the 1980s were full-fledged nurses before they emigrated, but their qualifications were not recognized here and language problems stood in the way of passing the requisite licensing exams to practice nursing in New York (see Foner, 1994).

In a time-worn pattern, women in each immigrant group gravitate in large numbers to particular occupations. As among men, English language ability and work skills help women in some groups gain a foothold in certain jobs; lack of English and specific job skills limit the employment possibilities of others. Once a beachhead is established, co-ethnics are likely to follow through a process of network hiring and referrals as well as employer preferences. Thus, for example, West Indian women are heavily concentrated in health care. Indeed, in 1990, close to a third of employed Jamaican women in New York were nurse's aides, orderlies, and attendants and registered or practical nurses (Kasinitz and Vickerman, 1995; see also Waldinger, 1996). Garment work has drawn in Dominican and Chinese women because it requires no English language ability, is quickly learned, and is often close at hand, in factories owned and managed by their compatriots. In the early days of the migration, Dominicans' entry into garment factories was also facilitated by the fact that the industry had already adjusted itself to Puerto Ricans, using bilingual supervisors and employee mediators (Grasmuck and Grosfoguel, 1997). Although the proportion of Dominican women in manufacturing has dramatically declined since 1980, substantial numbers still work in this sector. Chinese women remain the garment workers par excellence. Over half of all immigrant Chinese women workers in New York City are in the needle trades, virtually all as sewing machine operators. In recent years, new groups of immigrant women have also been drawn to the garment trades. The growing number of Korean-owned sewing shops—about 200 opened in midtown Manhattan in the late 1980s and early 1990s—are filled with Mexican and Ecuadoran workers, who are primarily women. Korean owners have had to look beyond the ethnic labor market for a source of cheap labor because Korean women are relatively well educated and have better opportunities elsewhere (Chin, 1997).

Wage Work: The Benefits

Wage work has, in many ways, improved the position of substantial numbers of migrant women in New York. This is not just the perception of the women themselves. From the outside looking in, it is clear that migrant women often gain greater independence, personal autonomy, and influence as a result of earning a regular wage for the first time, earning a higher wage than in the sending society, or making a larger contribution to the family economy than previously. How much improvement women experience depends to a large degree on their role in production and their social status in the home country as well as their economic role in New York. What is important is that, for the vast majority, the move to New York—and their involvement in work here—lead to gains in some domains of their lives, particularly in the household.

In cases where women did not earn an income, or earned only a small supplementary income, prior to migration, the gains in New York that come with a shift to regular wage work are especially striking. The much-cited case of Dominican immigrant women fits this pattern. Now that so many Dominicans work for wages—often for the first time—and contribute a larger share of the family income, they have more authority in the household and greater self-esteem. They use their wages, anthropologist Patricia Pessar observes, "to assert their rights to greater autonomy and equality within the household" (1995).[5]

In New York, Dominican women begin to expect to be co-partners in "heading" the household, a clear change from more patriarchal arrangements in the Dominican Republic. "We are both heads," said one woman, echoing the sentiments of many other Dominican women in New York. "If both the husband and wife are earning salaries then they should equally rule the household. In the Dominican Republic it is always the husband who gives the orders in the household. But here when the two are working, the woman feels herself the equal of the man in ruling the home" (Pessar, 1987: 121). In a telling comment, a Dominican migrant visiting her home village told her cousin about New York: "Wait till you get there. You'll have your own paycheck, and I tell you, he [your husband] won't be pushing you around there the way he is here" (Grasmuck and Pessar, 1991: 147).

The organization of the household budget is in fact more equal in New York. In the Dominican Republic, men generally controlled the household budget even when wives and daughters put in income on a regular or semi-regular basis. Commonly, men doled out an allowance to their wives, who were responsible for managing the funds to cover basic household expenses. The men had the last word when it came to decisions about long-term and costly outlays. When women contributed income, it was used for "luxuries" rather than staples, reinforcing the notion that the man was the breadwinner. In New York, Pessar found that husbands, wives, and working children usually pool their income; they each put a specific amount of their wages or profits into a common fund for shared household expenses. Often, they also pool the rest of what they earned for savings and special purchases. With this kind of arrangement, women's contributions are no longer seen as "supplementary" and men's as "essential." As men become more involved in developing strategies for stretching the food budget, they begin to more fully appreciate the skills women bring to these tasks. How critical women's wage work is to these new arrangements is brought out by what happens when women significantly reduce their contributions to the household budget, either in New York or when they return to the Dominican Republic. The man usually asserts his dominance once again by allocating a household allowance to his wife and reducing her authority over budgetary decisions.

No wonder that Dominican women are eager to postpone or avoid returning to the Dominican Republic where social pressures and an unfavorable job market would probably mean their retirement from work and a loss of new-found gains. One reason women spend large amounts of money on expensive durable goods like new appliances and home furnishings is to root their family securely in the United States and deplete the funds needed to return to the Dominican Republic.

Of course, many immigrant women, including some Dominicans, had regular salaries before emigration. Even these women often feel a new kind of independence in New York because jobs in this country pay more than most could ever earn at home and increase women's contribution to the family economy. For example, many Jamaican women I interviewed had white-collar jobs as secretaries, clerks, nurses, or teachers before they emigrated. Still, they said they had more financial control and more say in family affairs in New York where their incomes are so much larger. "We were brought up to think we have to depend on a man, do this for a man, listen to a man," said a New York secretary. "But here you can be on your own, more independent." Many told me that in Jamaica women usually have to depend on their husbands, whereas in New York they can "work their own money." Also, for those with training, there is a wider range of good jobs available. And there are better opportunities for additional training and education than in Jamaica, something that holds true for those from other Latin American and Caribbean countries as well (see Foner, 1986).

The sense of empowerment that comes from earning a regular wage—or a higher wage—and having greater control over what they earn comes out in studies of many different groups. Paid work for Chinese garment workers, according to one report, not only contributes to their families' economic well-being, but also has "created a sense of confidence and self-fulfillment which they may never have experienced in traditional Chinese society." "My husband dares not look down on me," one woman said. "He knows he can't provide for the family by himself." Or as another put it: "I do not have to ask my husband for money, I make my own" (Zhou and Nordquist, 1994: 201). For many Salvadoran women, the ability to earn wages and decide how they should be used is something new. As one woman explained: "Here [in the U.S.] women work just like the men. I like it a lot because managing my own money I feel independent. I don't have to ask my husband for money but in El Salvador, yes, I would have to. Over there women live dependent on their husbands. You have to walk behind him" (Mahler, 1996). Or listen to a Trinidadian woman of East Indian descent: "Now that I have a job I am independent. I stand up here as a man" (Burgess and Gray, 1981).

The female-first migration pattern involving adult married women that is common in some groups reinforces the effects of wage-earning on women's independence. Many women who initially lived and worked in New York without their husbands change, as one Dominican woman put it, "after so many years of being on my own, being my own boss" (Pessar, 1995: 60). One study suggests that Asian men who move to the United States as their wives' dependents often have to subordinate their careers, at least at first, to those of their wives since the women have already established themselves in this country (Espiritu, 1997: 70).

Work outside the home in New York brings about another change that women appreciate. Many men now help out more *inside* the home than before they moved to New York. Of course, this is not inevitable. Cultural values in different groups as well as the availability of female relatives to lend a hand influence the kind of household help men provide. A study of the division of labor in Taiwanese immigrant households found that, as in Taiwan, men who held working-class jobs or owned small businesses did little around the house (Chen, 1992: 77–78).[6] Korean men, staunch supporters of patriarchal family values and norms, generally still expect their wives to serve them and resist performing household chores like cooking, dishwashing, and doing the laundry. Such resistance is more effective when the wife's mother or mother-in-law lives in the household, a not infrequent occurrence in Korean immigrant families. Yet much to their consternation, Korean men in New York with working wives often find themselves helping out with household work more than they did in Korea—and that wives make more demands on them to increase their share (Min, 1998; Park, 1997; see also Lim, 1997, on Korean women in Texas).

Research on a number of Latin American and Caribbean groups shows that when wives are involved in productive work outside the home, there is a change in the organization of labor within it (cf. Lamphere, 1987). We are not talking about a drastic change in the household division of labor or the emergence of truly egalitarian arrangements. Indeed, Latin American and Caribbean women strongly identify as wives and mothers and they like being in charge of the domestic domain. What they want—and what they often get—is more help from men. Mainly, men oblige because they have little choice. Evidence also suggests that women's, and men's, conceptions of what men should do in the household begin to shift in the immigrant context.

West Indian men are definitely more helpful in the household than they were in the Caribbean. There, men hardly ever did housework, even when their wives had cash-earning activities. Work back home did not always take women out of the house for long periods of time. In the West Indies, neighbors and kin, especially mothers and sisters, frequently helped with childminding. Those with salaried jobs employed domestics and nannies to cook, clean, and mind their children.

Although West Indian women in New York still do most of the cooking, cleaning, shopping, and washing, men often help out with this "women's work." However much they resent pitching in, men recognize that there is no alternative when their wives work and children (particularly daughters) are not old enough to lend a hand. "If she's working, we both chip in," is how one Trinidadian man put it (Burgess and Gray, 1981: 102). Working women simply cannot shoulder all of the domestic responsibilities expected of them, and they do not have relatives to help. Even if close kin live nearby, they are usually busy with work and their own household chores. Wives' wages are a necessary addition to the family income, and West Indians cannot afford to hire household help. "In order to have a family life here," said a middle-class Trinidadian woman, "[my husband] realizes he has to participate not only in the housework but in the childrearing too. It's no longer the type of thing where he comes home and the maid is there, having prepared the dinner.... Here if you're going to have a household, he has to participate. He has to pick up the children, or take them to the babysitter, or come home and begin the dinner" (Burgess and Gray, 1981: 102). Several Jamaican men I met in New York—exceptions to be sure—even served as the main family cooks.

West Indian couples with young children often arrange their shifts so that the husband can look after the children while the wife works. I interviewed a number of Jamaican men in New York who worked night shifts and were at home during the day minding the children. "In Jamaica, oh, please," a Jamaican nurse told me. "That was slavery. Bring the man his dinner and his slippers, do the laundry, you're kidding. Not anymore." In New York, her husband does the laundry, makes the children's breakfast and, in the past, got up at night to feed and change the babies.

More than behavior changes. As men become accustomed to doing more around the house, their notions of what tasks are appropriate—or expected—often also shift. Research shows that Dominican and Jamaican men and women believe that when both partners have jobs, and daughters are too young to help, husbands should pitch in with such tasks as shopping, washing dishes, and childcare. Women tend to view their husband's help as a moral victory (Pessar, 1984); men accept their new duties, however reluctantly.

While the exigencies of immigrant life—women working outside the home, a lack of available relatives to assist, and an inability to hire help—are mainly responsible for men's greater participation in household tasks, American cultural beliefs and values play a role, too (see Foner, 1997). Many of the Dominicans whom Sherri Grasmuck and Patricia Pessar spoke to claimed that they self-consciously patterned their more egalitarian relations on what they believed to be the dominant American model. They saw this change as both modern and a sign of progress. One Dominican man and his wife said that soon after they were both working, they realized that "if both worked outside the house, both should work inside as well. Now that we are in the United States, we should adopt Americans' ways" (Grasmuck and Pessar, 1991: 152). Whatever men think, immigrant women may feel they can make more demands on their husbands in this country where the dominant norms and values back up their claims for men to help out.

In addition to the independence, power, and autonomy that wages bring, there are intrinsic satisfactions from work itself. Women in professional and managerial positions gain prestige from their positions and often have authority over others on the job. Certainly, this was true of the immigrant nurses in the nursing home I studied. The registered nurses were proud of their professional achievements, received deference from nursing aides below them, and exercised enormous authority in their units (Foner, 1994).

Many women in lower-level jobs also get a sense of satisfaction from doing their job well and from the new skills they have learned in New York. Dominican garment workers take pride in meeting the rigorous demands of the workplace (Pessar, 1995), and many immigrant women who do "caregiving work" in private homes or institutions get enormous pleasure from giving good care and from feeling needed and becoming close to their charges. "I like to help people," said a Jamaican woman who cared for a frail elderly couple on a live-in basis. "People don't realize how hard it is to work in the home and deal with sick people. Have to please them, make them comfortable, keep them happy. I like to work and I love my job. I may not be an R.N., but I help people" (Foner, 1986: 145). Deep attachments often develop between West Indian babysitters and the children they look after, and I found that many immigrant nursing home aides were close to elderly patients whose needs they saw to day after day (Foner, 1994).

An important aspect of work is the sociability involved. In factories, hospitals, and offices, women make friends and build up a storehouse of experiences that enriches their lives and conversations. Indeed, when women are out of work, they often complain of boredom and isolation. A Chinese garment worker said that when she was laid off "I had too much housework to do and I felt even busier than when I worked. Sometimes I get frustrated if I am confined at home and don't see my coworkers" (Zhou, 1992: 178). Dominican women say that when they are laid off they feel isolated at home; they not only miss the income, but also socializing with workmates and the bustle of the streets and subways (Pessar, 1995).

Typically, informal work cultures develop on the job that make work more interesting and liven up the day. Workers often chat and joke while they work, and they socialize at lunch and on breaks. Sometimes, they celebrate weddings or birthdays during free time or take up collections for sick co-workers. In the nursing home I studied, workers had formed a number of savings groups among themselves, with regular weekly contributions. Nursing aides also routinely lent each other a hand in difficult chores. In general, friendships formed on the job may extend outside the bounds of the workplace as women visit and phone each other or go to parties and on shopping jaunts with co-workers (see Foner, 1994).

Other Gains

Although the focus in this article is on the benefits that immigrant women reap from working outside the home, the move to New York has improved their status as women in other ways. In fact, women from some countries see the chance *not* to work as a gain. According to Fran Markowitz (1993), many Jewish emigre women from the former Soviet Union are freed from the triple role of worker, wife, and mother in New York because their husbands earn enough for them to stay at home or they are eligible, as refugees, for government assistance. While some Soviet emigre women feel depressed and useless because they no longer need to work full-time, others are glad to be able to take time off to care for young children. Couples who would never have dreamed of having more than one child in the old country may now have two or three (1993: 190).

For immigrants in some groups, welfare programs available in New York have provided new options for women on their own with young children to stay out of the paid labor force—or at least until the 1996 welfare reforms severely restricted noncitizens' access to welfare benefits. In the Dominican Republic, the lack of a system of public assistance increased the pressure on women without a man in the household to enter the labor force; in New York in the 1980s and early 1990s,

Dominican women on their own, with young children and no spouse in residence, often preferred to seek public assistance than take the low-paying jobs available, since they could then care for their children (rather than spend a significant part of their wages on child care) and perhaps advance their own education and obtain future marketable skills (Gurak and Kritz, 1996).

Housework and other domestic chores are easier in New York for many immigrant women. In the case of Russian Jewish emigres, cooking, cleaning, and shopping, among other tasks, are less time-consuming than in the old country where keeping a family fed often meant standing on lines for hours each day just to purchase basic foodstuffs, bribing grocery store workers, and keeping abreast of news about special black market shipments (Markowitz, 1993; Orleck, 1987). In general, access to modern appliances like washing machines, vacuum cleaners, and microwave ovens makes life much easier for women who could never have afforded such luxuries in the countries they came from.

In New York, women may be able to engage in certain activities that were unacceptable or at least unusual for women in their home countries, which contributes to their sense that living abroad offers a new kind of freedom. Maxine Margolis describes a scene she observed in a Queens nightclub one Friday night, where a group of five Brazilian women in their forties and fifties sat at the bar drinking, smoking, and talking among themselves. Occasionally, the women were asked to dance by male patrons of the establishment. "What was so memorable about the scene is that it could not have occurred in these women's native land. In Brazil, it would be unthinkable for 'respectable' middle-aged women from the middle strata of society to go to a bar or a nightclub 'alone,' meaning without appropriate escorts" (1994: 237). Several Jamaican women in my study spoke of the new opportunities to expand their cultural horizons in New York through the theater, concerts, and films—and of the opportunity to pursue their interests and lead their lives without the eyes, and censure, of the local community so closely upon them (Foner, 1986). Dominican women, too, say they feel liberated in their ability to travel widely on their way to and from work or to other activities without people gossiping that "they spend too much time away from their homes . . . [and] think the woman is up to no good" (Pessar, 1995: 81–82).

Divorce is often easier and more acceptable in New York than it was back home. Despite the increasing prevalence of divorce in Taiwan, Chen (1992: 254) explains, it is still very embarrassing for a divorced woman to face family and friends. In New York, Taiwanese divorced women can take care of themselves: "no one will question your past, and you can restart life here." Divorce, of course, is a risky business for immigrant women since, without the husband's financial contributions, their standard of living is in jeopardy and it is more of a struggle to make ends meet. Female-headed households typically have lower incomes and higher poverty rates than those with two working partners.

Still, better wage-earning opportunities in this country and, until recently, the widespread availability of welfare benefits to noncitizens, have meant that women can often manage on their own more easily in this country. Women may be more willing to make demands on their husbands than they would have done back home—and insist on more egalitarian relations—because they know these economic supports are on hand if the union breaks up. Also, they are spurred on by American norms that emphasize that husbands should be marriage partners who help out around the house and make decisions in concert with their wives—and by an American legal and social welfare system that supports them in cases of severe spouse abuse (cf. Kibria, 1993; Repak, 1995).

Wage Work: The Burdens

If wage work enables many immigrant women to expand their influence and independence, these gains often come at a price. Indeed, wage work in New York brings burdens as well as benefits to immigrant women and may create new sets of demands and pressures for them both on the job and at home. Moreover, despite changes in women's status in New York, pre-migration gender-role patterns and ideologies do not simply fade away; they continue to affect the lives of migrant women, often in ways that constrain and limit them.

Wage work, as immigrant women commonly explain, is not an option but a necessity for their family's welfare. As one Korean woman put it: "Without me helping out economically, it is absolutely impossible to survive in New York City" (Min, 1998: 38). Wage work typically brings a host of difficulties for women. On the job, women's wages are generally lower than men's. Moreover, women are limited in their choice of work due to gender divisions in the labor market—often confined to menial, low-prestige, and poorly paying jobs that can be described as industrialized homework. Working in the ethnic economy does not help most women either. Recent studies of Chinese, Dominican, and Colombian women in New York who work in businesses owned by their compatriots show that they earn low wages and have minimal benefits and few opportunities for advancement (Gilbertson, 1995; Zhou and Logan, 1989). Indeed, sociologist Greta Gilbertson argues that some of the success of immigrant small-business owners and workers in the ethnic enclave is due to the marginal position of immigrant women. The many Korean women who work in family businesses are, essentially, unpaid family workers without an independent source of income. Although many are working outside the home for the first time, they are typically thought of as "helpers" to their husbands; the husband not only legally owns the enterprise but also usually controls the money, hires and fires employees, and represents the business in Korean business associations (Min, 1998).[7]

For many immigrant women, working conditions are extremely difficult. Among the worst are those endured by garment workers who often have to keep up a furious pace in cramped conditions in noisy lofts. Despite federal and state laws, some sweatshops they work in are physically dangerous, located in windowless buildings with sealed fire exits and broken sprinkler systems. Often paid by the piece, many do not even make the minimum wage and are forced to work overtime at straight-time wages if they want to keep their jobs. Slow workers may make as little as $20 a day, fast workers more than $60 (Sung, n.d.). In the early 1990s, according to one account, Chinese women in unionized shops averaged $200 a week (Chin, 1997).

Domestic workers often have to deal with humiliating or demeaning treatment from employers as well as long hours, low pay, and lack of benefits (Colen, 1989). For those who clean houses, there are the dangers that come with using noxious and often toxic substances as well as the sheer physical strenuousness of the job. House cleaners, like many Salvadoran women, have to piece together a number of daily cleaning jobs so they can keep busy all week. Some immigrant women with full-time jobs have more than one position to make ends meet. I know many West Indian women, for example, who care for an elderly person on the weekend to supplement what they earn from a five-day child-care job. Others supplement their income through informal economic activities like selling homemade food or beauty products in various cosmetic lines.

Added to this, of course, are the demands of child-care and burdens of household work. Only very affluent immigrants can afford to hire maids or housekeepers; female relatives, if present in New York, are often busy at work themselves. Occasionally, women can juggle shifts with their husbands so one parent is always around and sometimes an elderly mother or mother-in-law is on hand to help out.[8] Many working women pay to leave their children with babysitters or, less often, in day-care centers.[9] Child-care constraints are clearly a factor limiting women to low-paid jobs with flexible schedules; they may prevent women from working full-time or, in some cases, at all. Sometimes, women leave their young children behind with relatives in the home country so they can manage work more easily, a common pattern among West Indian live-in household workers (Colen, 1989; Soto, 1987).

Immigrant women in all social classes have the major responsibilities for household chores as well as childrearing so that a grueling day at work is often followed or preceded by hours of cooking, cleaning, and washing. "I'm always working," is how Mrs. Darius, a Haitian nursing home aide with eight children put it. Although her husband, a mechanic, does not help much around the house ("some men are like that"), Mrs. Darius gets assistance from her mother, who lives with her. Still, there is a lot to do. "I have to work 24 hours. When I go home, I take a nap, then get up again; sometimes I get up at two in the morning, iron for the children, and go back to sleep" (Foner, 1994).

Korean working wives, according to sociologist Pyong Gap Min, suffer from overwork and stress due to the heavy demands on their time. After doing their work outside the home, they put in, on average, an additional twenty-five hours a week on housework, compared to seven hours done by their husbands. Altogether, working wives spend seventy-six hours a week on the job and housework—twelve more hours than men do. Although professional husbands help out more around the house than other Korean men, their wives still do the lion's share (Min, 1998). Kim Ai-Kyung, the wife of a physician, has run a boutique in New Jersey for more than thirteen years. She explained that she has not visited her family in Korea for many years because she cannot leave her husband and children alone:

> [T]he older boy is in medical school, and the younger one is working at a bank in New York City. But, when they come home, they still don't even open the refrigerator to get their own food or drink. I always serve them. And my husband—he does not know anything about the house. He doesn't even know how to make ... instant noodle soup. If I went to Korea, he would starve to death. (Kim, 1996)

Or take the case of Antonia Duarte, a Dominican mother of three children, who put in a seventeen-hour day. At 5:00 A.M., she was up making breakfast and lunch for the family. She woke her three children at 6:00, got them dressed, fed, and ready for school, and then took them to the house of a friend, who cared for the four-year-old and oversaw the older children's departure to and return from school. By 7:15, Antonia was on the subway heading for the lamp factory where she worked from 8:00 A.M. to 4:30 P.M., five days a week. She collected her children a little after 5:00 and began preparing the evening meal when she got home. She didn't ask her two oldest children to help—the oldest is a twelve-year-old girl—because, "I'd rather they begin their homework right away, before they get too tired." Her husband demanded a traditional meal of rice, beans, plantains, and meat, which could take as long as two hours to prepare. She and the children ate together at 7:00, but her husband often did not get back from socializing with his friends until later. He expected Antonia to reheat the food and serve it upon his arrival. By the time she finished her child care and other domestic responsibilities, it was 11:30 or 12:00. Like other Dominican women, she explained that if she did not manage the children and household with a high level of competence, her husband would threaten to prohibit her from working (Pessar, 1982).

Women in groups where strong "traditional" patriarchal codes continue to exert an influence may experience other difficulties. In some better-off Dominican families, wives are pressured by husbands to stay out of the work force altogether as a way to symbolize their household's respectability and elevated economic status (Pessar, 1995). In many groups, working women who are now the family's main wage earners may feel a special need to tread carefully in relations with their husbands in order to preserve the appearance of male dominance. Indeed, one study shows professional Korean women making conscious attempts to keep their traditional lower status and to raise the position of their husbands by reducing their incomes. A nurse explained: "My basic salary exceeds his. If I do overtime, my income will be too much—compared to his—and so, when overtime work falls on me, I just try so hard to find other nurses to cover my overtime assignments. . . . By reducing my income, I think, my husband can keep his ego and male superiority" (Kim, 1996: 170).

Finally, there is the fact that women's increased financial authority and independence can also lead to greater discord with their spouses. Conflicts often develop when men resent, and try to resist, women's new demands on them; in some cases, the stresses ultimately lead to marital break-ups. There are special difficulties when men are unemployed or unsuccessful at work, and become dependent on women's wage-earning abilities, yet still insist on maintaining the perquisites of male privilege in the household (see Margolis, 1994; Min, 1998; Pessar, 1995). In extreme cases, the reversal of gender roles can lead to serious physical abuse for women at the hands of their spouses (Lessinger, 1995; Mahler, 1995). Indeed, in some instances, increased isolation from relatives in the immigrant situation creates conditions for greater abuse by husbands, who are freer of the informal controls that operated in their home communities.[10]

Conclusion

Wage labor, as one scholarly observer puts it, both oppresses and liberates immigrant women (Espiritu, 1997: 117; see also Brettell and Simon, 1986; Morokvasic, 1984). On the positive side, women's regular access to wages—and to higher wages—in the United States frequently gives them greater say in household decision making and more control over budgeting. Because immigrant working mothers are often absent from the home for forty to forty-five hours a week, or sometimes longer, someone must fill their place—or at least help out. Often, it is husbands. Women's labor force participation, in other words, frequently increases husband's participation in household work and leads to changes in the balance of power in many immigrant families. Working outside the home also broadens migrant women's social horizons and enhances their sense of independence. "A woman needs to work," said one Cuban sales worker. "She feels better and more in control of herself. She doesn't have to ask her husband for money. It seems to me that if a woman has a job, she is given more respect by her husband and her children" (Prieto, 1992). Many contemporary immigrant women would heartily agree. For a good number, the opportunities to work—and earn more money—represent a major gain that has come with the move to New York.

Yet, if migration has been liberating for women in some ways, it is clear that they are far from emancipated. Not only do they suffer from gender inequalities that are a feature of American society generally, but important vestiges of premigration gender ideologies and role patterns may place additional constraints on them. Like their native-born counterparts, immigrant women continue to experience special burdens and disabilities as members of the second sex. Many work in low-status, dead-end positions that pay less than men's jobs. Immigrant working wives in all social classes experience a heavy double burden since the household division of labor remains far from equal. If husbands help out with domestic burdens, they may do so only grudgingly, if at all, and it is women, more than men, who make work choices to accommodate and reflect family—and childcare—needs. Indeed, while many—perhaps most—immigrant women feel that the benefits of wage work outweigh the drawbacks, others would, if they could afford it, prefer to remain at home. As a Korean woman who worked as a manicurist in a nail salon fifty-four hours a week said, "If my husband makes enough money for the family, why should I take this burden?"(Min, 1998: 38).

If, as this article makes clear, studies of migrant women must consider the complex combination of gains and losses they experience in this country, additional research is needed to further specify the dynamics of these changes among different groups in a variety of domains, including the household, workplace, and community. Among the challenges ahead, as Patricia Pessar (1998) has recently pointed out, is to investigate how a host of interrelated factors—age, class, employment history, and legal status as well as family structures and gender ideologies (both prior to and after emigration)—affect the benefits as well as losses that migrant women experience. We have come a long way from the days when immigration scholars lamented that women were ignored in migration studies. Yet there is still

Benefits and Burdens

much research to do to clarify and deepen our understanding of the complex and often contradictory ways that migration affects women.

Notes

1. I am completing a book, *From Ellis Island to JFK*, that compares immigrants in New York today with immigrants at the turn of the century. In addition to analyzing the role of immigrant women then and now, it also examines such topics as education, transnationalism, race and ethnicity, and residence and work patterns.

2. My research among Jamaicans in New York in the early 1980s was based on in-depth interviews with forty immigrants (twenty men and twenty women) and participant observation. I also conducted research among health care workers, largely Jamaican immigrant women, in a New York nursing home in the late 1980s (Foner, 1994).

3. These same factors, according to Grasmuck and Grosfoguel (1997), also account for the fact that Dominican female householders have a poverty rate almost twice that of Jamaican female heads.

4. Immigration and Naturalization Service data are the best we have for getting an idea of immigrants' occupational background, but they are not without problems. "Current" occupation asked on the immigrant visa can refer to last occupation held back home before immigrating but also, in some cases, to a job held in the United States or, for those entering under occupational preferences, to the occupation in the U.S. for which certification is being sought.

5. Pessar has developed her analysis of Dominican women in a number of publications. See Pessar, 1982, 1984, 1986, 1987, 1995, as well as Grasmuck and Pessar, 1991.

6. In his study of one hundred Taiwanese households in Queens, Hsiang-Shui Chen (1992: 77–79) found that men were most likely to help with garbage disposal and vacuuming, jobs seen as requiring physical strength. Taiwanese professional men helped out slightly more around the house than men in the working and business-owner classes. Chen links this to the work schedules of the different classes of men. He suggests that because professional men had shorter working hours, usually nine to five work schedules, they could spend more time at home than business owners, who put in longer hours in their stores, or working-class men, who worked long hours at restaurant jobs. On the distribution of housework in Korean immigrant households in New York City see Min (1998) and Park (1997).

7. A 1988 survey, based on telephone interviews with a randomly selected sample of Korean married women in New York City, found that 38 percent of the women in the labor force worked together with their husbands in the same business; 12 percent ran their own businesses independently of their husbands; and 36 percent were employed in co-ethnic businesses (Min, 1998).

8. It is not infrequent for Korean immigrant couples to ask their mothers or mothers-in-law to come to New York to live with them to help out with child-care (Min, 1998).

9. Day-care centers are in short supply, and they are often more expensive than babysitters in the immigrant community. Zhou notes that in 1988 there was only one subsidized day-care center for garment workers in Chinatown and a few home day-care services sponsored by the city government and some quasi-governmental organizations. The New York City Chinatown Daycare Center only had space for eighty children, chosen by lottery from among the families of the approximately 20,000 members of the International Ladies Garment Workers Union who worked in Chinatown's garment industry. The fee for subsidized day care in the late 1980s ranged from $8–$10 a week for each child from a low-income family (Zhou, 1992: 178–79).

10. Hagan suggests a link between domestic violence among the Maya in Houston and the absence of the "watchful eyes of parents and other elderly kin" (1994: 58–59). Also see Ong's (1995) account of marital abuse experienced by two migrant Chinese women in San Francisco, one from an elite Beijing family, the other from a working-class Hong Kong background.

References

Brettell, Caroline and Rita Simon. 1986. "Immigrant Women: An Introduction." In: Rita Simon and Caroline Brettell (eds.). *International Migration: The Female Experience.* Totowa, NJ: Rowman and Allenheld.

Burgess, Judith and Meryl Gray. 1981. "Migration and Sex Roles: A Comparison of Black and Indian Trinidadians in New York City." In: Delores Mortimer and Roy Bryce-Laporte (eds.). *Female Immigrants to the United States: Caribbean, Latin American, and African Experiences.* Washington, D.C.: Research Institute on Immigration and Ethnic Studies.

Chen, Hsiang-Shui. 1992. *Chinatown No More: Taiwan Immigrants in Contemporary New York.* Ithaca, NY: Cornell University Press.

Chin, Margaret. 1997. "When Coethnic Assets Become Liabilities: Mexican, Ecuadorian, and Chinese Workers in New York City." Paper presented at conference on Transnational Communities and the Political Economy of New York in the 1990s, New School for Social Research.

Colen, Shellee. 1990. "'Housekeeping' for the Green Card: West Indian Household Workers, the State, and Stratified Reproduction in New York." In: Roger Sanjek and Shellee Colen (eds.). *At Work in Homes: Household Workers in World Perspective.* Washington, D.C.: American Ethnological Society Monograph Series, Number 3.

———. 1989. "Just a Little Respect: West Indian Domestic Workers in New York City." In: Elsa Chaney and Mary Garcia Castro (eds.). *Muchachas No More: Household Workers in Latin America and the Caribbean.* Philadelphia: Temple University Press.

Donato, Katharine. 1992. "Understanding U.S. Immigration: Why Some Countries Send Women and Others Send Men." In: Donna Gabaccia (ed.). *Seeking Common Ground: Multidisciplinary Studies of Immigrant Women in the United States.* Westport, CT: Praeger.

Espiritu, Yen Le. 1997. *Asian American Women and Men.* Thousand Oaks, CA: Sage.

Foner, Nancy. 1997. "The Immigrant Family: Cultural Legacies and Cultural Changes." *International Migration Review* 31: 961–74.

———. 1994. *The Caregiving Dilemma: Work in an American Nursing Home.* Berkeley: University of California Press.

———. 1986. "Sex Roles and Sensibilities: Jamaican Women in New York and London." In: Rita Simon and Caroline Brettell (eds.). *International Migration: The Female Experience.* Totowa, NJ: Rowman and Allenheld.

———. 1983. *Jamaican Migrants: A Comparative Analysis of the New York and London Experience.* Center for Latin American and Caribbean Studies, New York University, Occasional Paper 36.

Gilbertson, Greta. 1995. "Women's Labor and Enclave Employment: The Case of Dominican and Colombian Women in New York City." *International Migration Review* 19: 657–71.

Grasmuck, Sherri and Ramon Grosfoguel. 1997. "Geopolitics, Economic Niches, and Gendered Social Capital Among Recent Caribbean Immigrants in New York City." *Sociological Perspectives* 40: 339–64.

Grasmuck, Sherri and Patricia Pessar. 1991. *Between Two Islands.* Berkeley: University of California Press.

Gurak, Douglas and Mary Kritz. 1996. "Social Context, Household Composition and Employment Among Migrant and Nonmigrant Dominican Women." *International Migration Review* 30: 399–422.

Hagan, Jacqueline. 1994. *Deciding to Be Legal: A Maya Community in Houston.* Philadelphia: Temple University Press.

Hondagneu-Sotelo, Pierrette. 1994. *Gendered Transitions.* Berkeley: University of California Press.

Houston, Marion, Roger Kramer, and Joan Mackin Barrett. 1984. "Female Predominance of Immigration to the United States since 1930: A First Look." *International Migration Review* 18: 908–63.

Kasinitz, Philip and Milton Vickerman. 1995. "Ethnic Niches and Racial Traps: Jamaicans in the New York Regional Economy." Paper presented to the Social Science History Association, Chicago, Illinois.

Kibria, Nazli. 1993. *Family Tightrope: The Changing Lives of Vietnamese Americans.* Princeton, NJ: Princeton University Press.

Kim, Ai Ra. 1996. *Women Struggling for a New Life: The Role of Religion in the Cultural Passage from Korea to America.* Albany: State University of New York Press.

Lamphere, Louise. 1987. *From Working Daughters to Working Mothers: Immigrant Women in a New England Industrial Community.* Ithaca, NY: Cornell University Press.

Lessinger, Johanna. 1995. *From the Ganges to the Hudson: Asian Indians in New York City.* Boston: Allyn and Bacon.

Lim, In-Sook. 1997. "Korean Immigrant Women's Challenge to Gender Inequality at Home." *Gender and Society* 11: 31–51.

Lobo, Arun Peter, Joseph Salvo, and Vicki Virgin. 1996. *The Newest New Yorkers, 1990–1994.* New York: Department of City Planning.

Mahler, Sarah. 1996. "Bringing Gender to a Transnational Focus: Theoretical and Empirical Ideas." Unpublished manuscript.

———. 1992. "Tres Veces Mojado: Undocumented Central and South American Migration to Suburban Long Island." Unpublished doctoral dissertation, Columbia University.

Margolis, Maxine. 1994. *Little Brazil: An Ethnography of Brazilian Immigrants in New York City.* Princeton, NJ: Princeton University Press.

Markowitz, Fran. 1993. *A Community in Spite of Itself: Soviet Jewish Emigres in New York.* Washington, D.C.: Smithsonian Institution Press.

Min, Pyong Gap. 1998. *Traditions and Changes: Korean Immigrant Families in New York.* Needham Heights, MA: Allyn and Bacon.

———. 1996. *Caught in the Middle: Korean Communities in New York and Los Angeles.* Berkeley: University of California Press.

Mollenkopf, John, Philip Kasinitz, and Matthew Lindholm. 1995. "Profiles of Nine Immigrant Categories and their Sub-Groups and of Island-Born Puerto Ricans." In: *Immigration/Migration and the CUNY Student of the Future.* New York: The City University of New York.

Morokvasic, Mirjana. 1984. "Birds of Passage are also Women." *International Migration Review* 18: 886–907.

Moss, Mitchell, Anthony Townsend, and Emanual Tobier. 1997. "Immigration is Transforming New York City." Taub Urban Research Center, Robert F. Wagner School of Public Service, New York University.

Ong, Aihwa. 1995. "Women Out of China: Traveling Tales and Traveling Theories in Postcolonial Feminism." In: Ruth Behar and Deborah Gordon (eds.). *Women Writing Culture.* Berkeley: University of California Press.

Orleck, Annelise. 1987. "The Soviet Jews: Life in Brighton Beach, Brooklyn." In: Nancy Foner (ed.). *New Immigrants in New York.* New York: Columbia University Press.

Park, Kyeyong. 1997. *The Korean American Dream.* Ithaca, NY: Cornell University Press.

Pedraza, Silvia. 1991. "Women and Migration: The Social Consequences of Gender." *Annual Review of Sociology* 17: 303–25.

Pessar, Patricia. 1998. "The Role of Gender, Households, and Social Networks in the Migration Process: A Review and Appraisal." In: Josh DeWind, Charles Hirschman, and Philip Kasinitz (eds.). *Immigrants and the Transformation of America.* New York: Russell Sage Foundation.

———. 1996. *A Visa for a Dream: Dominicans in the United States.* Needham Heights, MA: Allyn and Bacon.

———. 1995. "On the Homefront and in the Workplace: Integrating Immigrant Women into Feminist Discourse." *Anthropological Quarterly* 68: 37–47.

———. 1987. "The Dominicans: Women in the Household and the Garment Industry." In: Nancy Foner (ed.). *New Immigrants in New York*. New York: Columbia University Press.

———. 1986. "The Role of Gender in Dominican Settlement in the United States." In: June Nash and Helen Safa (eds.). *Women and Change in Latin America*. South Hadley, MA: Bergin and Garvey.

———. 1984. "The Linkage between the Household and Workplace of Dominican Women in the United States." *International Migration Review* 18: 1188–1211.

———. 1982. "Kinship Relations of Production in the Migration Process: The Case of Dominican Emigration to the United States." Occasional Paper, No. 32. New York: Center for Latin American and Caribbean Studies, New York University.

Prieto, Yolanda. 1992. "Cuban Women in New Jersey: Gender Relations and Change." In: Donna Gabaccia (ed.). *Seeking Common Ground*. Westport, CT: Praeger.

Repak, Terry. 1995. *Waiting on Washington: Central American Workers in the Nation's Capital*. Philadelphia, PA: Temple University Press.

Salvo, Joseph and Ronald Ortiz. 1992. *The Newest New Yorkers: An Analysis of Immigration into New York City During the 1980s*. New York: Department of City Planning.

Simon, Rita. 1992. "Sociology and Immigrant Women." In: Donna Gabaccia (ed.). *Seeking Common Ground*. Westport, CT: Praeger.

Soto, Isa Maria. 1987. "West Indian Child Fostering: Its Role in Migrant Exchanges." In: Constance Sutton and Elsa Chaney (eds.). *Caribbean Life in New York City*. NewYork: Center for Migration Studies.

Sung, Betty Lee. n.d. "The Chinese: Creating Their Own Jobs." Unpublished manuscript prepared for Regional Plan Association.

Waldinger, Roger. 1996. *Still the Promised City?* Cambridge, MA: Harvard University Press.

Zhou, Min. 1992. *Chinatown: The Socioeconomic Potential of an Urban Enclave*. Philadelphia: Temple University Press.

Zhou, Min and John Logan. 1989. "Returns on Human Capital in Ethnic Enclaves: New York City's Chinatown." *American Journal of Sociology* 86: 295–319.

Zhou, Min and Regina Nordquist. 1994. "Work and Its Place in the Lives of Immigrant Women: Garment Workers in New York City's Chinatown." *Applied Behavioral Science Review* 2: 187–211.

2

Gender and Citizenship in the Restructuring of Janitorial Work in Los Angeles

Cynthia Cranford

Abstract: The author examines intersections of gender and citizenship with a study of building services janitors in Los Angeles County. Changes in the industry using 1970, 1980, and 1990 censuses, union reports, and field work are analyzed. The author finds that restructuring facilitated the entrance of Latinas into janitorial work. In Los Angeles County in the 1980s, building managers switched from employing union janitors to contracted, nonunion janitors. The contractors hired Latina/o immigrants to do the lower-paid, restructured work. The share of Mexican and Salvadoran women increased during the 1980s. In addition, Mexican and Salvadoran women moved into janitorial work at higher rates than men. Furthermore, Latinas who arrived during the 1980s entered janitorial work at higher rates than the 1970s arrivals.

Since the late 1960s, the U.S. economy has been characterized by a crisis in production as employers strive to maintain high profit levels amidst increasing global competition. Employers have restructured work to cut labor costs by shedding in-house, long-term, union employees and adopting flexible work schedules using subcontracted, part-time or temporary, nonunion employees. One way employers have restructured work has been to recruit immigrant women (Sassen-Koob, 1984; Smith, 1984). The "new," post-1965 immigration is overwhelmingly from Latin America and Asia and is increasingly female (Tyree and Donato, 1986). In Los Angeles County, by 1990 roughly half of Salvadoran (51 percent) and Guatemalan (49 percent) immigrants were women, while 46 percent of Mexican immigrants were women. The majority of these women came to the U.S. to work; labor force participation rates in 1990 were 66 percent, 63 percent, and 51 percent, respectively.[1] In Los Angeles, Latina immigrants have moved into the low-paid service and factory jobs—such as janitorial, paid domestic, and sewing—that have grown with economic restructuring (Sassen-Koob, 1984; Morales and Ong, 1991).

The importance of immigrant women in these fundamental changes in the U.S. economy has prompted considerable scholarship, indicated by several review essays (Pedraza, 1991; Tienda and Booth, 1991) and edited volumes (Simon and Bretell, 1986; Gabaccia, 1992; Buijs, 1993) on the topic. However, women remain largely excluded from immigration theory (Massey et al., 1993; Basch, Glick Schiller, and Szanton Blanc, 1994; Portes, 1995) and widely read empirical work (Massey, 1987; Borjas, 1990; Portes and Rumbaut, 1990; Waldinger, 1996; Waldinger and Bozorgmehr, 1996). Although scholars are beginning to examine gender as a set of social relations that structure the work lives of immigrant women and men (Bretell and Simon, 1986; Hondagneu-Sotelo, 1992; Romero, 1992; Chang, 1994), this exclusion has meant that too many scholars focus on merely writing women into the literature (Handagreu-Sotelo and Cranford, forthcoming).

In this article, I examine the links between gender, immigration, and economic restructuring. I bring together two literatures that generally do not speak to one another: the literatures on gendered occupational change and on economic incorporation of immigrants. I draw on scholarship concerned with how these inequalities intersect, reinforce and contradict one another. I argue that employers draw on inequalities of class, gender, race, and citizenship in their attempts to guarantee a low-paid, unorganized labor force.

To illustrate this argument, I use census data to examine Latina/o janitors in Los Angeles who work in business services. This industry switched from employing union janitors to nonunion janitors in the 1980s as building owners contracted with the lowest-bidding cleaning companies. Restructuring has allowed Latina immigrants to move into what was previously an African American male-dominated job. Yet the restructuring of janitorial work has generated an unintended consequence: Latina/o immigrants are struggling to reunionize Los Angeles janitors.

The article proceeds in the following way. After a review of the literature and a discussion of the data and methods, I place the restructuring of janitorial work within the broader industrial shifts in Los Angeles and examine Latinas' place within these changes. Next, I describe the restructuring of janitorial work and analyze the shifting demographics this restructuring brought about. I then trace cohorts of Latinas as they move into janitorial work and examine the extent to which the occupation is feminizing. Finally, I summarize what we have learned from this case study and conclude with a discussion of the contradictions that have come with the struggle to reunionize the industry in the 1990s and Latinas' participation in this struggle.

Literature Review

Gender and Occupational Change

The literature on gender and occupational change shows that women workers are recruited to de-skill and restructure previously well-paid union jobs. Scholars argue that in competitive industries, employers cut labor costs by recruiting women who are seen as supplemental workers who will accept a lower wage than men due to inequalities within the family. This literature finds little evidence of genuine integration of women and men workers because when pay and prestige go down, men leave these downgraded occupations (Hartmann, 1976; Milkman, 1987; Reskin and Roos, 1990; Cockburn, 1991).

Three changes in the organization of work have led men to exit jobs and women to enter since in the 1970s. The first is the move from in-house production to contracted work, as occurred in real estate sales (Thomas and Reskin, 1990). The second is a decline in union shops, as occurred with bartenders (Detman, 1990). The third is a change in technology. For example, Roos (1990) argues that the switch to electronic compositing in the printing industry was a deliberate strategy by the owners to eliminate high-paid, union, male hot metal printers and replace them with women to do the new, lower-paid, clericalized work.

This literature reveals how employers draw on relations of gender in the home and in the labor market to restructure work. However, these studies fail to note differences *between* women, due to race, class and/or citizenship. Immigrant women are recruited for the least-paid, most insecure jobs. In addition, immigrant *men* are also recruited to cut labor costs in competitive industries. The immigration literature suggests that these men lack the opportunities that would allow them to leave a job when it is restructured. In short, immigrant women and men share disadvantages based on nation, race/ethnicity, and class even while immigrant women are affected by gendered power relations and ideologies.

Immigrants and the Economy

The immigration literature recognizes that the labor force is structured along the lines of race and citizenship (Moore and Pinderhughes, 1993; Morales and Bonilla, 1993; Lamphere, Stepick, and Greiner, 1994; Ong, Bonacich, and Cheng, 1994; Romero, Hondagneu-Sotelo, and Ortiz 1997). Yet scholars differ on whether they emphasize the supply of immigrants willing to work for low wages, or employer recruitment of a nonunion workforce. For example, a debate over whether immigrants are substitutes for U.S.-born workers, displacing them and depressing wages (Borjas, Katz, and Freeman, 1991; Winegarden and Khor, 1991) or whether they are recruited for different jobs than, and are thus complements to, the U.S.-born (Bean, Lowell, and Taylor, 1988; Marcelli and Heer, 1997) continues among economists and other scholars.

One reason why these scholars are at odds is their use of static, regression analyses of aggregate sites that fail to capture the dynamics of immigrant incorporation into a restructuring economy. Using case studies, sociologists and anthropologists have found that the dynamics of restructuring are context specific (Portes and Stepik, 1993; Lamphere, Stepick, and Greiner, 1994). For example, in the LA automobile industry immigrants are recruited by the nonunion firms while the U.S. born are concentrated in union firms, thus the former do not displace the U.S. born (Morales, 1983). Yet in the Georgia poultry processing industry employers are actively trying to replace U.S. workers with Mexican immigrants (Bach and Brill, 1991).

Clearly, we need more dynamic case studies to understand the process of immigrant incorporation into a restructuring economy. Roger Waldinger's case studies of several industries in New York (1996) and Los Angeles (1996) are a considerable contribution to this project. Waldinger shows that in many industries, including garment, hotel, retail, and construction, employers have recruited recently arrived immigrants, rather than African Americans, to ensure a low-wage, flexible labor force. Continual immigration from Latin America and Asia allows employers to use the networks of their current workers to reproduce what they see as a docile, vulnerable, labor force. On the supply side, the newly arriving immigrants turn to their relatives and *paisanos*,[2] who arrived in the U.S. earlier, to help in their job search.

While this literature is critical to the understanding of the importance of race and citizenship in employers' recruitment strategies (and employees' willingness to accept a given job), it says little about gender. Yet we are left with the question of under what circumstances immigrant women are recruited to the same jobs as immigrant men, as in the case of janitorial work in Los Angeles. The gender and occupational change literature suggests that immigrant men might be leaving janitorial work, causing it to feminize. Yet, their ability to do so will likely depend on men's citizenship and class status as well as the availability of traditionally immigrant "male" jobs—such as construction and gardening. The movement of Latinas/o immigrants into janitorial work necessitates a framework that is able to consider relations of class, nation, gender, and citizenship simultaneously.

Intersecting Relations of Gender, Class and Citizenship

These two literatures hold either gender or nationality/citizenship as *the* primary power relation structuring one's labor market experience. This is, in part, because the subject of these studies have been white women and immigrant men, respectively. However, Latina immigrants cannot categorically separate their gender, class, race, and citizenship identities.

In the 1980s, scholars began to theorize gender, race, and class as power relations that intersect by analyzing working class, racial-ethnic women whose lives make these intersections visible (Glenn, 1985; Collins, 1990; Zinn and Dill, 1996). In doing so, they have shown that intersecting social relations are embedded in our key institutions, like the economy, family, and state. Conceptualizing privilege and oppression as "relational" (Zinn and Dill, 1996), they have shown that a given individual can both be oppressed and privileged in varying degrees and in different contexts. Domestic work is a good case for illustration. As white, married women moved into the labor force, few of their husbands began to share equally in the housework and child care. This resulted in a "second shift" of housework and child care for working women (Hochschild, 1989). Yet many middle-class women are able to get out of this "second shift" by hiring racial/ethnic women. Racial/ethnic women are in the labor force out of necessity as the men in their lives are rarely able to earn a living wage. However, ideologies of breadwinning husbands and homemaking moms are extended to racial/ethnic working-class families, and the employment of racial/ethnic women in domestic work and other low-paid jobs is viewed as a choice and the low pay is justified. Even as white, middle-class women are earning less pay than white men, the racialized labor market mitigates some of the gender inequalities in the (white, middle-class) home (Rollins, 1985; Romero, 1992; Glenn, 1992).

In addition to race and class, inequalites based on *nation*—the set of social relations surrounding the position of one's nation in the global economy—are gendered. The literature on women workers in less-developed nations shows that subcontracting, union busting, and changing technology are not just used to replace "women" for "men" workers, or "third-world" for "first-world" workers. These scholars argue that Latin American and Asian women are the new proletariat in an international division of labor that is made possible by the position of these women in intersecting inequalities of class, gender, and nation (Nash and Fernández-Kelly, 1983; Ward, 1990).

In addition to the place of one's nation in the world capitalist system, citizenship or legal status is a central part of the experience of immigrant women workers in the United States (Hondagnu-Sotelo, 1993). Contrary to popular opinion, many

Latina immigrants come to the United States specifically to work, while others move into the labor force after arrival to contribute to family income (Fernández-Kelly, 1989; Repak, 1994). One study found that 70 percent of undocumented Mexican women surveyed came to the United States for "economic reasons" (Simon and DeLey, 1986:129). Anti-immigrant sentiment has taken a decisively gendered turn as undocumented Latinas, like black women on welfare, are blamed for the fiscal crisis of the state (Chang, 1994; Hondagneu-Sotelo, 1995). This case study of Latina/o janitors in Los Angeles will further inform our theorizing of the ways in which power relations and ideologies surrounding gender and citizenship are intertwined.

Data and Methods

This article is part of an ongoing project examining gender relations among Los Angeles janitors as Latinas move into what was once a African American male-dominated job. In this article, I use census data to examine the changing demographic make-up of janitorial work as it has restructured and the movement of Latinas into this job. When appropriate, I also draw on secondary studies, and reports and data from my ongoing field work.[3]

In this article, "Los Angeles" refers to Los Angeles County. While other scholars have operationalized the Los Angeles region as the entire five counties of Southern California (Myers, 1995; Waldinger, et al., 1996; Allen and Turner, 1997), limiting the sample to Los Angeles County allows me to better link the qualitative and secondary data to the census-based analysis. At the same time, Los Angeles County better captures the sprawling region that overlaps and intersects with the city limits as well as adjacent cities that the janitor's union, SEIU local 1877, has begun to organize. I use three samples in this analysis drawn from the 1970, 1980, and 1990 census Public Use Microdata Samples. I have limited the samples to those currently holding a paid job.

The analysis of the industrial and occupational structure of the region only uses 1980 and 1990 data. The PUMS codes for industry and occupation are listed on the tables.

I conduct two analyses of the role of Latina/o immigrants in the restructuring of janitorial work. I expand these analyses to include 1970 to add a point of reference before restructuring. I first examine the job of janitorial work itself by describing the changing demographic composition of janitors. The coding for janitors is 903 in 1970 and 453 in 1980 and 1990. This part of the analysis compares the business services industry, which experienced the most restructuring, with all janitors. The business services industry is operationalized as "services to dwellings and other buildings," PUMS codes 728 in 1970 and 722 in 1980 and 1990. The other industries include grocery stores, hospitals, schools, and universities. In this demand-side analysis the denominator is either all janitors, or all building services janitors. This analysis is graphically displayed with a series of line and bar graphs.

The second analysis focuses on the people moving into janitorial work. The denominator in this supply side analysis is the persons in a given cohort. Cohorts are defined on two levels following a "double cohort" method that has recently been used to examine the mobility of immigrants (Myers and Lee, 1996; Myers and Cranford, 1998). The first level is birth cohorts, defined by ten-year age groups. The second level is immigration cohorts, defined by the decade of arrival in the United States or U.S.-born status. Cohorts are analyzed separately by race, nationality, and gender. A new variable called "racespan" was created that separates race and ethnicity so that "Latinos" is defined by all Hispanics of any race while the other categories are non-Hispanic Asian, White, Black, and other. The "other" category is very small and is not shown in the graphs.

The cohort analysis is graphically displayed in order to visualize the movement of birth cohorts into or out of janitorial work over time. In the graphs, the white triangle represents the 1970 data point; the white dot denotes the 1980 data point, and the black dot represents the 1990 data point. These birth cohorts are traced separately for immigration arrival cohorts or U.S.-born. I trace African American cohorts over three decades. For example, one cohort is defined by African American women who were fifteen to twenty-four years old in 1970, twenty-five to thirty-four years old in 1980, and thirty-five to forty-four years old in 1990. I trace immigrants cohorts only over two decades because I focus on recent arrivals, as will be explained in more detail below. The 1970s arrivals were not here yet when the 1970 census was taken.

Because janitorial work is only 2 percent of all work in Los Angeles County and because the cohorts are broken down by race, nationality, gender, immigration cohort, and birth cohort, the percent of a given cohort who are janitors is necessarily small. Therefore, this supply-side analysis includes janitors in all industries. The cohort graphs are here used for analyzing trends of change. It is the demand-side analysis that allows us to see the share of the occupation that has gone to a given race, nationality, gender group.

In both analyses I focus on "recently arrived" immigrants. I operationalize recent immigrants as those who arrived one to ten years prior to their measurement in the census. For example, recent immigrants in 1980 are those who arrived at any time during the decade of the 1970s. I also compare recent arrivals in 1980 (1970s arrivals) to recent arrivals in 1990 (1980s arrivals) to determine whether cohorts of recent arrivals have entered janitorial work in greater numbers with restructuring. In the graphs, the 1980s arrivals who were recent in 1990 are represented by an x. Since we have not yet collected the census for the year 2000, we cannot trace these workers over time.

Combining an analysis of changing cohorts of workers within an analysis of the changing occupation itself allows me to examine the complex dynamics that accompany economic restructuring. I interpret the census based figures based on the theoretical framework outlined above, previous studies, and ongoing field work.

Latina Immigrants in the Restructuring Los Angeles Economy

In this section I place Latina immigrants within the general shifts in the Los Angeles economy in order to contextualize their movement into janitorial work. The growth in distributive and producer services in the 1980s are evidence that Los Angeles is increasingly one of the "global cities" that have emerged to manage and coordinate global transactions (Sassen, 1991; Soja, 1996). Distributive services, which include transportation, communication, and trade, make the daily movement of capital and workers possible. The convergence of financial transactions between Los Angeles and other Pacific Rim cities in Asia and Latin America can be seen in the growth of producer services, which include the finance, real estate, and business service industries (Figure 1). Business services include janitorial and security services to buildings as well as personnel supply, computer and data processing, and advertising services. The growth in finance services necessitated a boom in commercial real estate. In turn the increase in finance and real estate fueled a growth in business services and produced a demand for janitorial workers. This growth in producer services combined with the changing business culture, which rescinded the Fordist social contract (Soja, 1996), to facilitate the restructuring of janitorial work. As will be discussed below, by the 1980s building owners no longer believed that the best workers were those with job security. Instead they turned to more flexible relationships with a host of competing cleaning contractors who in turn hired (and fired) the janitors.

The growth in producer and distributive services also indirectly produced a demand for low-wage workers by producing a large professional class of financial advisors, managers, and agents. The professional classes, many of whom are women, demand domestic workers, hand-washed cars, designer garments, and pre-packaged dinners spurring an increase in personal services as well as nondurable or light manufacturing (Sassen, 1991). In contrast, heavy or durable manufacturing, such as steel, stone, and metal, declined during the 1980s.

FIGURE 1
The Changing Industrial Structure
Los Angeles County, 1980–1990

	1980	1990	Growth
Extractive	40,240	56,199	28.4
Construction	148,400	239,239	38.0
Non-Durable Manufacturing	273,440	297,670	8.1
Durable Manufacturing	584,620	537,181	-8.8
Distributive Services	770,500	925,559	16.8
Personal Services	381,200	539,307	29.3
Producer Services	450,620	677,196	33.5
Business Services	*14,740*	*34,257*	57.0
Social Services	682,580	784,538	13.0
Total Workers	3,331,600	4,056,889	17.9

Source: 1980 and 1990 Census PUMS. 1980 was made compatible to the following 1990 codes. Extractive includes agriculture, forestry, fisheries and mining 10–50; Construction 60; Non-durable manufacturing includes light industry like apparel and food 100–222; Durable manufacturing includes heavy industry like steel and metals 230–392; Distributive services include transportation, communication, wholesale and retail trade, except food and drinking establishments 400–640, 642–691; Personal services includes personal services, entertainment, repairs and eating and drinking establishments 641, 742–810; Producer services includes financial, real estate and business services 700–712, 721–741, 841, 882–893; Social services includes medical, education, welfare, religious and non-profit organizations, miscellaneous professional and social services and government 812–840, 842–881, 900–932.

Saskia Sassen argues that these industrial transformations accompanying globalization are "inextricably linked" to the proletarianization of Latina and Asian women (Sassen-Koob, 1984). This certainly seems to be the case in Los Angeles where Latina immigrants are concentrated in the low-paid service and factory jobs created by the shifting industrial structure (Figure 2). Both Latina and Latino immigrants are under-represented in managerial and professional work, while white and Asian women and men have high representation in these occupations. The percent of Latina immigrant operators and laborers rivals that of Latino men and surpasses that of black, white, and Asian men.

FIGURE 2
Percent Distribution of Workers by Occupation
Los Angeles County, 1990

Females Occupation	Native-Born	Latina* Immigrant Recent	Latina* Immigrant Established	Native-Born	Asian Immigrant Recent	Asian Immigrant Established	Black Total	White Total	Total Workers
White Collar	29.55	8.13	17.44	46.65	31.95	45.89	36.60	47.40	37.00
Sales	10.70	8.43	8.18	9.67	12.73	9.49	7.19	10.55	8.80
Administrative Support	38.13	9.39	19.84	31.36	27.08	25.58	35.43	29.16	16.60
Service	12.11	36.24	22.60	6.82	14.68	9.60	13.65	8.73	11.70
Janitors	*0.63*	*4.65*	*3.01*	*0.43*	*0.93*	*0.23*	*1.42*	*0.32*	*1.16*
Craft	1.73	4.29	4.71	1.66	3.30	2.43	1.76	1.10	9.30
Operators and Laborers	7.58	32.77	26.80	3.48	10.11	6.89	5.21	2.70	15.40
Farm, Fishing and Forestry	0.21	0.75	0.45	0.36	0.14	0.13	0.15	0.36	1.20
	100	100	100	100	100	100	100	100	100
Total Women	187,264	148,578	189,958	42,755	86,445	83,496	182,683	724,802	1,645,981

Males Occupation	Native-Born	Latino Immigrant Recent	Latino Immigrant Established	Native-Born	Asian Immigrant Recent	Asian Immigrant Established	Black Total	White Total	Total Workers
White Collar	27.28	8.61	17.33	51.07	40.56	55.70	31.08	53.44	37.00
Sales 7.16	4.25	4.62	8.63	11.20	8.32	6.26	10.12	8.80	
Administrative Support	11.84	4.70	5.64	9.98	12.89	9.71	14.22	7.30	16.60
Service	10.02	18.24	12.58	7.26	11.65	7.10	15.33	6.20	11.70
Janitors	*2.50*	*5.10*	*3.85*	*1.30*	*2.00*	*1.08*	*4.73*	*0.95*	*2.38*
Craft	16.46	19.55	20.58	10.21	10.57	9.45	11.51	12.58	9.30
Operators and Laborers	25.67	40.11	35.25	10.42	12.54	8.63	20.47	10.61	15.40
Farm, Fishing and Forestry	1.56	4.53	4.01	2.43	0.60	1.09	1.13	0.75	1.20
	100	100	100	100	100	100	100	100	100
Total Men	216,350	320,740	296,328	46,559	103,355	90,571	164,752	893,891	2,132,546

Latina immigrants are more highly concentrated in service occupations than all other workers. While U.S.-born Latinas and black women are more likely to be in service occupations than white women, their percentages do not come close to those of Latina immigrants and are far lower than Latina who arrived recently (in the 1980s). In 1990, 36 percent of recently arrived Latina immigrants were employed in service occupations, which include domestic workers, food servers, and cleaners of hotels and buildings. Nearly 5 percent of recently arrived Latina immigrants were janitors. A slightly higher percent of recently arrived men were janitors in 1990. Both Latinas and Latino men were over-represented in this occupation compared to total workers. In addition, a study that estimated the legal status of immigrants found that undocumented Latinas and Latino men were more highly concentrated in janitorial work than other women and men workers (Marcelli and Heer, 1997).

In sum, Latina immigrants, more than any other group, are concentrated in the low-paid service and factory jobs that have grown with recent industrial and occupational shifts. Undocumented Latinas are concentrated in the least-paying service sector and factory jobs, including janitorial work (Marcelli and Heer, 1997). The differences among women show that inequalities of race and citizenship intersect with those of gender. It is this intersection that has made the restructuring of janitorial work possible.

The Restructuring of Janitorial Work

The Recruitment of Immigrant Janitors

The restructuring of janitorial work has resulted in a change in the organization of work, a drastic decline in union power and plummeting wages. This restructuring has taken place most rapidly within the business services sector. Business services janitors were once direct employees of building owners who controlled hiring, firing, and the management of labor relations. Today, most janitors are

---

FOOTNOTES TO FIGURE 2

Note: *Latina and Latino refer to all "hispanic" women and men, respectively; the other racial/ethnic categories are non-Hispanic Asian and Pacific Islander, Black and White.

Source: 1990 Census PUMS for the following occupation codes. White Collar includes managerial, professional specialty, technical and all supervisors 3–199, 203–235, 243, 303–307, 413–415, 433, 488, 456, 503, 553–558, 613, 628, 633, 803, 843, 864; Sales 253–285; Administrative Support 308–389; Service 403–407, 416–427, 434–444, 445–447, 449–455, 457–469, Craft includes precision production, craft, and repair 505–549, 563–799, 614–617, 634–699; Operators and Laborers include operators, fabricators and laborers 703–779, 783–795, 796–799, 804–834, 844–859, 865–889; Farm, Fishing and Forestry 473–499.

employees of contractors that specialize in cleaning and maintenance of office buildings. While this move from "in-house" to contract workers began in the late 1950s (Waldinger et al., 1996), competition among many small cleaning companies intensified in the 1980s (SEIU, 1995).

During the 1980s real estate boom, developers made a united effort to reduce cleaning costs. One union report describes this as a "bidding war" between cleaning contractors that resulted in a 42 percent reduction in cleaning costs between 1979 and 1993 (SEIU, 1995:10). As the growing number of new building owners contracted with these competing cleaning companies, even long-time building owners turned to the new contractors.

Most of the newer cleaning contractors were nonunion and their proliferation led to a decline in the number of janitors with union representation. By the 1970s, SEIU local 399 (now local 1877) had organized Los Angeles janitors and the largest cleaning companies had union contracts. As a result, wages and work conditions were good, especially downtown which was nearly all union (Mines and Avina 1992). This changed in the 1980s. By 1987, nonunion contractors controlled 83 percent of the business services market (SEIU, 1998).

Since wages and benefits make up the greatest share of cleaning costs, competition between contractors led to declining wages and benefits for janitors as union contractors could not compete. An organizer who was a janitor from 1972 to 1991 explains the situation well.[4] She was one of the few janitors who worked directly for the building manager in a union building throughout the 1980s. Yet she was forced to take a pay cut from $8 an hour to $5.50 due to nonunion competition. When she and her co-workers did a delegation to the building manager he told them, "I'm the laughing stock of BOMA (Building and Owners Maintenance Association) because I'm paying you these kind of wages." In 1983 union janitors earned slightly over $7.00/hr, compared to below $4.00/hr for nonunion janitors. With such fierce competition, even unionized janitors experienced wage and benefits cuts. Their wages fell below $6.00/hr by 1985 and to $5.00/hr in 1989.

The decline in unionization not only led to lower wages but to greater work load for janitors. Total office space doubled in the 1980s, yet the number of building service workers only increased by 25 percent, according to a 1994 national survey done by *Cleaning and Management Magazine*, the leading trade journal for cleaning contractors. Violation of labor laws have also increased with restructuring. Workers I have spoken to report many wage and hour violations in nonunion buildings.

The dynamics of the restructuring of business services janitorial work are summed up well by one union researcher. "As commercial building owners primed themselves for the unprecedented building boom, they capitalized on the contracting process, using it to plunge wages and benefits for janitors to minimum levels" (SEIU, 1998:15).

Demographic Change with Restructuring

Which workers did the nonunion, cleaning contractors hire to do the restructured work? Figure 3 shows that they hired recently arrived immigrants.

The relationship between decade of arrival and restructuring is nearly a linear one. While the share of recently arrived janitors increased substantially in the 1970s, it rose more rapidly in the 1980s, the decade of the most rapid restructuring in the building services industry. In 1970, 7 percent of janitors in business services were recently arrived immigrants (1960s arrivals). By 1990 the share of recent immigrants (1980s arrivals) was over 46 percent. The share of janitors in all industries who were recent arrivals in 1990 is lower because this group includes industries—such as grocery stores, schools, and universities—where restructuring has only begun in the 1990s. Thus, the comparison of building services and all janitors confirms the strong positive correlation between economic restructuring and the employment of recently arrived immigrants.

FIGURE 3
Change in Percent of Janitors who are Recent Immigrants
Los Angeles County, 1970–1990

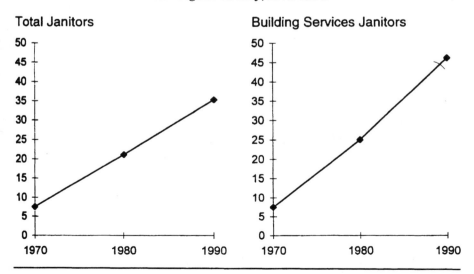

Source: 1979, 1980, 1990 Census PUMS. The code for janitor is 903 in 1970 and 453 in 1980 and 1990. The code for building services is 728 for 1970 and 722 for 1980 and 1990.

Because immigration is so closely correlated with race in the United States, the rising share of recently arrived janitors resulted in a changing racial make-up as well. The building services industry also experienced the most dramatic racial change. The share of Latino business services janitors grew from 13 percent in 1970 to 68 percent by 1990 with the largest growth occurring in the 1980s (Figure

**FIGURE 4
Change in Percent of Janitors by Race and Nationality
Los Angeles County, 1970–1990**

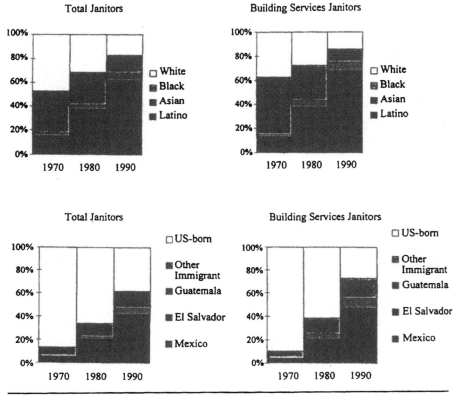

Note: *Latino refers to all "hispanic" women and men. The other racial/ethnic categories are non-hispanic Asian and Pacific Islander, black and white.

Source: 1970, 1980, 1990 Census PUMS. The code for janitor is 903 in 1970 and 453 in 1980 and 1990. The code for building services is 728 for 1970 and 722 for 1980 and 1990. Nativity is defined by the place of birth variable. The code for Guatemala is 62 in 1970, 434 in 1980 and 313 in 1990; for El Salvador is 66 in 1970, 433 in 1980 and 312 in 1990; for mexico is 61 in 1970, 436 in 1980 and 315 in 1990.

4). The share of Latinos is made up of immigrants from Mexico, El Salvador, and Guatemala. While the share of Mexican immigrants rose significantly between 1970 and 1980 as well as between 1980 and 1990, Salvadorans and Guatemalans began to move into this occupation in the 1980s. It was during this decade that many Salvadorans and Guatemalans left their nations due to civil war and the resulting economic depression (Hamilton and Chinchilla, 1991).

The rising share of immigrants from Mexico, El Salvador, and Guatemala coincided with a falling share of U.S.-born blacks and whites. In 1970, 48 percent of janitors were African Americans. Their share fell significantly during the 1970s and 1980s to reach 29 percent in 1980 and a low of 14 percent by 1990.

While the falling share of African Americans has been a topic of academic debate (Mines and Avina, 1992; Waldinger, et al., 1996), the falling share of white janitors has received less attention. By 1980 the share of white workers had declined to 27 percent, making it nearly equal with the share of black workers. In 1990 only 11 percent of business services janitors were white.

The correlation between economic restructuring and the changing racial and nationality make-up of janitors is further shown by comparing the racial breakdown among business services janitors and janitors in all industries. The slightly greater share of African Americans and smaller share of Latinos among all janitors reflects the fact that African Americans continue to clean federal and state buildings in Los Angeles, including public schools and universities. Janitorial work in schools and universities has not restructured like private industry.[5]

The rising share of Latino immigrants and the declining share of whites and blacks suggests a clear relationship between immigration and the economic restructuring of business services janitorial work. Yet Figure 4 shows that Asian immigrants did not move into janitorial work in significant numbers, even while the 1970s and 1980s were a period of increasing immigration to Southern California from South Korea, Vietnam, Cambodia, the Philippines, and other Asian nations.

There are two possible explanations for this difference between the share of Asian and Latino immigrants in janitorial work. First, Latino immigrants might have more access to networks that, as Waldinger (1996) suggests, could be important to the "Latinoization" of janitorial work. My field work confirms the importance of networks for entry into janitorial work. Second, Latino immigrants are more likely to be undocumented compared to Asian immigrants (Warren and Passel, 1987) making them more likely recruits in employers' restructuring strategies. An estimation of the proportion of Latino janitors who are undocumented is beyond the scope of this paper. However, previous studies (Loucky, Hamilton, and Chinchilla 1989; Mines and Avina, 1992; Marcelli and Heer, 1997) suggest that the employment of undocumented Latinos is widespread in janitorial work. My ongoing field work supports the assertion that many Latino janitors are undocumented. I have rarely had to ask about legal status because in informal conversations, usually in public spaces, Latina janitors frankly tell me about their undocumented status, often in the form of a joke. In addition, at union meetings, both with members and with newly organizing janitors, legal status is openly discussed. The workers are assured that the union is not the INS and that they will not ask for papers. The low share of Asian immigrants in janitorial work suggests a complex intersection of nation, citizenship, and race.

In sum, the restructuring of business services janitorial work coincided with the entrance of recently arrived Mexican, Salvadoran, and Guatemalan immigrants, many of whom were undocumented. Many of these recently arrived immigrants were women.

We can see a strong relationship between the economic restructuring that occurred in building services in the 1980s and the rising share of women janitors. Figure 5 shows that the share of women in this industry increased from 28 percent in 1980 to nearly 40 percent in 1990. A comparison with the percent of total janitors who are women indicates that women are employed in much lesser proportions in other industries.[6]

FIGURE 5
Change in Percent of Janitors who are Women
Los Angeles County, 1970–1990

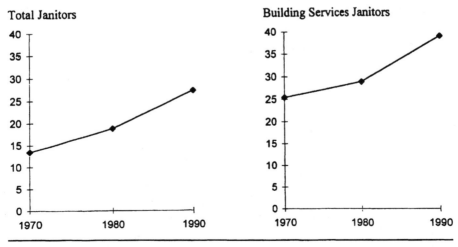

Source: 1970, 1980, 1990 Census PUMS. The code for janitor is 903 in 1970 and 453 in 1980 and 1990. The code for building services is 728 for 1970 and 722 for 1980 and 1990.

Gender and Citizenship in the Restructuring of Janitorial Work 37

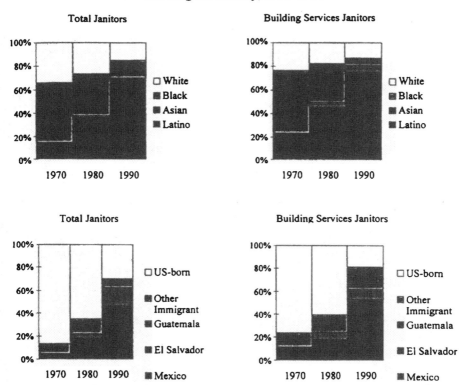

FIGURE 6
Change in Percent of Women Janitors by Race and Nationality
Los Angeles County, 1970–1990

Note: *Latina refers to all "hispanic" women. The other racial/ethnic categories are non-hispanic Asian and Pacific Islander, black, and white.

Source: 1970, 1980, 1990 Census PUMS. The code for janitor is 903 in 1970 and 453 in 1980 and 1990. The code for building services is 728 for 1970 and 722 for 1980 and 1990. Nativity is defined by the place of birth variable. The code for Guatemala is 62 in 1970, 434 in 1980 and 313 in 1990; for El Salvador is 66 in 1970, 433 in 1980 and 312 in 1990; for mexico is 61 in 1970, 436 in 1980 and 315 in 1990.

It is clear from these data that gender has been central to the restructuring of the commercial real estate industry. But which women moved into janitorial work? Restructuring coincided with a decline in the share of white and black U.S.-born women. Asian women made up only a small share of women building services janitors in 1990 (Figure 6).

The declining share of U.S.-born white and black women coincided with a rising share of Mexicanas, Salvadoreñas, and Gutemaltecas. Among women janitors we see a sharp rise in the share of Salvadoreñas and a less pronounced increase in the share of Mexicanas and Guatemaltecas. By 1990, the percent of women who were from El Salvador was 23 percent, compared to 9 percent from Guatemala and 29 percent from Mexico. Their share is significant given the size of the Salvadoran and Guatemalan populations in Los Angeles.[7]

The most dramatic difference between women janitors and all janitors is that the share of *Latina* immigrants did not rise until the 1980s, while the share of total Latino immigrants began to rise in the 1970s (Figure 4 vs. Figure 6). In short, Latino immigrant men moved into this occupation before Latina immigrants.

In this demand-side analysis, I have found a strong correlation between the restructuring of business services janitorial work and the rising share of recently arrived Latina immigrants in this occupation. This analysis, coupled with informal discussions, previous research, and theory, suggests that during the 1980s developers, building managers, and cleaning contractors increasingly recruited Latina immigrants to do the restructured, low-paid, cleaning work. In doing so, employers drew on relations of gender that intersect with race, citizenship, and class in complex ways. In the next section, I switch to the supply side and trace cohorts of Latina recent immigrants as they move into janitorial work. I also examine the extent to which these trends suggest feminization of the occupation.

The Movement of Latinas into Janitorial Work

The decade of the 1980s was characterized by a movement of recently arrived Latina immigrants into janitorial work. Figure 7 shows that Mexican and Salvadoran women who arrived in the United States in the 1970s moved into janitorial work in the 1980s. The rate of increase for middle-aged Salvadoran women was very high in this decade. By 1990, 11 and 12 percent of women in the oldest two cohorts, respectively, were janitors. In contrast, older Guatemalan women moved out of janitorial work in the 1980s, while the young moved in. By 1980, however, the percent of Guatemalan women who were janitors was much higher than it was for Salvadoran or Mexican women. This suggests that older Guatemalan women moved into janitorial work in the previous decade only to be moving out by the time they were measured by the census in 1980.[8]

Latino men who arrived in the 1970s did not realize as much movement into janitorial work in the 1980s as did Latinas. Only the oldest cohort of Mexican men increased their representation in janitorial work from 1980 to 1990, while the others realized little change. The greater rates of increase for cohorts of Mexican women

Gender and Citizenship in the Restructuring of Janitorial Work 39

FIGURE 7
**Cohorts of Recently Arrived Latina/o Immigrants and African Americans
Los Angeles County, 1970–1990**

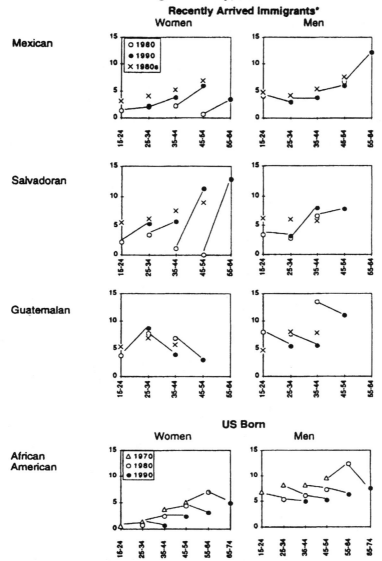

Note: *Recent arrivals are defined as those who arrived 1–10 years before the census in which they were measured. 1970s arrivals, who were recent in 1980, are traced from 1980 to 1990. They are compared to 1980s arrivals (represented by the x) who were recent in 1990.

1970s arrivals meant that by 1990 their participation in janitorial work reached that of Mexican men, except among the oldest cohort. Among Salvadoran men who arrived in the 1970s only one cohort (those twenty-five to thirty-four in 1980 and thirty-five to forty-four in 1990) increased their percentage in janitorial work, while the next oldest cohort and the youngest cohorts nearly held steady. The participation rate of Salvadoran men 1970s arrivals was well below that of Salvadoran women who arrived in the same decade. In contrast, Guatemalan men, like women, were moving out of janitorial work by the 1980s.

The increasing participation of Latina/os throughout the decade of the 1980s was combined with a succession of immigration arrival cohorts. A comparison between the white dot and the x shows whether cohorts of recent arrivals entered janitorial work in greater numbers in 1990 than in 1980. For Mexican men, recent arrivals are nearly entering at the same level in 1980 and 1990. Among the youngest cohorts of Salvadoran men the percent of recent arrivals in 1990 (1980s arrivals) was much higher than those in 1980 (1970s arrivals), indicating immigration cohort succession. For Guatemalan men, however, the recent arrivals in 1990 entered below the recent arrivals in 1980 for both the youngest and oldest birth cohort.

The succession of recent arrivals is greater for the women than it is for the men. Unlike Mexican men, the percent of recently arrived Mexican women was significantly higher in 1990 (1980s arrivals) than it was in 1980 (1970s arrivals). Similarly, succession of recently arrived cohorts is more pronounced for Salvadoran women, compared to men. For Guatemalans this pattern holds for younger cohorts but neither older Guatemalan women or men moved into janitorial work at a higher level in 1990 compared to 1980.

The high rates of succession for Latino/as, compared to the low rates of movement out for African Americans suggests that Latino/as took the newly created jobs, rather than directly displacing African Americans. In addition, the degree to which the participation of African Americans declined differs for women and men and for different age groups. Furthermore, older African American men and each cohort of African American women moved into janitorial work during the 1970s. Younger African American women seemed to benefit from the restructuring that began in the late 1970s and did not suffer from the intensified competition among contractors in the 1980s.

In sum, a cohort analysis of janitors shows that gender intersected with race and nation to produce complex patterns of change with restructuring. By the 1980s, Latina immigrants were driving the racial/national demographic change. The increasing participation of Salvadoran women is the most noticeable. In addition, the higher percent of Mexican and Salvadoran women who arrived in the 1980s suggest that the occupation is feminizing as it is becoming increasingly dominated by Latinos.

Discussion

This analysis provides strong evidence that the restructuring of janitorial work in the 1980s has allowed recently arrived Latina immigrants to move into this occupation. Nevertheless, causality is difficult to infer when social structures, social relations, and individuals' lives are all changing. However, by analyzing both the changing job and the changing workers moving into the job, we can better understand how the demand for nonunion, controllable workers intersects with the willingness of these workers to take low-paid jobs. The demand side analysis reveals a strong correlation between the decade of most intensive restructuring (1980s) and the rising share of recently arrived immigrant women from El Salvador, Guatemala, and Mexico. The supply-side analysis shows that the participation rates of these women in janitorial work increased substantially during the 1980s. In addition, Latinas arriving in the 1980s are entering janitorial work at even higher rates than the recent arrival did a decade earlier. These trends suggest a feminization of the occupation. Given race and citizenship inequalities in the labor market, if feminization occurs it will likely happen over several decades as newly arrived Latino men no longer enter this job due to declining salary, work speed up and perhaps declining prestige. Yet, the ability of Latino men to leave this job depends on the labor market opportunities available to them.

The quantitative data coupled with previous studies and field work suggest that Latina immigrants initially benefited from networks with their husbands, brothers, and uncles. The quantitative data show that the growing share of Latina immigrants occurred primarily in the 1980s (Figure 6). Because there was a significant increase in the number of all janitors who were Latino immigrants in the 1970s (Figure 4), Latino immigrant men must have moved into janitorial work in larger numbers before women. Yet in the 1980s few Latino men increased their participation in janitorial work. In contrast, the increased participation of Latinas in this period was substantial (Figure 7). Analysis not shown here finds that the higher participation rates of Latino men in 1980 are due to their movement into this job in the late 1970s.[9] Discussions with janitors and union organizers confirm that it is common for a wife and husband to work as janitors. In addition, employers could have increased their recruiting of women as part of a restructuring strategy. My field work shows that women are being recruited to do the vacuuming work previously done by men, as well as the cleaning work traditionally done by women.

It is likely that both employer recruitment of women and the use of men's networks were occurring in the early 1980s. Yet with the growing numbers of Latinas entering janitorial work we might expect a snowball effect leading to even higher participation rates of Latinas in the future. By the 1990s, enough Mexican women were in the United Sates to sponsor the migration of women kin, often with the husbands' disapproval (Hondagneu-Sotelo, 1992), while Central American migration includes large numbers of single women (Hamilton and Chinchilla, 1991; Repak, 1994). As migration networks become resources for finding jobs, we might expect more women to move into janitorial work in the 1990s. In addition, Waldinger's theory of network recruitment leads us to expect that if indeed employers view Latinas as a controllable, docile workforce they will use networks to try to reproduce this labor force. Many of the women I have met found their job through women kin, or *paisanos*.[10] Clearly, more research must be done to learn exactly how the rising share of Latina immigrant janitors came about.

Continuities and Contradictions in the 1990s

This analysis has shown a strong correlation between the restructuring of janitorial work in Los Angeles and the entrance of Latina immigrants into this occupation. Informed with a theoretical perspective that conceptualizes gender, race, class, and citizenship as intersecting social relations we can see that these inequalities influence not only the willingness of the workers to accept these jobs, but also the—often incorrect—assumptions that the employers make in recruiting them. We must recognize that these intersecting relations are embedded in the organization of our (global) economy and society so that their use generates common sense approval. Yet the given set of social relations are always susceptible to change, and intersections of gender and citizenship at the workplace produce contradictions that can be exploited.

Scholars concerned with economic restructuring too often end their story with a portrait of immigrant workers recruited as victims of a changing political economy. Yet, in the 1990s the very immigrant women who were used to restructure the work have begun to organize with the help of SEIU's *Justice for Janitors* campaign. By 1995, 81 percent of Los Angeles janitors had won back union representation, resulting in rising wages (SEIU, 1998). This success is due to a combination of commitment from the SEIU to organizing immigrants and women, radical community based organizing tactics, sophisticated market research, and past experiences of Latina/o immigrants (Banks, 1997; Waldinger et al., 1996). Their success, however, is occurring within a context of continual restructuring and a general atmosphere hostile to unions that is best conceptualized as hegemonic.[11] Nevertheless, the continual restructuring of the industry has resulted in the politicization of janitors, which is in turn fueling the reorganization of the industry. It is the workers who lose their jobs when a building changes from union to nonunion hands that actively participate in organizing the unorganized.

Latina immigrants are central players in the struggle to reunionize the janitorial workforce. Informal counts of the number of women on picket lines reveal that their numbers are comparable to their percentage in the occupation (generally 40 percent women). In addition, while housework, child responsibilities, and husbands' dissent are generally seen as obstacles to union participation in the literature (Tilly, 1981), I see enough women leading the chants, handing out flyers during pickets, leading delegations, and blocking traffic to question this assertion. Women tell me that they love to yell (*gritar*) at the marches, that they yell better and louder than the men, and that their union listens to women. Many of these women are pushing strollers on the line and bouncing young children on their laps at shop steward meetings. Only future research can determine whether Latinas' unionism subverts or reinforces gendered power relations and ideologies. In addition, the ways in which the movement of Latinas into this previously male-dominated job change work and gender relations will have to await future study.

Notes

I would like to thank Rob Wilton, Shari Dworkin, and David Heer for their comments on earlier drafts of this article. I would also like to acknowledge the support of the University of Southern California Department of Sociology.

1. Original analysis by author of 1990 Census.
2. *Paisano* is a Spanish term used to distinguish one who is from the same country or even from the same town.
3. I have conducted both participant and nonparticipant observation for the last twelve months in Los Angeles. I have observed and talked with women and men janitors and union organizers in buses, cars, their homes, and at union meetings. I have participated with janitors in many union actions including picket lines, delegations to employers, and handing out leaflets. In addition, I have conducted twenty-two semi-structured interviews.
4. Personal interview with the author.
5. However, private universities, like my very own University of Southern California, are beginning to sub-contract with cleaning contractors in an effort to reduce labor costs.
6. By 1990 the percentage of janitors who were women was 22 percent in schools and universities, 24 percent in hospitals, and 7 percent in grocery stores.
7. In 1990 the Los Angeles County foreign-born Guatemalan and Salvadoran populations were 107,966 and 212,788, respectively, compared to 1,174,185 for the Mexican population.
8. Because the census surveys behavior reported about the previous decade, I cannot trace 1970s arrivals over three decades.
9. This analysis is available upon request.
10. For example, one Guatemalan women found her janitorial job through a fellow Guatemalan

woman who she met on the bus. Upon learning her *paisano* was unemployed, the latter suggested they go directly to her employer where she would tell him the two were old friends. One Mexican women I spoke with got her job through her sister-in-law. A third woman found out about janitorial work from a fellow Salvadoreña who often visits this woman's (female) cousin's store. And a fourth woman was referred to janitorial work by a close female friend of the family from back home in El Salvador.

11. My use of the term *hegemony*, as a set of practices distributed through cultural apparatuses like journals or newspapers, is drawn from Gramsci.

Bibliography

Allen, James P. and Eugene Turner. 1997. *The Ethnic Quilt: Population Diversity in Southern California*. Northridge, CA: The Center for Geographical Studies, California State University, Northridge.

Bach, R. and H. Brill. 1991. "Shifting the Burden: The Impacts of IRCA and U.S. Labor Markets." Unpublished Interim Report to the Division of Immigration Policy and Research, U.S. Department of Labor, November.

Banks, Andy. 1991. "The Power and Promise of Community Unionism." *Labor Research Review* 18:16–31.

Basch, Linda, Nina Glick Schiller, and Cristina Szanton Blanc. 1994. *Nations Unbound: Transnational Projects, Postcolonial Predicaments and Deterritorialized Nation-States*. Gordon and Breach.

Bean, Frank D., B. Lindsay Lowell, and Lowell J. Taylor. 1988. "Undocumented Mexican Immigrants and the Earnings of Other Workers in the United States." *Demography* 35(1):35–52.

Bretell, Caroline B. and Rita James Simon. 1986. "Immigrant Women: An Introduction." In *International Migration: The Female Experience*, ed. Rita James Simon and Caroline B. Bretell. New Jersey: Rowman and Allanheld.

Borjas, George. 1990. *Friends or Strangers*. New York: Basic Books.

Borjas, George, Lawrence Katz, and Richard Freeman. 1991. "On the Labor Market Effects of Immigration and Trade." Working Paper. Washington, D.C.: National Bureau of Economic Research.

Buijis, Gina, ed. 1993. *Migrant Women: Crossing Boundaries and Changing Identities*. Oxford: Berg.

Chang, Grace. 1994. "Undocumented Latinas: The New 'Employable Mothers.'" In *Mothering: Ideology, Experience and Agency*, eds. Evelyn Nakano Glenn, Grace Chang, and Linda Rennie Forsey. New York: Routledge.

Cockburn, Cynthia. 1991. *In the Way of Women: Men's Resistance to Sex Equality in Organizations*. Ithaca, NY: ILR Press.

Collins, Patricia Hill. 1990. *Black Feminist Thought: Knowledge, Consciousness and the Politics of Empowerment*. New York: Routledge.

Detman, Linda A. 1990. "Women Behind Bars: The Feminization of Bartending." In *Job Queues Gender Queues: Explaining Women's Inroads into Male Occupations*, eds. by Barbara Reskin and Patricia Roos. Philadelphia: Temple University Press.

Fernández-Kelly, María Patricia. 1989. "International Development and Industrial Restructuring: The Case of the Garment and Electronics Industries in Southern California." In *Instability and Change in the World Economy*, ed. Arthur MacEwan and William K. Tabb. New York: Monthly Review Press.

Gabaccia, Donna, ed. 1992. *Seeking Common Ground: Multidisciplinary Studies of Immigrant Women in the United States*. Westport, CT: Praeger.

Glenn, Evelyn Nakano. 1992. "From Servitude to Service Work: Historical Continuities in the Racial Division of Paid Reproductive Labor." *Signs: Journal of Women in Culture and Society* 18 (11).

———. 1985. "Racial Ethnic Women's Labor: The Intersection of Race, Gender and Class Oppression." *Review of Radical Political Economy* 17, (3):86–108.

Gramsci, Antonio. 1971. *Selections from the Prison Notebooks*. Edited and translated by Quintino Hoare and Geoffrey Nowell Smith. New York: International Publishers.

Hamilton, Nora, and Norma Chinchilla. 1991. "Central American Migration: A Framework for Analysis." *Latin American Research Review* 26, (1):75–110.

Hartmann, Heidi. 1976. "Capitalism, Patriarchy, and Job Segregation by Sex." In *Women and the Workplace: The Implications of Occupational Segregation*, ed., Martha Blaxall and Barbara Reagan. Chicago: University of Chicago Press.

Hochschild, Arlie with Anne Manchung. 1989. *The Second Shift: Working Parents and the Revolution at Home.* New York: Viking.

Hondagneu-Sotelo, Pierrette. 1995. "Women and Children First: New Directions in Anti-Immigrant Politics." *Socialist Review* 25(1):169–90.

———. 1993. "Working 'Without Papers' in the U.S.: Toward the Integration of Legal Staus in Frameworks of Race, Class and Gender." In *Women and Work: Race, Ethnicity and Class*, eds. Elizabeth Higginbotham and Mary Romero.

———. 1992. *Gendered Transitions: Mexican Experiences with Immigration.* Berkeley: University of California Press.

Hondagneu-Sotelo, Pierrette and Cynthia Cranford. Forthcoming. "Gender and Migration." In *Handbook on Gender and Sociology*, ed. Janet Chafetz. Plenum Publishing.

Lamphere, Louise, Alex Stepick, and Guillermo Grenier, eds. 1994. *Newcomers in the Workplace: Immigrants and the Restructuring of the U.S. Economy.* Philadelphia: Temple University Press.

Loucky, James, Nora Hamilton, and Norma Chinchilla. 1989. "The Effects of the Immigration Reform and Control Act on the Garment, Building Maintenance, and Hospitality Industries in Los Angeles." Final Report to the Division of Immigration Policy and Research, U.S. Department of Labor.

Marcelli, Enrico and David M. Heer. 1997. "Unauthorized Mexicans in the 1990 Los Angeles County Labor Force." *International Migration* 35(1): 59–83.

Massey, Douglas. 1987. "Understanding Mexican Migration to the United States." *American Journal of Sociology* 92(6):1372–1403.

Massey, Douglas, J. Arango, G. Hugo, A, Kouaouci, A Pellegrino, and J.E. Taylor. 1993. "Theories of International Migration: A Review and Appraisal." *Population and Development Review* 19(3).

Milkman, Ruth. 1987. *Gender at Work: The Dynamics of Job Segregation by Sex During World War II.* Urbana and Chicago: University of Illinois Press.

Mines, Richard and Jeffrey Avina. 1992. "Immigrants and Labor Standards: The Case of California Janitors." In *U.S.-Mexico Relations: Labor Market Interdependence*, eds. Jorge A. Bustamante, Clark Reynolds, and Raul Hinojosa Ojeda. Stanford: Stanford University Press.

Moore, Joan and Raquel Pinderhughes, eds. 1993. *In the Barrios: Latinos and the Underclass Debate.* New York: Russell Sage.

Morales, Rebecca. 1983. "Transitional Labor: Undocumented Workers in the Los Angeles Automobile Industry." *International Migration Review* 17(4):570–96.

Morales, Rebecca and Frank Bonilla, eds. 1993. *Latinos in the Changing U.S. Economy: Comparative Perspectives on Growing Inequality.* Sage Series on Race and Ethnic Relations Volume 7. Newbury Park, CA: Sage Publications.

Morales, Rebecca and Paul Ong. 1991. "Immigrant Women in Los Angeles." *Economic and Industrial Democracy* 12:65–81.

Myers, Dowell. 1995. "The Changing Immigrants of Southern California." Research report LCRI-95-04R. Los Angeles: School of Urban and Regional Planning, University of Southern California.

Myers, Dowell and Cynthia Cranford. 1998. "Temporal Differentiation in the Occupational Mobility of Immigrant and Native-born Latina Workers." *American Sociological Review* 63, (1):68–93.

Myers, Dowell and Seong Woo Lee. 1996. "Immigration Cohorts and Residential Overcrowding in Southern California." *Demography*.

Nash June and María Patricia Fernandez-Kelly, eds. 1983. *Women, Men and the International Division of Labor.* Albany: State University of New York Press.

Ong, Paul, Edna Bonacich, and Lucie Cheng. 1994. *The New Asian Immigration in Los Angeles and Global Restructuring.* Berkeley: University of California Press.

Pedraza, Silvia. 1991. "Women and Migration: The Social Consequences of Gender." *Annual Review of Sociology* 17:303–25.

Portes, Alejandro. 1995. "Economic Sociology and the Sociology of Immigration: A Conceptual Overview." Pp. 1–41 in *The Economic Sociology of Immigration,* ed. Alejandro Portes. New York: Russell Sage.

Portes, Alejandro and Rubén Rumbaut. 1990. *Immigrant America: A Portrait.* Berkeley: University of California Press.

Portes Alejandro and Alex Stepick. 1993. *City on the Edge: The Transformation of Miami.* Berkeley: University of California Press.

Repak, Terry. 1994. *Waiting on Washington: Central American Workers in the Nation's Capital.* Philadelphia: Temple University Press.

Reskin, Barbara and Patricia Roos, eds. 1990. *Job Queues, Gender Queues: Explaining Women's Inroads into Male Occupations.* Philadelphia: Temple University Press.

Rollins, Judith. 1985. *Between Women: Domestics and Their Employers.* Philadelphia: Temple University Press.

Romero, Mary. 1992. *Maid in the U.S.A.* New York: Routledge.

Romero, Mary, Pierrette Hondagneu-Sotelo, and Vilma Ortiz. 1997. *Challenging Fronteras: Structuring Latina and Latino Lives in the U.S.* New York and London: Routledge.

Roos, Patricia. 1990. "Hot Metal to Electronic Composition: Gender Technology and Social Change." In *Job Queues Gender Queues: Explaining Women's Inroads into Male Occupations,* eds. Barbara Reskin and Patricia Roos. Philadelphia: Temple University Press.

Sassen-Koob, Saskia. 1984. "Notes on the Incorporation of Third World Women into Wage-Labor Through Immigration and Off-Shore Production." *International Migration Review* 18(4):1144–65.

Sassen, Saskia. 1991. *The Global City: New York, London, Tokyo.* Princeton, NJ: Princeton University Press.

Service Employees International Union (SEIU), local 1877. 1998. Untitled Report.

Service Employees International Union (SEIU), local 399. 1995. "A Penny for Justice: Janitors and L.A.'s Commercial Real Estate Market." Los Angeles. March.

Simon, Rita James and Caroline Bretell, eds. 1986. *International Migration: The Female Experience.* New Jersey: Rowman and Allanheld.

Simon, Rita James and Margo Corona DeLey. 1986. "Undocumented Mexican Women: Their Work and Personal Experiences." In *International Migration: The Female Experience,* eds. Rita James Simon and Caroline B. Bretell. New Jersey: Rowman and Allanheld.

Smith, Joan. 1984. "The Paradox of Women's Poverty: Wage-earning Women and Economic Transformation." *Signs: Journal of Women in Culture and Society* 10, (2):291–310.

Soja, Edward. 1996. "Los Angeles, 1965–1992: From Restructuring-Generated Crisis to Crisis-Generated Restructuring." In *The City: Los Angeles and Urban Theory at the End of the Twentieth Century,* eds. Allen Scott and Edward Soja. Berkeley: University of California Press.

Tienda, Marta and Karen Booth. 1991. "Gender, Migraton and Social Change." *International Sociology* 6:51–72.

Tilly, Louise. 1981. "Paths of Proletarianization: Organization of Production, Sexual Division of Labor and Women's Collective Action." *Signs* 7 (Winter): 400–17.

Thomas, Barbara and Barbara Reskin. 1990. "A Woman's Place is Selling Homes: Occupational Change and the Feminization of Real Estate Sales." In *Job Queues Gender Queues: Explaining Women's Inroads into Male Occupations,* eds. Barbara Reskin and Patricia Roos. Philadelphia: Temple University Press.

Tom, Dominic and Sean Cummings. 1998. "The Benefits of Workfare Elude the Cleaning Industry." *Cleaning and Maintenance Management,* February, 39–45.

Tyree, Andrea and Katharine Donato. 1986. "A Demographic Overview of the International Migration of Women." In *International Migration: The Female Experience*, eds. Rita James Simon and Caroline B. Bretell. New Jersey: Rowman and Allanheld.

Waldinger, Roger. 1996. *Still the Promised City?: African Americans and New Immigrants in Post-Industrial New York*. Cambridge: Harvard University Press.

Waldinger, Roger. 1996. "Who Makes the Beds? Who Washes the Dishes?: Black/Immigrant Competition Reassessed." In Harriet Orcutt Duleep and Phanindra V. Wunnava, eds. pp. 265–88. *Immigrants and Immigration Policy: Individual Skills, Family Ties and Group Identities*. Greenwich, CT: JAI Press.

Waldinger, Roger and Mehdi Bozorgmehr, eds. 1996. *Ethnic Los Angeles*. New York: Russell Sage.

Waldinger, Roger, Chris Erickson, Ruth Milkman, Daniel J.B. Mitchell, Abel Valenzuela, Kent Wong, and Maurice Zeitlin. 1996. "Helots No More: A Case Study of the Justice for Janitors Campaign in Los Angeles." Working Paper No. 15. The Lewis Center for Regional Policy Studies, School of Public Policy and Social Research. University of California, Los Angeles.

Ward, Kathryn, ed. 1990. *Women Workers and Global Restructuring*. Ithaca, NY: Cornell University, ILR Press.

Warren, Robert and Jeffrey Passel. 1987. "Counting the Uncountable: Estimates of Undocumented Aliens Counted in the 1980 United States Census." *Demography* 24:375–93.

Winegarden, C.R. and Lay Boon Khor. 1991. "Undocumented Immigration and Unemployment of U.S. Youth and Minority Workers: Econometric Evidence." *The Review of Economics and Statistics* 73(1):105–12.

Zinn, Maxine Baca and Bonnie Thornton Dill. 1996. "Theorizing Difference from Multiracial Feminism." *Feminist Studies* 22 (2):321–31.

3

The Impact of Resources and Family-Level Cultural Practices on Immigrant Women's Workforce Participation

M.D.R. Evans and Tatjana Lukic

Abstract: This article aims to assess the extent to which women's labor force participation reflects culturally or situationally induced family strategies above and beyond the well-known effects of opportunities and constraints associated with education and the life cycle. We focus particularly on women immigrants from the former Yugoslavia in Australia, and explore the family strategies by comparing the Yugoslav women systematically to immigrant women from other parts of the Mediterranean world and to immigrant women from other parts of the Slavic world. To this end, we use data from the one percent public use sample of individual records of the 1981 Australian Census. We find that the labor force participation patterns of immigrant women from the former Yugoslavia are more shaped by education and less shaped by the life course than is true of other groups, although the life course matters for all of them. Indeed, in the impact of education on labor force they closely resemble the Eastern Europeans across most of the range of education. But in the impact of life cycle stage on participation they more closely resemble the Greeks and the Italians. This emphasizes how important it is that statistical agencies release data at the greatest possible level of detail: A country may belong in one group for some purposes, but in a different group for other purposes. We assess a number of explanations for birthplace differences in participation patterns, and find most wanting. We suggest that they may reflect culturally conditioned intergenerational wealth flows and patterns of time investment in children and the elderly.

Introduction

Early debate on the impact of immigration on women focused on the costs and benefits of life in poor agrarian or early industrializing societies from which many immigrant women came as compared to the rich mature industrial or post-industrial societies that were their destinations. In this sense it has formed a special case of the assessment of modernization on gender roles. Research revealed a complex picture within some clear broad outlines. For nearly all immigrants, the loss of community is quite substantial (e.g., Appleyard and Amera, 1986; Foner, 1986; Prieto, 1986, Simon and Corona, 1986; Bhachu, 1986; Lamphere, 1986). Women's paid work is typically more separated from the home in the mature industrial societies; men's authority over women is typically less in the mature industrial societies; and conflict over the legitimate extent of that authority is more common (e.g., Brettell and Simon, 1986; Caspari and Giles, 1986; Davis and Heyl, 1986; Lamphere, 1986). The logistics of childrearing, especially with respect to babies and toddlers, are typically much more burdensome in the mature industrial societies (e.g., Appleyard and Amera, 1986; Foner, 1986; Mirdal, 1984). It is also noteworthy that the affluence that immigrants experience in mature industrial societies comes with (and generates) a wide range—indeed sometimes a bewilderingly wide range—of options (e.g., Boyd, 1986; Evans, 1984; Muenscher, 1984; Pessar, 1986).

The strategies that families employ with regard to these options continue to form the focus of research on gender and immigration up to the present day. In contrast to earlier research that tended to assume that the interests of men and women were opposed, we are now still following through the more nuanced framework that began to emerge in the mid-1980s, exploring both commonalities and opposition of interests of men and women, family strategies, and individual strategies (e.g., Brettell and Simon 1986; Evans, 1984; Manderson and Inglis, 1984).

The focus on family strategies is also, in part, a response to the (then) surprising result that global gender ideologies associated with the country of origin bear little relation to patterns of workforce participation in the new country (for example, some groups of women from extremely patriarchal countries have high labor force participation rates). This turned some researchers altogether against cultural explanations of immigrants' gender roles, but that rejection goes far beyond the evidence. Instead, it may be that we need to treat as problematic the degree to which immigrants endorse the "maxi-culture" of global gender role ideologies in their home countries. And, equally important, we need to begin to explore the "mini-culture" zone of cultural practices at the familial level.[1]

We would like to suggest that cultural practices at the familial level form important resources and constraints in their own right. Several that appear immediately crucial are the availability of grandmothers as major childcare providers with sanctioning authority. Grandmothering roles vary tremendously among cultures, especially in the authority dimension. We will show that immigrants from several societies that are very conservative on gender roles in the "maxi-culture" sense but that also enjoy traditions of committed grandmothering with full sanctioning authority have high rates of labor force participation. Another family level issue we will explore is whether the maternal role strongly emphasizes a "good provider" component—note that this is not a rarity, but occurs in some peasant societies, as well as many hunting and gathering societies. Finally, we explore the importance of intergenerational wealth flows and their timing, in particular assessing the possibility that women's labor force participation will be elevated during the period when there are dependent children in the home among immigrants from cultures that enjoin the accumulation of wealth in order to establish children in neo-local residences upon marriage (with the version in the destination country involving the parents making a substantial payment towards the purchase of a house, furnishing that house, acquiring appliances, etc.). The existing evidence suggests that the division of labor by gender in the home tends to show a lot of continuity between the old country and the new; when women go out to jobs they typically retain nearly all their household chores, and it is important to remember that going out to work for them involves a major "second shift" at home.

This paper takes up this issue by examining labor force participation patterns of immigrant women from the former Yugoslavia in Australia.[2] These women hail from a country at the intersection of two major culture areas—the Slavic world and the Mediterranean, and we systematically compare them to women from other countries in each of these culture areas. These women were all subject to the same regime of immigration policies, so although those are important for many issues (e.g., Caspari and Giles, 1986; Davis and Heyl, 1986; de Wenden and DeLey, 1986), they are effectively held constant in our analysis. The emergence of ethnic politics is a sufficiently distinct issue (Kelley, 1996) that we will not attempt to deal with it here.

Is there any point assessing the common experiences of immigrants from a country that has now fractured into separate pieces? We think so, at least for the purposes of an analysis of labor force participation—it might be different if we were studying ethnic identity or politics. For the purposes of analyzing labor market experiences, several society-wide institutions are crucial: Social capital formation took place under the Yugoslav self-management system and human capital formation took place under the Yugoslavia-wide educational system.

An important question in comparative work on immigrants is how to group the sending countries so that the comparisons are manageable and theoretically interesting. Good answers to this question, in turn, will enable us to begin going beyond the nominal approach to country difference (which, correctly and necessarily, dominates exploratory research) by developing hypotheses about which social forces affect the adaptation process and reception in the host country. The eventual goal would be to assess what underlying dimensions give rise to the groupings, but the first task is to begin developing the groupings.

Our purpose here is to assess this grouping problem for immigrants from the former Yugoslavia in Australia: The former Yugoslavia was ruled by a Communist government for most of the postwar period and so many political scientists tend to treat it as an East European country (together with Poland, Hungary, etc.), a placement which gains an extra rationale from the fact that its people are mostly Slavs. But many of the immigrants who came to Australia from the former Yugoslavia were more like Mediterranean immigrants (mostly Italians, Greeks, Maltese, and Lebanese) in their rural origins, limited human capital endowments, and unskilled occupational experiences than like Eastern European immigrants (Kelley and McAllister, 1984).

We assess systematically the impact of educational and life cycle stage on workforce patterns of women to assess whether immigrants from the former Yugoslavia should be grouped with the Eastern Europeans or the Mediterraneans. This builds on prior research using aggregate data that used factor analysis to demonstrate Yugoslavs' greater proximity to the Mediterranean group (McAllister and Kelley, 1983). Their proximities to and distances from these other groups may help illuminate the family strategies being pursued, as well as the resources and constraints that impinge on these groups.

The History of Yugoslav Immigration

Australia is an advanced industrial society structurally similar to Western Europe and the United States, but with 21 percent of the population foreign born (at the time of this study) it is much more dramatically an immigrant society. Note that this is far in excess of the 10 to 15 percent foreign born that the U.S. experienced during its heyday of immigration earlier in this century (Zubrzycki, 1964). Levels of education are intermediate—lower than the U.S., but higher than Britain.

At the end of 1995, Australia's population included more than 183,000 people born in the former Yugoslav republics. They form one of the largest immigrant groups in Australia, accounting for 1 percent of the total population and 4.3 percent of the overseas-born population. The only countries contributing more immigrants are the UK, Ireland, New Zealand, and Italy. The Yugoslav influence on the composition of Australia's population is even greater if we include the "second generation"—the Australian-born children of immigrants—then 1.4 percent are of recent Yugoslav extraction (Department of Immigration and Ethnic Affairs, 1995). An ancestry-based measure of origins yields similar estimates (Jones, 1991); in the 1986 Australian Census, 230,204 people reported their ancestries as Croatian, Serbian, Slovene, Macedonian, or Yugoslavian—first, second, and third generation.

A trickle of immigration from the Yugoslav region started even before the first major wave of immigrants from non-English-speaking countries came to Australia immediately after World War II. Just under 4,000 immigrants from the Yugoslav region already lived in Australia in 1933 (BIR, 1990). These first arrivals came mostly from the Croatian areas of Dalmatia, the Dalmatian islands, and Istria—areas that have long been sources of immigrants, especially for distant countries such as the U.S., New Zealand, and Australia. Macedonians from the region of Bitola, Slovenes, Montenegrans, and immigrants from Medigurje also started to swell the ranks of these settlers especially after 1920 (Price, 1963). At this period, many fewer immigrants from all these groups came to Australia than went to the U.S.—then a target country for most Dalmatian villagers (Zivkovic, Sporer, and Sekulic, 1995)—but for pre-War Australian society, with its tiny population, their societal impact may have been greater. As with Greeks and Italians, whose Australian presence was even larger than that of the Yugoslavs before World War II (Borrie, 1954; Tsounis, 1975), the first Yugoslav immigrants mainly came from poor farming or coastal areas, with little education and few skills, perhaps not surprisingly since Australia faced tough competition from the U.S. as a destination for skilled workers (Cobb-Clark and Connolly, 1997). Farmers, gardeners, and laborers predominated, with some Macedonians also working in restaurants and as timber workers, and Dalmatians working as seamen and miners (Price, 1963). Many of them continued their traditional family occupations brought from the country of origin. Almost a third of all southern Europeans in Australia were farmers by 1946 (Price, 1963). Children of these first Yugoslav immigrants often joined their parents working on their farms.

A large portion of the Yugoslavs who came in the 1920s later left Australia (Price, 1963), so that their communities had dwindled by the end of World War II, when a fresh wave of immigration renewed them. In the late 1940s and early 1950s, the war refugees coming to Australia under the Displaced Persons Scheme included many from Yugoslavia (Martin, 1965; Kunz, 1988). Twenty-three thousand, eight hundred sixteen displaced persons born in Yugoslavia came to Australia between 1947 and 1951 (McArthur, 1983). It was then that their communities became firmly established in Australia (Tkalcevic, 1980a, 1980b), although their effectiveness as communities was sometimes hampered by bitter political divisiveness (Cox, 1975). The same period also saw waves of Polish, Hungarian, Czech, and other East-Central European immigrants. Many of the women who arrived in this period worked within ethnic enclaves as either paid or unpaid workers, a situation which may have been a mixed blessing for them, as contemporary work on women's employment in other ethnic enclaves indicates many drawbacks (Gilbertson, 1995).

There is some uncertainty about the educational and occupational profiles of the immediate post-war immigrants from Yugoslavia, because analyses of them relied on small samples or case studies (Kunz, 1988). Even allowing for the fact that some of the highly educated concealed their prior occupations in order to facilitate governmental permission to come to Australia under the Displaced Person Scheme, the educational attainments of the Yugoslav groups were probably low, with only Poles less educated than they. The majority of Yugoslavs had little education, averaging less than nine years of schooling. Only a tiny group of 3 percent were tertiary educated, mainly in military fields. By way of comparison, approximately 85 percent of Polish men who arrived under the same Displaced Person Scheme had only primary education, and only 2 percent were tertiary graduates (Kunz, 1988). The educational profile of Yugoslavs reflects the fact that pre-war Yugoslavia was an extremely rural country with peasants constituting more than 70 percent of the population, and with 45 percent of adults illiterate (Savezni Zavod za Statistiku 1974, 1984). The provision of public education was, at best, patchy. As a result of such conditions in Yugoslavia, many Yugoslav immigrants who grew up before the Communist period had little education. Although these immigrants had (by the standards of an advanced industrial society) low-status social origins, established members of their communities nonetheless noticed that these newcomers were more educated, and that these new arrivals, despite holding jobs as unskilled laborers, saw themselves as middle class and had middle-class aspirations for their children (Tkalcevic, 1980a). In sum, the refugees who fled Yugoslavia at the end of World War II had broadly similar labor market resources and experiences to the previous and later waves of Yugoslavs who migrated for economic reasons (Telisman, 1978; Klemencic, 1978). Among Yugoslav immigrants in Australia more than three decades later, the same educational and occupational patterns continue to hold (BIR, 1990). By contrast, among Poles, subsequent waves were more highly educated, so that the migration stream changed drastically (Sussex and Zubrzycki, 1985).

For other Slavic groups immigration to Australia peaked soon after the war, but for immigrants from Yugoslavia it was just the beginning. An economic crisis and stagnation of the Yugoslav economy led to growing unemployment all round

Yugoslavia in the 1960s and 1970s. The ranks of the unemployed swelled to almost 400,000 in Yugoslavia. Of the unemployed, more than 60 percent had no academic qualification (Savezni Zavod za Statistiku, 1984). This pushed the Communist government to allow emigration from Yugoslavia, even to establish special migration programs with some foreign governments.

It was a period of notable emigration from the former Yugoslavia, especially to West European countries whose proximity to the motherland enabled most migrants to combine the hope of high pay with the possibility of home visits and eventual return. In almost all Western and Northern European countries the immigrants of these days were supposed to be temporary, even though, as they set out, only a tiny fraction of them expected to move back to their homeland (Morokvasic, 1972). Yugoslav immigrant women's high rates labor force participation were striking in Germany, Sweden, France, and other European countries, and their migratory behavior, labor market experience, socioeconomic status, and life styles in these countries have formed the focus of abundant research (Morokvasic, 1979, 1982, 1988).

The economic crisis also led many other Yugoslavs to seek jobs further afield in distant industrialized countries. In this context, Australia with its attractive pull factors now emerged as a major place to find a job and start a new life (Banovic, 1990). In 1970, the Yugoslav and Australian authorities signed the "Migration and Settlement Agreement" that preferred permanent settlement rather than guest-worker migration to Australia. Between the 1966 and 1971 Australian Censuses, the Yugoslav-born population rose by 58,539—the largest single intercensal gain in the history of Yugoslav immigration to date. In that period the population of Yugoslav immigrants almost doubled to 130,000. Yugoslav immigrants amounted to 5 percent of the total overseas-born population in 1971.

During the 1980s, immigration from Yugoslavia declined drastically. Yugoslavia's economy appeared to prosper, creating more jobs and promising future prospects that attracted back many guest workers from Germany and other Western European countries. Although most had been unqualified and unemployed when they left Yugoslavia, returnees became a great resource to the Yugoslav economy: Abroad they had gained work experience, Western working habits, sometimes additional education and training, and, in many cases, savings that they then invested in the Yugoslav economy. No policies prevented people from leaving the country, but Yugoslavia's improved economic conditions substantially reduced the number of emigrants throughout the 1980s. As a result, the number of Yugoslav-born Australians in the 1980s remained almost static (BIR, 1990). The story since the end of the 1980s is closely tied up with the eruption of ethnic conflicts, and people's flight from them, but they are beyond the scope of this paper with its focus on immigrants at the beginning of the 1980s.

As in other countries (Houstoun, Kramer, and Barrett, 1984; Tyree and Donato, 1986), women formed a very large fraction of this migration, although in many phases women were rather less than half the migration stream (Young, 1990). That led to an unusually favorable marriage market position for Yugoslav women and left an unusually large fraction of permanent bachelors among the men (Young, 1990).

Data and Methods

This paper uses data from the Public Use Sample of individual records from the 1981 Australian Census (N=144,365), the first—and still the best—unit-record data available from an Australian census. These, unfortunately, remain the only unit-record data in which birthplaces are identified by individual countries. Later, misplaced anxiety about confidentiality led the Australian Bureau of Statistics to release only unit record data with the countries lumped into broad regional groupings. This same wonderfully detailed dataset has been used in previous studies that assessed discrimination against immigrants in the Australian labor market (Evans and Kelley, 1986; 1991) and that described labor market resources of Yugoslav immigrants in Australia (Evans, 1990). The large sample size of the data and their fine-grained detail of measurement on key labor-market variables (birthplace, age, duration of residence in Australia, age of leaving school, and tertiary education) make it possible to undertake separate analyses at the single-country level for the largest groups of immigrants. The policy of the ABS to group countries of origin makes the task of finding sociologically sensible groupings all the more important.

We use these raw variables to construct our measures of years of education, and level of English language proficiency, and a series of variables to represent life cycle stage (married or not, number of children aged 0–5, number of children aged 6–18, and dummy variables for age categories since exploratory analysis showed no linear relationship to age).

The measurement of education follows Evans and Kelley (1991), computing primary and secondary education from the Census information on the age at which respondent left primary or secondary school and on the common age to start school in the respondent's home country. Years of tertiary education are estimated from information about the highest degree, diploma, or certificate, and added to years of previous schooling. These typical years of education required for diverse tertiary certificates and degrees were developed with the kind help of an expert on Australian education, Don Anderson. Comparable information was not available for most of the other countries, so we have imputed to foreign degrees and qualifications the years of study that an equivalent Australian qualification would require.

The English fluency scale that we use was scored as follows: "Speaks only English" and "Speaks English very well" were scored 100, "Speaks English well" was scored 67, "Speaks English not well" was scored 33, while "Speaks no English at all" was scored zero.

In order to assess processes of labor market adaptations, we have sought a compromise that allows us as fine-grained detail as possible in birthplace, but provides large enough numbers of cases in the groups to have confidence in the statistical results. Northwestern European immigrants, except Britons (N=1,065); Eastern European immigrants (prior research sometimes calls this group "Eastern European," sometimes "East-Central European," sometimes "Eastern Bloc" Europeans), except the Yugoslav-born (N=625). Going into more detail than prior research, we differentiate the Mediterranean group into the Yugoslav-born (N= 656), Greek immigrants (N=599), Italian immigrants (N=1,136), and "other Mediterraneans"—small numbers each from Turkey, Lebanon, Egypt, Malta, Cyprus, and the like (N=832). The analysis is based on men and women age sixteen to sixty-four. Let us note that this Census preceded the massive expansion of secondary education in the 1980s to early 1990s, so that early age at school leaving was common even among childhood immigrants who completed their schooling in Australia. We focus on the comparison between the Yugoslavs, the Eastern Europeans, and the various Mediterranean groups, so we do not consider the Anglophone immigrants, nor the Third World immigrants.

We use ordinary least squares regression techniques. The model and methods that are used here closely follow previous research (Evans and Kelley, 1986, 1991). However, the smaller size of the groups that we study in this paper makes a few simplifications necessary. The regression equations are presented in Appendix 1. In text we present the predicted values from the regression equations. These can be read as percentages of women in the labor force at different levels of a given causal variable while adjusting for compositional differences in the other causal variables by holding them constant. This conveys the same information as in the regression coefficients, but in a more widely accessible way. To simplify the exposition in the section on the regression results we will refer to percents on the understanding that this is shorthand for "predicted percents, all else equal."

Descriptive Overview

We begin with an overview of the key resources that women immigrants bring to the labor market: education, work experience, and host-language fluency. Note that the Australian labor market was highly segregated by gender in this period—gender differences in pay were substantially smaller than in the United States, but occupational segregation was much more extreme in Australia than in the United States (e.g., Charles, 1992). To place the Yugoslav immigrants' resources in context, we compare them with the labor market resources of eleven other immigrant groups.

Labor Force Participation

Women's labor force participation rates held steady for about a century at about one-third up to the middle 1950s.[3] Across this period, employed women were mostly young and single. Paid employment formed part of the transition to adulthood for women, a period of about ten to fifteen years accumulating a "nest egg," often used as a substantial down payment for a house to be bought upon marriage (in the middle to late twenties). There was a major shift in the character of employment across the period: Even at the end of the nineteenth century domestic service absorbed the labor of many of these young women, but by the time of the Second World War servants were almost unknown and young women were working in offices, stores, and factories. Beginning in the 1950s, there was a substantial rise in women's labor force participation to about one-half by the period of this study. This was almost entirely a rise in married women's labor force participation, with the most striking changes occurring in the 1950s and 1960s.

Other societal features that impinged on immigrant women's opportunities and constraints in this period include: (1) sharp liberalization of divorce laws in the middle 1970s, with an attendant upward leap in divorce rates (which have since stabilized or may be drifting very slowly up); (2) centralized wage setting, which results in pay for women's jobs being more nearly equal to pay for men's jobs; and (3) legislation and industrial agreements mandating job security and benefits for part-time jobs which probably greatly increased the attractiveness of those jobs compared to the insecure situation and exclusion of benefits which characterizes much part-time work in the United States, for example.

In 1986, 69 percent of the Yugoslav-born men were employed, as were 45 percent of females (BIR, 1990). The size of the gap in labor force participation—24 percent higher for men than women—is surprisingly close to that prevailing in their country of origin. According to the Yugoslav 1981 Census, 55 percent of Yugoslav men and 33 percent of Yugoslav women participate in the labor market, so the gender gap there is 22 percent.

Turning back to our focal year of 1981, the Census Public Use Sample shows that 53 percent of Yugoslav women participated in the labor market, as did 48 percent of Italians, 59 percent of Greeks, 52 percent of Eastern Europeans and 51 percent of Northwestern Europeans (Figure 1). This puts the labor force participation rate for Yugoslav women in the upper middle portion of the range of the other groups. Whether the observed group differences reflect different underlying propensities to engage in market work, or whether they simply reflect compositional differences in resources and constraints—notably, the aging of some of the populations, differences in educational attainments, and the like—forms the focus of the multivariate analysis below. Before deciding whether compositional differences entirely account for differences in behavior, it is worthwhile sketching the social composition of the immigrant populations.

FIGURE 1
Women's Labor Force Participation
Percent in Labor Force by Birthplace, Australia 1981

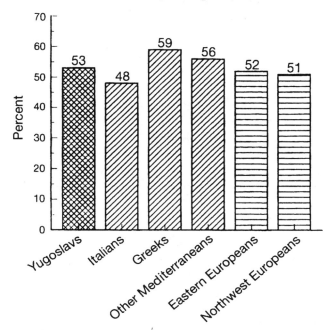

Education

As background, let us sketch the educational system that was established in Yugoslavia by the 1950s and persisted in substantially the same form throughout the period relevant to this study. Note that education was free at all levels.

After WWII, primary education (which children entered the autumn after they had turned age seven) was extended to eight years of compulsory schooling. A central federal core of compulsory education was used in all republics from 1959 until the collapse of the Yugoslav federation. It was extended in many republics or communes by supplementary programs. Core subjects covered by primary schooling included: natural and social sciences, native languages and literature, modern foreign languages, mathematics, physical and health education, aesthetic and artistic education, musical education, general technical education, and civic and moral education. Ethnic minorities had the opportunity to be taught and learn in their mother tongue, having additional programs on their specific cultures as well (OECD, 1973, 1981).

At age fifteen, the end of eight years of compulsory primary schooling, Yugoslavs could leave the educational system or pursue a variety of further education and training programs. Although some minor differences in form, curriculum, and methods of organization of secondary schools existed among republics before an educational reform was introduced in 1977, it is possible to provide a broadbrush sketch of secondary education. Teenagers seeking further education could, if their academic performance was good enough, choose among three main types of secondary schools in Yugoslavia: the three-year vocational training school; the four-year technical school; and the four-year gymnasium.

Vocational schools provide specialized, formal technical training that prepared students directly for skilled and semi-skilled jobs (such as carpentry, pipe fitting, machinist). They certified their training with vocational proficiency qualifications. The technical schools prepared students for middle technical, semi-professional, and management occupations, such as dental assistant, nurse, technical draughtsman, and the like. They also served as preparation for further study in the same field in a university. Finally, the gymnasia were similar to the gymnasia in many Northern and Central European countries: They are academic secondary schools whose main goal is to prepare students for university.

Two-year "higher schools" (similar to American Junior Colleges) have been growing in popularity throughout Yugoslavia since the 1960s. They offered secondary school graduates two years of intensive higher vocational education and training, especially as assistants to professionals in the fields of medicine, engineering, agriculture, economics, law, education, social work, management, and the like. They educated for technical and semi-professional occupations, and they have been closely linked to the labor market. More than half the students attending higher schools in 1977/78 studied part-time because they already had jobs. However, slow completion and high rates of drop out characterized Yugoslav tertiary education in the 1970s. The average number of years spent at higher schools and universities was seven (OECD 1973, 1981).[4]

As a result of the establishment and expansion of schools and universities illiteracy has fallen from 51 percent in 1921 to 25 percent in 1948 and, further, to 10 percent in 1981 (Statisticki Godisnjak Jugoslavije, 1984). All in all in 1981, 14 percent of Yugoslavs had no education at all, and another 30 percent had left school before completing eight years (some, but not all, of them having passed their childhood before the educational expansion of the communist era), 24 percent had eight years of schooling, another 26 percent had twelve years of education, and 6 percent were tertiary educated (Savezni Zavod za Statistiku, 1984). Education continued to expand during the 1980s, especially higher education: approximately 10 percent of the total Yugoslav population was tertiary educated by 1987 (Yu-Survey, 1987).

Despite the enormous expansion of education, a few children slipped through the educational net: 0.7 percent of boys and 1.2 percent of girls age ten to fourteen were illiterate in 1981 (Statisticki Godisnjak Jugoslavije, 1984). These percentages do not exclude the institutionalized population, so some of these may be severely retarded children. But if that were the whole story, there would be more boys than girls in the illiterate category because boys are more often afflicted with genetically based mental handicaps than girls.

Importantly, despite the notable gains in educational attainment of both men and women, a substantial educational gender gap persisted in Yugoslavia. For example, behind the figure of 10 percent illiterate in the total population in 1981 there is a stark gender gap: only 4 percent of men were illiterate, compared to 15 percent of women (Savezni Zavod za Statistiku, 1984). Thus, almost 1.5 million Yugoslav women had no literacy skills at all.

Interestingly, the gender gap is not constant at different levels of education. At the base of the educational system is a stark difference in the opportunity to get any schooling at all. Almost 20 percent of Yugoslav women have never been to school compared with 7 percent of men. Those who acquired a little schooling— who attended primary school but did not complete it—are a substantial portion of both sexes: 34 percent of women and 28 percent of men. Another 24 percent of women and 25 percent of men completed primary school. Another major difference is at the secondary school level: 19 percent of women and 33 percent of men completed secondary school; 4 percent of women and 7 percent of men completed a tertiary course (Statisticki Godisnjak Jugoslavije, 1984). Note that these dramatic differences shape the home environment of children, too. Most children grow up in homes where the father is clearly more educated than the mother.

Ever since the Displaced Persons program, the level of education has held mostly steady among the Yugoslav-born in Australia. Most emigrants from Yugoslavia who arrived during the 1960s and 1970s were poorly educated; indeed, many were peasants. Even though, over time, educational changes in Yugoslavia led to a more highly educated population there and Australian immigration policies increasingly have favored better educated immigrants, nonetheless the educational level of Yugoslav immigrants in Australia has not greatly changed, in part because immigration policies allowed immigration on both family reunion and employer sponsorship grounds in this period, both of which tend to perpetuate chain migration at the skill level of the existing immigrant population. It seems likely that Australia was especially attractive to less educated and qualified Yugoslavs in this period, because of new American policies that increasingly excluded unqualified immigrants (Telisman, 1978; Cobb-Clark and Conolly, 1997).

In the light of these facts, the low educational attainment of Yugoslav-born immigrants in the 1981 Census of Australia is not a surprise (Figure 2). On average, Yugoslavia-born men have 9.1 years of education, while women's education attainment is even lower, averaging 8.0 years. In detail, 27 percent of Yugoslavia-born women had 6 years of education or less, another 8 percent had completed 7 years of education, 26 percent had 8 years of education, 12 percent had completed 9 years of education, 9 percent finished 10 years of education, 12 percent had completed 11 years of education, 4 percent had 12 years of education, 2 percent had 13 years, 1 percent had completed 14 years, and only 1 percent had completed 15 or more years.

Thus, Yugoslav women were highly concentrated at the low end of the educational spectrum. Indeed, fully 61 percent of Yugoslav women had only 8 years of education or less. Although this indicates a relatively low level of education, Yugoslav women who immigrated to Australia were more highly educated than Yugoslav women who stayed behind. Seventy-eight percent of the nonimmigrant women had just primary school education or less (Statisticki Godisnjak Jugoslavije, 1984). That is 17 percent more concentrated at the low end of the educational spectrum among the home-staying women than among the immigrant women.

The educational attainments of Yugoslav immigrants in Australia are similar to other Mediterranean groups. Italian immigrant women averaged 7.9 years,

FIGURE 2
Educational Attainment of Immigrant Women
Mean Years of Education by Birthplace, Australia 1981

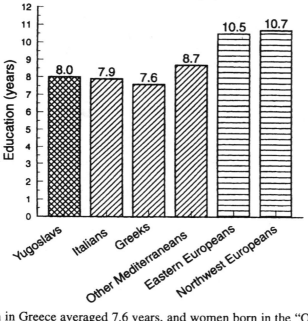

women born in Greece averaged 7.6 years, and women born in the "Other Mediterranean" countries averaged 8.7 years.

These educational attainments are much lower than those of other immigrants. The Eastern European immigrants, to whom Yugoslavs are linked by history, political system, and some aspects of culture differ sharply from the Yugoslav immigrants in their educational patterns. The Eastern Europeans have substantially more education—10.5 years of education, on average, for Eastern European immigrant women. That is two and a half years higher than Yugoslav immigrant women, and a two and a half year difference in educational outcomes is very large indeed (roughly equivalent to the difference in educational outcomes between coming from an only child family and a family with ten or twelve children, or the difference between coming from a family where the parents only completed elementary school and a family where the parents were university graduates). The Eastern Europeans also have smaller educational differences by gender (0.3 of a year, on average) than do the Yugoslavs (1.1 years). The attainments of the Yugoslavs are also less than those of the Northwestern Europeans (who are broadly similar to the Eastern Europeans in their educational endowments).

Life Cycle Considerations

Most Yugoslav immigrants came to Australia as young adults (Telisman, 1978; Evans, 1990), some at the very start of their careers, others after working for some years in their home country, others after some years of sojourner employment in Western Europe during 1960s and 1970s (Tkalcevic, 1980b). The slowing of Yugoslav immigration to Australia in the 1970s led to the aging of the Yugoslav immigrant population at the beginning of the 1980s (Young, 1990).

Language Fluency

Language fluency is important at work (Evans, 1986; Tienda and Neidert, 1984), and for many other aspects of life as well. Research on diverse countries has shown that immigrants' fluency in the language of the host country is important in the success of settlement in the new society (Esser, 1986; Evans, 1986, 1987; McManus, Gould, and Welch, 1983; Schmitter, 1983).

Earlier research has shown that Mediterranean immigrants tend to be less proficient English speakers than members of other immigrant groups (Evans, 1986; Evans, 1990; Jupp, 1966; Zubrzycki, 1964). This reduced fluency comes about in part because on average they have less education than do members of other immigrant groups (Evans, 1986). This connection with education may come about through direct language instruction in secondary schools, through the greater cognitive flexibility that education generally imparts, and through the greater verbal abilities of the highly educated.

Most Yugoslav immigrants have some substantial command of English. Thirty-nine percent of them speak English "very well," and another 36 percent of them speak English "well." Twenty-three percent speak English "not well," and just 2 percent have no English skills at all. Scored on a points-out-of-100 basis, the average fluency score is 71 (75 for men and 67 for women). Even though so many of them speak English "well" or "very well," they are among the least proficient groups (Evans, 1990), very close to the Greeks and Italians. Poles, Czechs, Hungarians, and other Eastern Europeans in Australia have acquired much more English language fluency. With language skill scores averaging 85 for men and 82 for women, Eastern Europeans' language skills typically rate ten to fifteen points higher than do Yugoslavs'. Northwest Europeans have yet a bit more fluency in English.

Another striking point is a very high level of gender differences among the Yugoslav immigrants: Yugoslav women were 8 points out-of-100 lower in English language fluency than the men. Greeks, Italians, and "other Mediterraneans" are again very close to Yugoslavs in having quite a large gap between men's and women's English language skills.

In the event, English language fluency does not have consistent or clearly patterned effects on immigrant women's work force participation, in part, perhaps because of the availability of ethnic enclave employment in the Mediterranean groups (Appendix 1). So we merely note that this is a form of resource or constraint that is not yet fully understood, and we control for it in the multivariate analysis of education and life cycle stage.

Women's Labor Force Participation: Regression Analysis

Effects of Education

Education has long been one of the key forces leading women into the labor market in Australia (Evans, 1988; Evans, 1996). Prior research suggests that for the majority population the education effect includes both a wage pull—the more generous pay that more education commands—and a cultural pull—the fact that more highly educated women tend to adhere to modern, workplace-oriented norms about women's roles (Evans, 1988). But it is worth noting that family strategies of income maximization could involve less educated women contributing to the family coffers by working extra long hours to compensate for their lower hourly pay. It is also worth remembering that the "wage pull" does not affect the woman alone—the rest of the family, too, will share in the extra pay if the wife goes to work and that may affect their preferences concerning her employment.

But there has been a puzzling absence of an effect of education on participation reported in prior research for the Mediterranean group as a whole (Evans, 1984). Let us see if dividing the group into its origin countries clarifies the matter.

Highly educated Yugoslav immigrant women participate much more extensively in the labor force than do their less educated sisters. There is a yawning gulf of fully 30 percent in labor force participation between the few most highly educated Yugoslav women, 76 percent of whom would participate in the labor force and the many who have only 6 years of schooling, 46 percent of whom would participate, all else equal (Figure 3).

We might interpret these results as saying that for Yugoslav immigrant women with the least education, the choice of whether to concentrate one's energies on the home and to bet one's future on a highly specialized division of labor by gender within the family or to undertake paid employment and build one's life around a blend of job and family is a very finely balanced decision, with about half choosing one way and half the other (and indeed, there may be plenty of shifting

FIGURE 3
Effects of Education on Work Participation for Immigrants Australia, 1981

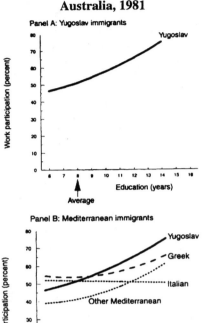

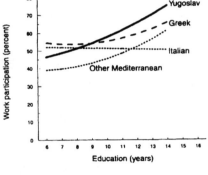

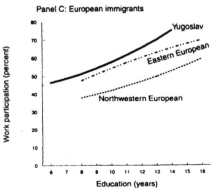

Note: Women, predicted values from regression.

between these paths). Note that for these women, "housewife" with its middling prestige ranking is a higher prestige (but obviously lower paid) job than the factory and low service jobs that people with their level of education can normally expect in Australia. By contrast, as one ascends the educational ladder, the attractions of jobs outside the home clearly come to predominate. Among women who completed secondary school, about three out of every five are in employment, as are about three out of every four who have some tertiary education.

Clearly, the relatively middling observed rate of Yugoslav women's labor force participation (53 percent, see the descriptive section, above) reflects their limited funds for education (rather than a propensity to refrain from utilizing one's education in the labor market). It also reflects the aging of the Yugoslav immigrant population, as we shall see below, and their limited English skills (see Appendix).

The workforce participation of Yugoslav women is much more differentiated by education than is true of the rest of the Mediterranean groups (Figure 4), so there appear to be some important cultural differences in the propensity to "cash in" one's education (recalling that these differences are adjusted for differences in language fluency and life cycle stage). Thus, at the bottom end of the educational spectrum—six years of education or less—Yugoslavs are in the middle of the Mediterranean group: 55 percent of Greek immigrant women participate, as do 52 percent of Italians, 46 percent of Yugoslavs, and 40 percent of "Other Mediterraneans." By about nine years of education, the Greeks and Italians and Yugoslavs are all tightly bunched at around 55 percent participating; the "Other Mediterraneans" are about ten points lower. Among those completing secondary school, the Yugoslavs, participating at 65 percent, exceed all the other groups by at least 5 percent. And among those with some tertiary education, the Yugoslavs, at 76 percent, are about 10 percent more likely to participate than the Greeks (65 percent), 16 percent more likely to participate than the "Other Mediterraneans" (60 percent), and 26 percent more likely to participate than the Italians (Figure 3).

What do these patterns mean? First of all, they mean that for the large majority with very little education in all these groups, costs and benefits are finely balanced between full-time homemaking and a more diverse life involving both employment and homemaking. But the balances of costs and benefits among the highly educated differ rather strongly among the groups. These differences are considerably larger than one would expect in light of prior research on men's workplace experiences which generally suggests that one is justified in treating all these country groups as a homogeneous Mediterranean group.

Why do they diverge among the more highly educated? This is, at this stage necessarily a more speculative matter. One possibility is that although chain migration is important in the history of the less-educated bulk of all these groups, that

FIGURE 4
Effects of Life Cycle Stage on Work Participation for Immigrants in Australia, 1981

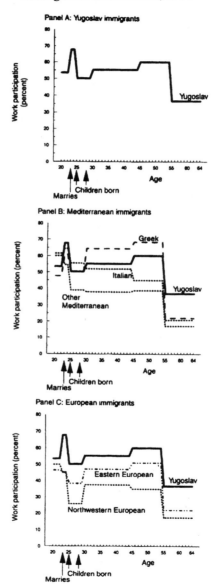

Note: Combined effects of age, marriage, and children. Women, predicted values from regression.

among the more highly educated folk, the Yugoslavs more often involve senior female relatives whose contribution to childcare and housework makes it possible for highly educated women in the prime working ages to go out to work without disturbing the traditional division of labor by gender within the home.

Alternatively, it may be that the Yugoslavs were less influenced by the widespread Mediterranean cultural ideal enjoining the confinement of women to home and church and moreover, that among the Italians, Greeks, and "Other Mediterraneans" this ideal either is more influential on the upper classes, or is experienced as a "luxury ideal"—not compulsory until one "can afford it."

Being "hard working" is a traditional virtue, sought after in Yugoslav wives in the country of origin (Tisay, 1985), and also lauded among the Greeks (Bottomley, 1979: 85–86) and hence perhaps influential. Placing a high value on diligence and on women's economic contribution is likely to encourage an instrumental attitude towards women's employment: Encouraging them to focus on homemaking when that affords the greatest economic contribution to the family, but to concentrate on market work among women who can get good jobs. Anthropological evidence suggests that, among Italians, diligence is not an especially sought-after virtue of women (Huber, 1977).

Possibilities that can safely be discounted include differences in local labor markets (since all these groups are heavily concentrated in the Sydney and Melbourne metropolitan areas, are not hugely segregated by neighborhood within these cities, and such industrial concentrations as exist offer more opportunities to the least educated).

Looking beyond the Mediterraneans, in comparison with the Eastern Europeans and the Northwestern Europeans, we find the Yugoslavs having the highest rates of women's labor force participation at each educational level, after adjusting for other compositional differences (Figure 4). Across most of the educational span, the Yugoslavs are quite close to the Eastern Europeans, diverging only at the higher levels of education. The Yugoslavs also stand out in having the strongest educational differentiation in participation, with the participation rates of the most and least educated differing by thirty points for the Yugoslavs and about twenty-five points for the other groups.

Effects of Life Course Stage

Yugoslav women's labor force participation depends strongly on their life course stage and family responsibilities (Figure 4). Among Yugoslav immigrants, 54 percent of young single women work, a figure that rises to 68 percent among young newlyweds. Participation drops to 50 percent with the birth of the children, and then rises to 55 percent and then 61 percent as the children reach school age and then begin to leave home. Participation drops drastically, by 24 points, to 37 percent in the middle fifties and it continues at that level to age 64. This drastic drop in later middle age has been noticed for long-established Anglo-Celtic Australians as well, and only a very small portion of it is explained by declines in health and by the achievement of a paid-off mortgage (Evans, 1988). Note that it may also reflect some of these women taking their turn at shouldering responsibility as deeply involved grandparents and some of them taking increasing responsibility for their and their husband's aging parents—a tradition of care very strong in traditional Yugoslav society that continues into modern times and forms an obligation enshrined in the Constitution of Yugoslavia during the communist period (Tisay, 1985: 103). This responsibility may be especially heavy because aging parents who do not speak English need extra help from their children (and strongly prefer help from children to help from strangers provided by social service agencies).

The life-course pattern of changes in labor force participation for Yugoslav women is broadly similar to the pattern for Italians, Greeks, and Other Mediterraneans (Figure 4). All four groups show a characteristic pattern of increase in women's labor force participation in the newlywed stage, probably associated with getting started on the purchase of a house. (Home ownership is very high in Australia.)

All these groups then experience a decline when the children are born, but these declines vary considerably in size, being about twenty points for the Yugoslavs, but only around ten points for the Italians and the Greeks. For all three of these groups, the drop in participation that occurs with the arrival of the children takes them back approximately to the level of participation that they experienced as young single women before marriage, so that half or more are still participating even when there are very young children in the home. Anecdotal evidence suggests that this is greatly facilitated by the baby-sitting by aunts and grandmothers, and that family care is seen by many of these immigrants as fine for babies and toddlers, in contrast to some other cultures which hold that babies and toddlers need to be almost entirely with their own mothers. (Daycare center care was cheap and fairly widely available in this period, before the marketization of the later 1980s and 1990s, but was not especially heavily used by employed women, and Mediterranean immigrant women were particularly loath to use it.)

The grandmothers contributing towards the family's financial advancement by undertaking extensive child care duties would be building on a long-established tradition of such care in all the major Yugoslav groups back in their home country

(Tisay, 1985: 80). Indeed the rapid expansion of industrial employment in the postwar period in Yugoslavia brought high wages, but such awkward hours and long commutes that many children lived with their grandparents during the week and with their parents on the weekends (Tisay, 1985: 88).

Thereafter the patterns diverge. When the children reach school age, Italian and "Other Mediterranean" women continue to participate at about the same rate. By contrast, Yugoslav women increase their participation at that stage, and Greek women very substantially raise their participation at that stage (so that Greek women at this stage actually reach their highest yet level of labor force participation). Clearly, the leading family strategies are different for these groups at this stage, with a substantial majority of the "Other Mediterraneans" opting for specialization as homemaker. The Italians are more nearly evenly divided, suggesting that the costs and benefits of market work and full-time homemaking are nearly evenly balanced for them. A small majority of Yugoslav women are in the market, suggesting more benefits than costs to market work, but not by a huge margin. But among the Greeks, a very substantial majority of women are in employment at this life cycle stage, suggesting that the benefits of employment are far outweighing the costs.

It is not immediately clear what lies behind these differences. The combination for the Italians of this flatness combined with the absence for them of an education effect suggests that the pull of a traditional sex role ideology may be very strong for them. That interpretation gains in plausibility from the fact that the "Other Mediterraneans" who mostly come from countries even more inclined to segregate women into the home also have low labor force participation in this stage. But it isn't an entirely satisfactory explanation because the Greeks who mostly came from the Greek Islands where gender roles are very traditional have such high labor force participation in this stage. Nor does it seem likely to be the differences in the availability of co-ethnic employment, because Italians, Greeks, and Yugoslavs all have thriving small business communities and social networks governing hiring into particular offices or occupations of large organizations. It is possible that the strong marriage market position of the Yugoslav women enables them to tilt their family strategies towards women's employment, but that doesn't help us account for the Greek women's very high participation.

Another, perhaps more compelling explanation may have to do with the wealth flows between generations (Caldwell, 1982). The parents of young couples throughout Yugoslavia have continued throughout the Communist period to make very substantial provision for the young couple's establishment of a home, including property transfers, household furnishings, and appliances (Tisay, 1985: 90). If this tradition continues in Australia, it may be that the wife's earnings are being saved towards buying and furnishing houses for their children upon marriage. If such a pattern of wealth accumulation and wealth flows also holds for the Greeks, but not the Italians whose maternal responsibilities are strongly focused on emotional rather than material provision (Huber, 1977) or the "Other Mediterraneans," that would account for the differences we observe at this stage of the life cycle.

Looking at things from a different angle, many of the jobs that these women hold are repetitive, closely supervised, and rather unpleasant, so it may be that some fraction of the women prefer to be home when that can be successfully incorporated into the family strategy. Why that should be more appealing to the Italians and the "Other Mediterraneans" than the Yugoslavs and the Greeks? We cannot be certain at this stage, but the Yugoslav and Greek emphasis on the wife's "hard working" economic contribution to family life may incline Yugoslav women to employment even in unpleasant jobs.

Despite the similarity of patterns of change in the early life course stages, the levels of participation are rather different at most life course stages. Among young single women, the participation rates range from a low of 47 percent for the Greeks to 53 percent for the Yugoslavs up to 60 percent for the Italians. Then all groups experience a short rise with marriage, and then a decline when the children begin to arrive. The size of the decline when the children come varies widely among the groups, from a high of eighteen points for the Yugoslavs, down to fourteen points for the "Other Mediterraneans" and to lows of about ten points for the Greeks and Italians. As their children grow, the participation of Yugoslav and Greek women rises again, but that of Italian and "Other Mediterranean" women continues flat or declines. Then, as the women move into their fifties and their children are grown, many leave the labor force in all groups, although Yugoslav women maintain the highest labor force participation rate at 37 percent. As we have mentioned before, these large drops remain almost entirely unexplained in the general population, but it seems likely that at least some women exit the labor force because they are taking their turns as baby-sitting grandmothers and some of them will be taking on responsibility for the care of their own and their husband's aging parents, responsibility which may weigh heavier than in the broader community when the parents dependency is increased because their English is very limited. In keeping with the wealth flows hypothesis mentioned earlier, it may also be that the incentive for Yugoslav women to work declines drastically once they have achieved the wealth accumulation target of establishing the children as newlyweds in their own homes.

The labor force participation patterns of women from the other groups, Eastern Europeans and Northwestern Europeans, are quite different, most notably in having a decline rather than a rise in participation right after marriage (Figure 4). All these groups begin in the middle range with 47–54 percent working. By contrast to all the Mediterranean groups, work participation among the Eastern and Northwestern Europeans drops after marriage, and again after the children begin to come. The onset of marriage and children makes a much bigger difference to the participation of Northwestern European women—the participation during the young single stage is thirty points higher than during the stage with young children in the home—than for the other groups. As the children grow, participation in all these groups rises again, but they maintain their different levels of participation— 35–39 percent for the Northwestern Europeans, 48–51 percent for the Eastern Europeans, and 55–60 percent for the Yugoslavs. As women move into their fifties, participation declines substantially in all three groups, with the Yugoslavs maintaining the highest level of participation at 37 percent, compared to 28 percent for the Eastern Europeans and 17 percent for the Northwestern Europeans. The fact that the Eastern European levels of participation would be lower by a very substantial margin than the Yugoslavs at all life cycle stages (if they had the same educational attainments and levels of English language fluency) is further evidence against the influence of a Pan-Slavic gender role ideology, and further evidence that research seeking substantively sensible groupings of birthplaces must not group the Yugoslav immigrants with the Eastern Europeans.

Discussion

The results show a wide range of labor force participation patterns among the birthplaces that form the Mediterranean group, a finding that buttresses earlier research suggesting that global gender ideologies in the country or region of origin are not necessarily highly pertinent to behavior in the country of destination. Although not strongly influenced at the "maxi-culture" level, we find strong suggestions of cultural effects at the "mini-culture" family level, in particular the results reveal that similar opportunities and constraints do not always have the same effects in the various groups. Patterns of specific values, and entrenched cultural practices noted by anthropologists are consistent with differences between origin countries that the regression analyses reveal in the census data.

All the Mediterranean groups seem to experience a division of labor by gender in the home that is felt as inevitable; the groups in which we observe high labor force participation propensities are those in which existing cultural practices and values enable women to undertake employment without disrupting the traditional division of labor in the home. Thus, for example, groups in which grandmothers traditionally play a large role in childrearing seem to integrate employment more readily into women's lives.

Many of the patterns described in the results section are consistent with the view that, in some groups, culturally patterned intergenerational wealth flows establish wealth accumulation goals that strongly encourage women to work until their children are married and established in a furnished house paid for by the parents (fully paid when possible, but failing that well started with a large down payment). The Yugoslavs and the Greeks, among whom this pattern is quite evident, have also been noted by anthropologists as placing a high value on women's diligence as providers for their families—a value that facilitates (or perhaps helps to generate) the practice of intergenerational wealth flows noted above.

Notes

Portions of this article were presented to a symposium on "Migrants from Yugoslavia in Australia" which was organized by Robert Miller and held at the Australian National University on 20–22 July 1988. We would like to thank participants in that symposium, many of whose comments led us in new directions. We would like to thank Jonathan Kelley, Gigi Santow, and Christabel M. Young for comments at various stages of this project.

1. Unfortunately, we have no way to measure immigrants' gender role ideologies with existing data. There are excellent, publicly available sample survey data on gender role ideologies (Evans, 1996 provides a guide to the relevant surveys), but the surveys have only been conducted in English and so would not be representative of the Yugoslav women.

2. The Australian Bureau of Statistics has used the terms "the Yugoslav-born" and "Yugoslav immigrants" both in collecting self-report data and in presenting census and survey data since 1921 (Bureau of Immigration Research, 1990), when immigrants from the region of south-eastern Europe, then constituting the Kingdom of the Serbs, Croats, and Slovenes, were separately enumerated for the first time. Since then, the Australian Census has used the same terminology, and so we follow their usage in this article for practical reasons, despite the complexity of the term and the diversity among the various included groups. Recently, the country of origin of immigrants from these same areas has been renamed "the former Yugoslavia" in the census. More substantively, all the "Yugoslav-born" immigrants that we analyze here, were born and raised in the geographical and political area that constituted the state of Yugoslavia. They were subject to many Yugoslavia-wide policies and programs, such the school system and the vocational training system, which we are interested in. Future research may be able to employ finer distinctions: For the very first time, the 1986 census asked a question about ancestry. If the Australian Bureau of Statistics were eventually to release unit-record data in sufficient detail, this could be used together with information on religion and language spoken at home more closely to approximate the various ethnic groups of the former Yugoslavia.

3. Many scholars have contributed to a rich literature on this topic. Evans (1996) gives a summary of it.

4. The main exception to the timing pattern described above is in the period immediately following the end of the war in 1945. Education had necessarily been extremely disorganized during the war, so cohorts whose schooling had been disturbed by the war were provided with accelerated schooling, passing 4 semesters, for example, during one student year. This provided many with education they would otherwise have missed, but widespread popular jokes suggest that the quality was not (or at least was perceived not to be) equivalent to regular schooling.

References

Appleyard, Reginald and Anna Amera. 1986. "Postwar Immigration of Greek Women to Australia: A Longitudinal Study." Pp. 215–228 in Rita James Simon and Caroline Brettell (eds.), *International Migration: The Female Experience*. Totowa, NJ: Rowman & Allanheld.

Australian Bureau of Statistics. 1983a. *Making Sense of Census '81* (Order No. 2140.0). Canberra: Australian Government Publishing Service.

———. 1983b. *Census '81: Language* (Order No. 2152.0). Canberra: Australian Government Publishing Service.

———. 1983b. *Census '81: Education, Qualifications* (Order No. 2149.0). Canberra: Australian Government Publishing Service.

Banovic, Branimir. 1990. "Potisni i privlacni faktori u iseljavanju iz Hrvatske u Australiju od konca 19. Stoljeca do recentnog vremena" [Push and Pull Factors in Emigration from Croatia to Australia from the End of the 19th Century to Present Times]. *Migracijske teme* 1:7–19.

Bhachu, Parminder. 1986. "Work, Dowry, and Marriage Among East African Sikh Women in the United Kingdom." Pp. 229–40 in Rita James Simon and Caroline Brettell (eds.), *International Migration: The Female Experience*. Totowa, NJ: Rowman & Allanheld.

Borrie, W.D. 1954. *Italians and Germans in Australia*. Melbourne: Cheshire.

Boyd, Monica. 1986. "Immigrant Women in Canada." Pp. 45–61 in Rita James Simon and Caroline Brettell (eds.), *International Migration: The Female Experience*. Totowa, NJ: Rowman & Allanheld.

Brettell, Caroline B. and Rita James Simon. 1986. "Immigrant Women: An Introduction." Pp. 3–20 in Rita James Simon and Caroline Brettell (eds.), *International Migration: The Female Experience*. Totowa, NJ: Rowman & Allanheld.

Bottomley, Gillian. 1979. *After the Odyssey: A Study of Greek Australians*. St. Lucia: University of Queensland Press.

Bureau of Immigration Research. 1990. *Community Profiles: Yugoslavia Born*. AGPS Cat No. 90-1187-3. Canberra: Australian Government Publishing Service.

Burnley, Ian H. 1982. "Lebanese Migration and Settlement in Sydney." *International Migration Review* 16: 102–32.

Caldwell, John C. 1982. *Theory of Fertility Decline*. London: Academic Press.

Caspari, Andrea and Wenona Giles. 1986. "Immigration Policy and the Employment of Portuguese Migrant Women in the UK and France: A Comparative Analysis." Pp. 152–77 in Rita James Simon and Caroline Brettell (eds.), *International Migration: The Female Experience*. Totowa, NJ: Rowman & Allanheld.

Charles, Maria. 1992. "Cross-National Variation in Occupational Sex Segregation." *American Sociological Review* 57(4): 483–502.

Cobb-Clark, Deborah and Marie D. Connolly. 1997. "The Worldwide Market for Skilled Migrants: Can Australia Compete?" *International Migration Review* 31: 670–93.

Cox, David. 1975. "The Role of Ethnic Groups in Migrant Welfare." In *Welfare of Migrants*, edited by Commission of Inquiry into Poverty, R.F. Henderson, Chair. Canberra: Australian Government Publishing Service.

Davis, F. James and Barbara Sherman Heyl. 1986. "Turkish Women and Guestworker Migration to West Germany." Pp. 178–96 in Rita James Simon and Caroline Brettell (eds.), *International Migration: The Female Experience*. Totowa, NJ: Rowman & Allanheld.

de Wenden, Catherine Wihtol, and Margo Corona DeLey. 1986. "French Immigration Policy Reform, 1981–1982, and the Female Migrant." Pp. 197–214 in Rita James Simon and Caroline Brettell (eds.), *International Migration: The Female Experience*. Totowa, NJ: Rowman & Allanheld.

Department of Immigration and Ethnic Affairs. 1995. "Migration from the Former Yugoslavia." *Fact Sheet* 1995–10:1. Available from: Public Affairs, Information and Publishing section, Department of Immigration and Ethnic Affairs, Canberra.

Donato, Katharine M. 1993. "Current Trends and Patterns of Female Migration." *International Migration Review* 27: 748–71.6

Esser, Hartmut. 1986. "Language, Intimacy, and Social Integration." *European Sociological Review* 2 (Dec.): 12–27.

Evans, M.D.R. 1996 "Women's labor force participation in Australia: Recent research findings." *Journal of the Australian Population Association 13* (May): 67–92.

———. 1995. "Norms on women's employment over the life course: Australia, 1989–1993." *WwA: Worldwide Attitudes* 1995-11–06:1–8.

———. 1990. "Labor Market Resources of Yugoslav Immigrants in Australia: Education, Work Experience, and Language Fluency." *Migracijske Teme* 6: 45–63.

———. 1988. "Working Wives in Australia: Influences of the Life Cycle, Education, and Feminist Ideology." Pp. 147–62 in *Australian Attitudes: Social and Political Analyses from the National Social Science Survey*, edited by J. Kelley and C. Bean. Melbourne: Allen & Unwin.

———. 1987. "Language skill, language usage, and opportunity: Immigrants in the Australian labor market." *Sociology: The Journal of the British Sociological Association 21* (May): 253–74.

Evans, M.D.R. 1986. "Sources of immigrants' language proficiency: Australian results with comparisons to the Federal Republic of Germany and the United States of America." *European Sociological Review* 2 (Dec.): 1–11.

———. 1984. "Immigrant Women in Australia: Resources, Family, and Work." *International Migration Review 18*: 1063–90.

Evans, M.D.R., and Jonathan Kelley. 1991. "Prejudice, Discrimination, and the Labor Market: Attainments of Immigrants in Australia." *American Journal of Sociology* 97:721–59.

———. 1986. "Immigrants' Work: Equality and Discrimination in the Australian Labor Market." *The Australian and New Zealand Journal of Sociology* 22:187–207.

Foner, Nancy. 1986. "Sex Roles and Sensibilities: Jamaican Women in New York and London." Pp. 133–51 in Rita James Simon and Caroline Brettell (eds.), *International Migration: The Female Experience*. Totowa, NJ: Rowman & Allanheld.

Gilbertson, Greta. 1995. "Women's Labor and Enclave Employment: The Case of Dominican and Cuban Women in New York City." *International Migration Review* 29: 657–70.

Gurak, Douglas and Mary M. Kritz. 1996. "Social Context, Household Composition, and Employment among Migrant and Non-migrant Dominican Women." *International Migration Review 30*: 399–422.

Haines, David. 1986. "Vietnamese Refugee Women in the U.S. Labor Force: Continuity or Change?" Pp. 62–75 in Rita James Simon and Caroline Brettell (eds.), *International Migration: The Female Experience*. Totowa, NJ: Rowman & Allanheld.

Houston, Marion F., Roger G. Kramer, and Joan Mackin Barrett. 1984. "Female Predominance of Immigration to the United States Since 1930." *International Migration Review 18*: 908–63.

Huber, Rina. 1977. *From Pasta to Pavlova: A Comparative Study of Italian Settlers in Sydney and Griffith*. St. Lucia: University of Queensland Press.

Jones, Frank. 1991. *Ancestry Groups in Australia: A Descriptive Overview*. Canberra: The Office of Multicultural Affairs, Department of the Prime Minister and Cabinet, and Wollongong: The Centre for Multicultural Studies, University of Wollongong.

Jupp, James. 1966. *Arrivals and Departures*. Melbourne: Cheshire-Longman.

Kelley, Jonathan. 1996. "Ethnic Sympathies and Politics In Australia, 1995." *WwA: Worldwide Attitudes* 1996–01–15:1–15

Kelley, Jonathan and Ian McAllister. 1984. "Immigrants, Socioeconomic Attainments and Politics in Australia." *British Journal of Sociology 35*: 387–405.

Kunz, Egon F. 1988. *Displaced Persons—Calwell's New Australians*. Canberra: Australian National University Press. Division of Pergamon Press Australia. Leichhardt: Pluto Press Australia.

Lamphere, Louise. 1986. "Working Women and Family Strategies: Portuguese and Columbian Women

in a New England Community." Pp. 266–83 in Rita James Simon and Caroline Brettell (eds.), *International Migration: The Female Experience*. Totowa, NJ: Rowman & Allanheld.
Landale, Nancy S. and Nimfa B. Ogena. 1995. "Migration and Union Dissolution Among Puerto Rican Women." *International Migration Review* 29: 671–92.
Manderson, Lenore and Christine Inglis. 1984. "Turkish Migration and Workforce Participation in Sydney, Australia." *International Migration Review* 18: 258–75.
Martin, Jean. 1975. "Family and Bureaucracy." In *Greeks in Australia*, edited by Charles A. Price. Canberra: Australian National University Press.
Martin, Jean. 1965. *Refugee Settlers—A Study of Displaced Persons in Australia*. Canberra: The Australian National University.
McAllister, Ian and Jonathan Kelley. 1983. "Contextual Characteristics of Australian Federal Electorates." *Australia and New Zealand Journal of Sociology* 19:113–35.
McArthur, Ian A. 1983. "The settlement history and experiences of Yugoslav and other European immigrants in Australian multicultural society." In *Australian Papers*, edited by Mirko Jurak, 13–21. Ljubljana: Edvard Kardelj University of Ljubljana.
McManus, W., W. Gould, and F. Welch. 1983. "Earnings of Hispanic men: The role of English language proficiency." *Journal of Labor Economics* 1:101–31.
Mirdal, Gretty M. 1984. "Stress and Distress in Migration: Problems and Resources of Turkish Women in Denmark." *International Migration Review* 18 : 984–1003.
Muenscher, Alice. 1984. "The Working Routine of Turkish Women in the Federal Republic of Germany." *International Migration Review* 18: 1230–46.
Morokvasic, Mirjana. 1988. "Jugoslavenke: Emigriranje, I Sta Potom?" [Yugoslav Women: Emigration and Afterward?]. *Migracijske teme* 4:477–95.
———. 1984. "Birds of Passage Are Also Women." *International Migration Review* 18: 886–907.
———. 1982. "Zene iz Jugoslavije na radu u Evropi. Analiticki okvir za tumacenje promijena" [Women from Yugoslavia at Work throughout Europe: An Analytical Framework for the Interpretation of Change]. *Socioloski Pregled.* 16(4):21–33.
———. 1979. "Jugoslavenke-migranti o sebi" [Yugoslav Women Migrants about Themselves]. *Sociologija Sela.* 17: 102–12.
———. 1972. "Yugoslav 'Temporary' Migrant Workers, Their Class Consciousness and Class Struggle of the Working Class in the Countries of Immigration." *Sociologija.* 15 (2).273–88.
Organisation for Economic Co-operation and Development (OECD). 1981. *Reviews of National Policies for Education—Yugoslavia*. Paris: OECD.
———. 1973. *Classification of Educational Systems—Canada, Greece, Yugoslavia*. Paris: OECD.
Pessar, Patricia. 1986. "The Linkage Between the Household and the Workplace in the Experience of Dominican Immigrant Women to the United States." *International Migration Review* 18: 1188–1211.
Price, C.A. 1963. *Southern Europeans in Australia*. London: Oxford University Press.
Prieto, Yolanda. 1986. "Cuban Women and Work in the United States: A New Jersey Case Study." Pp. 95–112 in Rita James Simon and Caroline Brettell (eds.), *International Migration: The Female Experience*. Totowa, NJ: Rowman & Allanheld.
Radcliffe, Sarah A. 1990. "Between Hearth and Labor Market: The Recruitment of Peasant Women in the Andes." *International Migration Review* 24: 229–49.
Savezni Zavod za Statistiku (SGJ-84). 1984. *Statisticki godisnjak Jugoslavije* [Annual Statistics of Yugoslavia]. Beograd: Savezni zavod za statistiku.
———(SGJ-74). 1974. *Statisticki godisnjak Jugoslavije* [Annual Statistics of Yugoslavia]. Pp. 105–09. Beograd: Savezni zavod za statistiku.
Schmitter, Barbara E. 1983. "Immigrant Minorities in West Germany: Some Theoretical Concerns." *Ethnic and Racial Studies* 6: 308–19.
Simon, Rita James and Margo Corona DeLey. 1986. "Undocumented Mexican Women: Their Work and

Personal Experiences." Pp. 113–32 in Rita James Simon and Caroline Brettell (eds.), *International Migration: The Female Experience*. Totowa, NJ: Rowman & Allanheld.

Simon, Rita James, Louise Shelley, and Paul Schneiderman. 1986. "The Social and Economic Adjustment of Soviet Jewish Women in the United States." Pp. 76–94 in Rita James Simon and Caroline Brettell (eds.), *International Migration: The Female Experience*. Totowa, NJ: Rowman & Allanheld.

Smolicz, J.J. and R. Wiseman. 1971. "European Immigrants and Their Children." *Quarterly Review of Australian Education* 1971:3.

Stephen, Elizabeth Hervey and Frank D. Bean. 1992. "Assimilation, Disruption, and the Fertility of Mexican-Origin Women in the United States." *International Migration Review* 26: 67–88.

Stevens, G. And G. Swicegood. 1987. "The Linguistic Context of Ethnic Endogamy." *American Sociological Review* 52:73–82.

Stier, Haya and Marta Tienda. 1992. "Family, Work, and Women: The Labor Supply of Hispanic Immigrant Wives." *International Migration Review* 26: 1291–1313.

Sussex Roland and Jerzy Zubrzycki. 1985. *Polish People and Culture in Australia. Departmental Monograph*. Canberra: Department of Demography, Australian National University.

Tienda, M., and L. Neidert. 1984. "Language, Education, and the Socioeconomic Achievement of Hispanic Origin Men." *Social Science Quarterly* 65:519–36.

Tkalcevic, Mato. 1980a. *Croats in Australian Society*. Melbourne: Melbourne City Government Printer.

———. 1980b. *Serbs in Australian Society*. Melbourne: Melbourne City Government Printer.

Trlin, Andrija. 1978. "Jugoslaveni na Novom Zelandu" [Yugoslavs in New Zealand]. Pp. 441–71 in *Iseljenistvo Naroda I Narodnosti Jugoslavije*. Zagreb: Zamin.

Tsounis, Michael P. 1975. "Greek Ethnic Schools." *International Migration Review* 9 (Fall): 345–359.

Tyree, Andrea and Katherine Donato. 1986. "A Demographic Overview of the International Migration of Women." Pp. 21–44 in Rita James Simon and Caroline Brettell (eds.), *International Migration: The Female Experience*. Totowa, NJ: Rowman & Allanheld.

Ware, Helen. 1974. "Fertility and Work Force Participation: The Experience of Melbourne Wives." *Population Studies* 30: 413–27.

Young, Christabel M. 1990. "The changing demographic and family relationships between Yugoslavs in Australia." *Migracijske Teme* 6:95–114.

Yu-Survey. 1987. "Classes and Class Structure of Yugoslav Society." Data obtained from Fakulteta za druzbene vede Ljubljana.

Zivkovic, Ilija, Zeljka Sporer, and Dusko Sekulic. 1995. *Asimilacija I Identitet, Studija O Hrvatskom Iseljenistvu U SAD I Kanadi* [Assimilation and Identity, A Study of Croats in the U.S. and Canada]. Zagreb: Skolska Knjiga

Zubrzycki, Jerzy. 1964. *Settlers of the La Trobe Valley*. Canberra: Australian National University Press.

APPENDIX 1

Regression models of occupational status, estimated for women labour force participation. The table provides metric regression coefficients; standard errors are shown in parentheses.

The model is estimated separately for each birthplace group.

Variable (units)	Yugoslavia	Italy	Greece	Other Mediterranean	Eastern Europe	North-Western Europe
1. Education (years)	0.036	-0.002	0.014	0.028	0.032	0.023
	(0.017)	(0.016)	(0.015)	(0.009)	(0.009)	(0.009)
2. Education squared (years–10)	0.002	-0.000	0.003	0.003	-0.001	0.001
	(0.002)	(0.002)	(0.002)	(0.001)	(0.001)	(0.002)
3. Educated in Australia (0 or 1)	-0.681	-0.643	-0.304	0.271	0.589	0.090
	(0.400)	(0.002)	(0.343)	(0.276)	(0.371)	(0.233)
4. Australian education (interaction of #1 and #3)	0.079	0.055	0.041	-0.028	-0.066	-0.017
	(0.041)	(0.026)	(0.035)	(0.027)	(0.035)	(0.023)
5. Australian education squared (interaction of #2 and #3)	-0.027	0.004	-0.008	0.005	0.011	0.007
	(0.012)	(0.006)	(0.006)	(0.006)	(0.006)	(0.004)
6. Trade qualification (0 or 1)	0.036	-0.015	-0.271	0.182	0.030	0.083
	(0.112)	(0.109)	(0.191)	(0.152)	(0.114)	(0.089)
7. Age 16 to 29 (0 or 1)2	0.309	0.435	0.387	0.376	0.232	0.275
	(0.1105)	(0.074)	(0.106)	(0.069)	(0.086)	(0.070)
8. Age 30 to 44 (0 or 1)2	0.360	0.399	0.529	0.366	0.032	0.392
	(0.095)	(0.059)	(0.087)	(0.068)	(0.072)	(0.034)

9. Age 45 to 54 (0 or 1)2	0.233 (0.093)	0.037 (0.051)	0.462 (0.086)	0.216 (0.069)	0.288 (0.059)	0.175 (0.054)
10. Married (0 or 1)	0.142 (0.063)	0.043 (0.047)	0.132 (0.068)	-0.069 (0.045)	-0.011 (0.049)	-0.059 (0.034)
11. Children present (0 or 1)	-0.175 (0.057)	-0.088 (0.040)	-0.106 (0.058)	-0.158 (0.040)	-0.070 (0.054)	-0.191 (0.041)
12. Adults other than spouse present	-0.011 (0.052)	0.098 (0.034)	-0.049 (0.046)	0.064 (0.037)	0.086 (0.045)	0.112 (0.038)
13. Australian citizen (0 or 1)	-0.041 (0.055)	0.026 (0.035)	0.049 (0.057)	-0.005 (0.035)	-0.023 (0.069)	0.019 (0.040)
14. Rural (0 or 1)3	-0.014 (0.111)	0.199 (0.067)	0.308 (0.124)	0.173 (0.091)	-0.143 (0.088)	-0.061 (0.055)
15. Small urban (0 or 1)3	-0.225 (0.117)	-0.019 (0.060)	0.098 (0.125)	-0.149 (0.078)	-0.119 (0.076)	-0.018 (0.047)
16. Speaks English very well (0 or 1)4	0.043 (0.096)	0.043 (0.066)	0.122 (0.128)	0.054 (0.053)	-0.060 (0.057)	-0.042 (0.038)
17. Speaks English well (0 or 1)4	0.540 (0.093)	-0.023 (0.069)	0.014 (0.125)	0.035 (0.058)	0.062 (0.066)	-0.099 (0.051)
18. Speaks English poorly (0 or 1)4	0.060 (0.10)	-0.116 (0.071)	-0.031 (0.062)	0.127 (0.113)	-0.153 (0.083)	-0.339 (0.108)
Constant	-0.078	0.189	-0.015	0.047	0.050	0.174
R-squared	0.110	0.120	0.110	0.190	0.153	0.124

Source: Australian Census 1981, 1% Public Use Sample.

4

The Family Investment Model: A Formalization and Review of Evidence from Across Immigrant Groups

Harriet Orcutt Duleep

Abstract: In what has become known as the Family Investment Model, several scholars have hypothesized that financing investment in host-country skills by immigrant husbands is a factor affecting the labor force decisions and human capital investment of immigrant married women. This paper reviews empirical evidence from one stream of research on the family investment model. I also formalize the family investment hypothesis and incorporate it into a traditional model of female labor force participation. The formalization provides a simple way to conceptualize the family investment hypothesis. Including it in a conventional model of female labor force participation emphasizes that the effect of a family investment strategy on the work behavior of immigrant women must be understood in the context of a woman's level of host country-specific skills, as well as all other factors generally included in models of female labor force participation.

Background

The term "family investment hypothesis" was first coined in a paper by Duleep and Sanders (1988, 1993) that sought to explain large differences across immigrant groups in the propensity of married immigrant women to work.[1] Controlling for factors commonly included in female labor force participation estimations, groups with the largest expected growth in immigrant men's earnings were found to have the highest labor force participation of married immigrant women, while groups with the smallest expected growth in men's earnings had the lowest female participation rates. The pattern suggested that financing their husbands' investments in host-country human capital is an important factor affecting the decision of married immigrant women to work.

Two streams of research have provided evidence of the Family Investment Model as a factor affecting the labor force decisions of immigrant married women.

One approach, exemplified in the work of Long (1980) and Beach and Worswick (1993), compares the patterns of work and earnings behavior of immigrant married women (relative to native-born immigrant women) with the patterns of work and earnings behavior of immigrant men (relative to native-born men). In an analysis of white immigrant women using 1970 U.S. census data, Long (1980, p. 628) observed that the earnings of married immigrant women—initially greater than those of native-born women—decreased with years in the United States. The estimated earnings decrease prompted Long to speculate that "wives in immigrant families that have recently entered the United States may have to work to help finance their husbands' initial investments in schooling or job skills required in U.S. labor markets. Later, as earnings of their spouses rise with time in the United States, foreign-born wives reallocate their time from market to nonmarket activities and their earnings are reduced."[2] Using Canadian data, Beach and Worswick (1993) found the initially higher hours worked of recently arrived immigrant women, versus Canadian-born women, decreased with years since migration. Beach and Worswick also found flatter wage profiles for immigrant married women than for native-born married women. They suggested that underlying the flatter wage profiles for immigrant married women was a family investment strategy in which immigrant women forego investment by pursuing work options that are initially higher paying, but offer less opportunity for career investment so as to finance their husbands' investment in host-country skills.

The other stream of empirical research providing evidence of the family investment model has used variation across immigrant groups in the likely extent to which immigrant husbands invest in host-country human capital, while holding constant a woman's own level of host-country skills as measured, for instance, by her own years since migration and level of host-country language proficiency. This is the approach that is used in Duleep and Sanders (1993) and Duleep, Regets, and Sanders (1998), whose work is reviewed below. In a study of Canadian data, Baker and Benjamin (1997) also provide across-group evidence on the existence of the

The Family Investment Model

family investment model by comparing the over time profiles of hours worked and wages of immigrant women married to foreign-born men versus immigrant women married to Canadian-born men. Consistent with the family investment hypothesis, they find that immigrant women married to foreign-born men work more upon arrival and have flatter wage profiles and a lower propensity to invest in schooling than do immigrant women married to native-born men.

In the next section, I formalize the family investment hypothesis and incorporate it into a traditional model of female labor force participation. Following this, Section III reviews analyses from Duleep and Sanders (1993) and Duleep, Regets, and Sanders (1998), which provide evidence of the family investment model from across immigrant groups. The paper concludes with directions for further research.

Incorporating the Family Investment Hypothesis into a Traditional Model of Female Labor Force Participation

The traditional model of female labor force participation posits that a woman works if her market wage (W_M)—the wage she can receive if she works, which is a function of factors such as education—exceeds her reservation wage (W_R)—the wage she must receive in order to work, which is a function of factors such as whether there is a baby in the home and the husband's income. Or, a woman works if $W_M > W_R$ at zero hours of work.

To the above model, the following concept may be added: *Family members can increase the future labor income of the family by either directly pursuing activities that increase their own skill levels, or indirectly, by engaging in activities that finance, or otherwise support, the investment activities of other family members.*

This line of thought leads to the following model reformulation of a woman's decision to work: A woman works if $W_M + E(q) > W_R$, where q is the return in terms of the change in the net present value of family income that results from the increased investment in U.S.-specific human capital by the husband which is financed by the wife working.

Specifically, let y_I be the husband's earnings stream that results from investment financed by the wife working and let y_{NI} be the husband's earnings stream that would exist if the wife did not work; r is the market interest rate and p_t is the probability that the family is in the United States in time period t (the probability that they have not emigrated). Then the expected family investment return to the wife working can be expressed as

$$E(q)=\Sigma\ 1/(1+r)^{t-1} \bullet (y_{I,t} - y_{NI,t}) \bullet p_t$$

Thus, the return to the wife-financed investment will depend on the net effect of the investment on the husband's earnings, and how long the family stays in the United States.

In this model, the price (or opportunity cost) of the wife's nonmarket activity is not only her market wage, as in the traditional model of a woman's decision to work, but also the lost investment in the husband's human capital and resulting gain in future family income that would be financed if she worked: the price of non-market activity includes the return to work in terms of the investment it finances. In this way, married immigrant women who are quite similar in terms of factors such as their child status, level of schooling, English proficiency, time in the United States, and husband's income, could be remarkably different in their labor force participation.

Empirically, we would expect that, controlling for factors that affect a woman's market wage and reservation wage, the higher the return to financing her husband's investment in U.S.-specific skills, the more likely she will work. This implies that across immigrant groups, the greater the average return to investment in U.S.-specific human capital for immigrant men, the greater the propensity should be for married immigrant women in these groups to work. Evidence consistent with this hypothesis from two studies—Duleep and Sanders (1993) and Duleep, Regets, and Sanders (1998)—is reviewed below using 1980 and 1990 census data, respectively.[3] Both studies use cross-group variations in the labor force participation of married immigrant women and focus on Asian immigrant groups relative to European and Canadian immigrants. Given that the source-country skills transferability to the United States of immigrant men in these groups varies, as evidenced by the divergence in their education-adjusted entry earnings, analysis of the labor force behavior of married women in these groups provides an interesting arena for testing expectations associated with the family investment model.[4]

Empirical Evidence of the Family Investment Model from Across Immigrant Groups

In both the analysis of 1980 census data, reflecting the work of Duleep and Sanders (1993), and in the analysis of 1990 census data, reflecting the work of Duleep, Regets, and Sanders (1998), we first estimate group effects on the propensity to work of married immigrant women adjusting for relevant personal characteristics. The labor force participation estimates for women, in both analyses, reflect

The Family Investment Model

the following conventional structural model of a woman's decision to work, modified to include concerns relevant to immigrants.

W_M=f(Level of Human Capital, U.S.-Specific Skills, Market Conditions)
W_R=f(the Cost of Working, the Need to Work)
A woman works if $W_M > W_R$ at zero hours of work.

In this model, a woman's market wage, W_M, is affected by two classes of factors: the skills she possesses and the employment opportunities in the area in which she lives. General skill levels are measured in our model by a woman's years of schooling (a two-part spline breaking at sixteen years of schooling), her potential years of work experience (approximated by age minus years of schooling minus 6), experience squared, and education x experience. Given the paucity of work history information on the census, we added two variables to our model to better approximate the extent of a woman's work experience—age at first marriage and the number of children ever born: the younger the age at first marriage and the greater the number of children ever born, the fewer the likely years of work experience. Of relevance to immigrant women, we measured U.S.-specific skills by years since migration, English proficiency, and whether a woman first migrated alone or as a tied mover.[5] To adjust for employment demand conditions, six regions (including California and Hawaii) and a set of metropolitan status codes were included. As health can potentially affect both the reservation wage and market wage, we controlled for health conditions by including a variable measuring the presence of a work-inhibiting disability.

The reservation wage, W_R, is also affected by two sets of factors: the cost of a woman working and the financial need for her to work. Variables that we used to capture the monetary and psychic costs of a woman working outside the home included the number and age structure of the family's children as well as the presence of live-in adult relatives.[6] Young children, particularly the presence of a baby, are believed to raise the costs of a woman working outside the home. To capture the potentially nonlinear effect of children's ages on the cost of immigrant women working outside the home we included a set of categorical variables that equal 1 when the family's youngest child is less than one, one to five, six to eleven, or twelve to seventeen years old. Since older children may help with the care of younger children, our model also included whether children twelve years of age and older are present in homes with children under twelve years of age. To control for financial need, we included variables measuring the availability and certainty of sources of income other than the wife's potential income from work. In particular, we included the husband's earnings, whether he had ever been unemployed in the preceding year, and a measure of the family's level of assets.

To examine whether group effects on the propensity to work of immigrant married women persist once personal characteristics are taken into account, we estimated a reduced-form labor supply model that included the explanatory variables discussed above. The estimating model took the following form:

$$P(w) = f(X, Z_1, Z_2, G)$$

where $P(w)$ is the probability that a woman works in paid employment (the dummy variable w, whether works, equals 1 if a woman reports positive earnings, positive weeks worked, and positive hours per week worked for the year preceding the census); X refers to variables, such as the presence of young children in the home and the husband's income, that are believed to affect a woman's reservation wage; Z_1 refers to general characteristics that affect a woman's market wage, such as her level of schooling and where she lives; Z_2 refers to a woman's level of U.S.-specific skills, as measured by her year of immigration and her proficiency in English, and G refers to a set of 0–1 group variables—Japanese, Chinese, Filipino, Korean, and Indian, with married immigrant women from Europe and Canada forming the reference group.

We then related the estimated group effects on immigrant women's propensity to work from the reduced-form labor supply model to estimates of the average return to investment in U.S.-specific capital by the husbands in each group. Details specific to the analyses of the 1980 and 1990 census data and the findings from these analyses are described below.

Group Effects on Immigrant Women's Propensity to Work and the Family Investment Return to the Wife Working: Evidence from the 1980 Census

According to the family investment model, the higher the return to investment in U.S.-specific skills by the husband, the more likely that married immigrant women will work to support that investment. Hence, across groups, the greater the average return to investment in U.S.-specific human capital for immigrant men, the greater the propensity should be for married immigrant women in those groups to work.

To measure the return to investment in husband's U.S. human capital, we would like to measure for each immigrant husband i the difference between the husband's full potential earnings, $y_{fpi}(h)$, if he were fully vested with U.S.-specific

The Family Investment Model

skills, and $y_{cpi}(h)$, his current potential income, if he fully applied his current set of skills. Neither is observed. As a proxy for the return to investment in U.S.-specific human capital for immigrant husbands, we used the difference between the earnings of recent immigrant men, and the earnings of otherwise statistically similar men in the same immigrant group who had been in the United States for thirty years or more.

The coefficients shown in Table 1 are derived from group-specific regression estimations for immigrant men in which the dependent variable is the natural logarithm of earnings and the explanatory variables include education, work experience, region, location, marital status, and disability. The first row shows the approximate proportionate difference between the earnings of men who immigrated during 1975–80 and the earnings of "otherwise similar" immigrants in the same group who have lived in the United States thirty years or more. Viewed from a human capital perspective, the growth in earnings with time in the United States, holding schooling and years of experience constant, likely reflects investment in human capital specific to the U.S. labor market, such as the development of job contacts, job training, and English proficiency. Assuming that the most recent immigrants could attain the earnings of earlier immigrants with investment in U.S. human capital, the difference between their earnings and those of the earlier cohort is one potential measure of the average return to investment in U.S.-specific human capital for each immigrant group. The larger the negative coefficient, the larger the likely return to investment in U.S.-specific human capital by immigrant men.

The first row in Table 1 could be interpreted as the potential return to investment in U.S.-specific capital for recently arrived immigrant men in each immigrant group shown. According to this measure, the return to investment in U.S.-specific human capital is largest for Filipino, Chinese, and Korean men, somewhat smaller but still large for Indian men, much smaller for European and Canadian immigrant men, and smallest for Japanese immigrant men.[7]

According to the Family Investment Hypothesis, we would expect that there would be a positive association across immigrant groups between the average return to U.S. human capital investment by immigrant husbands and the propensity of married immigrant women to work, controlling for factors that affect a woman's market and reservation wage. The coefficients on the group variables from the reduced-form women's labor supply model described above are shown in Table 2. These coefficients measure the effect on the labor force participation of married immigrant women of belonging to a particular immigrant group, adjusting for all the other variables in the model. Since European and Canadian immigrant women form the reference group, a positive coefficient implies that women in a specific

TABLE 1
Percentage Impact of Years since Migration on Annual Earnings of Immigrant Men Ages 25–64, by Group, 1980

Years Since Migration	Filipino	Chinese	Korean	Indian	Japanese	European/ Canadian
0- 5	-.74*	-.69*	-.76*	-.55*	-.09	-.27*
6-10	-.38*	-.36*	-.37	-.19	-.17	-.10
11-15	-.24*	-.25*	-.22	-.02	-.07	-.04
16-20	-.14*	-.14*	-.12	.04	-.07	-.07
21-30	-.11	-.12*	-.19	.04	-.12	.06

Notes: The results presented above indicate the approximate proportionate amount by which the earnings of immigrant men, who immigrated during a specified time period, differ from the earnings of immigrants in the same group who have resided in the U.S. thirty years or more. The coefficients are derived from group-specific regression estimations in which the dependent variable is the natural logarithm of earnings and the explanatory variables include education, work experience, region, location, marital status, and disability. *Significant at .05 level.

group are more likely to work than European and Canadian women, holding other variables constant.

Comparing the estimates in the first row of Table 1 with the adjusted source-country effects on the propensity of married immigrant women to work, shown in Table 2, reveals that the groups with the largest expected growth in immigrant men's earnings (Filipinos, Koreans, and Chinese, followed by Indians) are those with the highest unexplained labor force participation of married women; the groups with the smallest expected growth in men's earnings (the Japanese and the benchmark group of Europeans and Canadians) are those with the lowest female participation rates.

The pattern suggests a family investment strategy in which wives are more likely to work, ceteris paribus, the higher the return from their working in terms of the husband's investment in U.S.-specific human capital that their work finances. The higher the potential return to investments in U.S.-specific human capital by their husband, the higher the return to their financing that investment, and the more likely they are to work.

TABLE 2
Group Effects on the Labor Force Participation of Married Immigrant Women from a Pooled Logit Model

Immigrant Group	Estimated Logit Coefficients
Japanese	-.8459
Indian	.3077
Korean	.5103
Chinese	.5533
Filipino	1.5874
−2 Equation Log Likelihood	46299.099
Sample size	12,446

Notes: Model includes explanatory variables for a woman's child status, general skills, U.S. specific skills, and husband's income and unemployment experience: Married immigrant women ages 25–64. Other variables included in the estimation are location, whether married prior to migration, and the presence of adult relatives in the home. Based on asymptotic t-statistics, all of the estimated group effects shown above are statistically significant at the .05 level. For a more complete discussion of the model, refer to Duleep, Regets, and Sanders (1998).
Source: Estimates based on 1980 Census 5% Public Use "A" Sample.

Group Effects on Immigrant Women's Propensity to Work and the Family Investment Return to the Wife Working: Evidence from the 1990 Census

Further evidence from across immigrant groups of the family investment model using data from the 1990 census comes from a comparative study of Asian and European immigrants by Duleep, Regets, and Sanders (1998). Controlling for the above-described variables affecting an immigrant woman's reservation and market wage, we included in the women's labor force participation model categorical variables for the groups that dominated post-1965 nonrefugee Asian immigration as well as four reference groups of Europeans and Canadians. Separate estimations were run for each year-of-immigration category shown in Table 3.

The first column of each year-since-migration category in Table 3 shows the estimated logit coefficients on the group variables of the women's labor force participation model for each year-of-immigration cohort estimation. The corresponding marginal effects, evaluated at each cohort's pooled mean, are shown in the second column.[8] The group effects are relative to the reference group, married women from non-English-speaking Western Europe, and are measured adjusting for a woman's general skills, her U.S.-specific skills, and variables that are believed

TABLE 3
Relationship between Country-of-origin Effects on the Propensity of Married Immigrant Women, Aged 25–64, to Work and Each Group's Average Expected Return to the Husband's Investment in U.S.-Specific Skills.

Year of Immigration

Group	1985-1990 logit coef.	1985-1990 mar. effect	1985-1990 y_{fp}-y_c	1982-84 logit coef.	1982-84 mar. effect	1982-84 y_{fp}-y_c	1980-81 logit coef.	1980-81 mar. effect	1980-81 y_{fp}-y_c	1975-79 logit coef.	1975-79 mar. effect	1975-79 y_{fp}-y_c	1970-74 logit coef.	1970-74 mar. effect	1970-74 y_{fp}-y_c
Japanese	-1.536 (9)	-.384	-$17,833 (9)	-.786 (9)	-.170	-$18,186 (7)	-.2423 (9)	-.049	-$4,279 (7)	.0046 (7)	.0086	$3,625 (5)	.0025 (7)	.0005	$1,160 (4)
Indian	.522 (4)	.130	$20,186 (4)	.275 (4)	.060	$12,511 (4)	.291 (4)	.059	$7,569 (5)	.3099 (5)	.058	$1,724 (6)	.475 (4)	.092	-$3,789 (6)
Korean	.573 (3)	.143	$22,519 (3)	.226 (5)	.049	$13,653 (3)	.271 (5)	.055	$12,259 (2)	.5533 (3)	.104	$10,340 (2)	.599 (3)	.116	$1,832 (3)
Chinese	.790 (2)	.198	$25,743 (2)	.449 (3)	.097	$14,373 (2)	.784 (2)	.159	$11,930 (3)	.626 (2)	.118	$9,406 (3)	.939 (2)	.182	$4,256 (2)
Filipino	1.62 (1)	.405	$27,751 (1)	1.363 (1)	.295	$19,945 (1)	2.242 (1)	.455	$16,440 (1)	1.909 (1)	.359	$13,780 (1)	1.680 (1)	.325	$12,551 (1)
Canadian	.199 (7)	.050	-$9,332 (7)	-.135 (8)	-.029	-$22,045 (9)	.048 (7)	.0097	-$22,045 (9)	-.082 (9)	-.015	-$19,048 (8)	-.225 (9)	-.043	-$20,992 (9)
East European	.331 (5)	.083	$19,522 (5)	.556 (2)	.120	$9,962 (5)	.619 (3)	.126	$8,748 (4)	.517 (4)	.097	$7,753 (4)	.438 (6)	.085	$449 (5)
Eng. West European	.230 (6)	.058	-$11,260 (8)	-.056 (7)	-.012	-$18,827 (8)	.1798 (6)	.036	-$14,385 (8)	.1949 (6)	.037	-$19,195 (9)	.475 (5)	.092	-$14,304 (8)
Other W. European	0 (8)	0	-$4,420 (6)	0 (6)	0	-$7,146 (6)	0 (8)	0	-$3,576 (6)	0 (8)	0	-$3,402 (7)	0 (8)	0	-$3,929 (7)

Notes: Controls for education, experience, location, child status, proficiency in English, assets, husband's earnings and husband's unemployment. Estimates are relative to immigrant married women from non-English Speaking Western Europe. Relative ranking in parentheses.
Source: Duleep, Regets, and Sanders (1998). Estimates based on the 5% Public Use Sample of the 1990 Census of Population.

The Family Investment Model

to affect her reservation wage, such as the number and ages of children, the husband's income, his unemployment experience, the family's level of assets, and all of the other variables that have been previously discussed. The group of non-English West Europeans has the value of zero since this group is the reference group in the estimation.

According to the family investment model, the higher the return to investment in U.S.-specific skills by the husband, the more likely that married immigrant women will work to support that investment. Hence, across groups, the greater the average return to investment in U.S.-specific human capital for immigrant men, the greater the propensity should be for married immigrant women in those groups to work.

In our analysis of 1980 census data, we measured the return to investment in U.S.-specific human capital for immigrant husbands—the difference between the husband's full potential earnings, $y_{fpi}(h)$, if he were fully vested with U.S.-specific skills, and $y_{cpi}(h)$, his current potential income if he fully applied his current set of skills—by the estimated difference between the earnings of recent immigrant men and the earnings of immigrant men in the same group who had been in the United States for thirty years or more. A different measure was used in our 1990 analysis. As a proxy for $y_{fpi}(h)$, we used the earnings of U.S.-born men with comparable characteristics; as a proxy for $y_{cpi}(h)$, we used the immigrant husband's current earnings.[9] The difference between these two variables represents the difference between what each husband in our sample is currently earning, and what he could earn with U.S.-specific skills—the greater the gap, the greater the return to investment in U.S.-specific skills.[10] The average of the individual differences for each group/year-of-migration cohort provides an estimate of the average return to investment in U.S.-specific skills for married men in each source-country/year-of-immigration cohort. These averages are shown in the third column of each year-since-migration category in Table 3.

As we move across the different year-of-entry cohorts in Table 3, we see that the return to investment in U.S.-specific skills by immigrant men, as measured by the difference in earnings between immigrants and their U.S.-born counterparts, decreases for all groups with initially low entry earnings. With the exception of the Japanese, Asian immigrant men who have been in the United States for some years narrow the earnings gap considerably. For example, immigrant husbands who had arrived from China between 1985 and 1990 earned on average $25,743 less than comparably skilled U.S.-born non-Hispanic white Americans in 1990, while those who immigrated between 1970 and 1974 earned $4,256 less in 1990 than their U.S.-born counterparts. Korean husbands who immigrated between 1985 and 1990 earned $22,519 less than their U.S.-born statistical counterparts, while those who immigrated between 1970 and 1974 earned $1,832 less. For Asian Indian husbands, the U.S.-born/immigrant gap decreases from a positive $20,186 to a negative $3,789.

According to the family investment hypothesis, the greater the return if the husband invests in U.S.-specific skills, the higher the propensity for the wife to work in order to finance this investment. As such, we would expect a positive correlation between each cohort's group effects in the women's labor force participation model and the group/cohort-specific measure of the average gap between the husband's current earnings and his full potential earnings if vested with U.S.-specific skills.

For each year-of-immigration category in Table 3, the relative ranking of the magnitude of each group effect on the propensity to work of immigrant married women is shown in parentheses under the logit coefficient in the first column. In the third column, the relative ranking of the average return to investment for immigrant husbands is also shown in parentheses. Comparing the first and third columns, we see that there is a close correspondence, for all the cohorts, between the ranking in terms of the size of the potential return to U.S.-specific investment by the husband, and the size of the group effect on the probability that a woman works outside the home. Indeed, for the most recent cohort of immigrant women, the correspondence between the two rankings is perfect with one exception.

Figure 1 graphs the relationship shown in the second and third columns of Table 1 for the cohort of married immigrant women who immigrated in 1985–90. The y axis is the marginal group effect on the wife working, while the x axis is the potential return to investment by their husbands, standardized to a 0 to 100 scale.[11] This graph demonstrates the striking relationship between the estimated average return to investment in U.S.-specific skills by the husband for each group and the wife's propensity to work.[12] It also highlights two extreme values: the point for Japan is much lower and the point for the Philippines much higher than one would expect given the positions of the points for the other groups.

According to the family investment model presented in Section II, it is not only the size of the potential gain to the husband's income if he invests in U.S.-specific skills that affects the wife's propensity to work, but also the probability of actually attaining that return. An important factor affecting the expected gain is whether the family intends to stay in the United States or not. The expected gain can be denoted as $(y_{fpi} - y_{ci}) \times p_i$, where p_i is the probability that family i stays in the United States.

To incorporate permanence into our analysis, we weighted the husband's average return to investment by our estimates of the probability of staying in the

The Family Investment Model 93

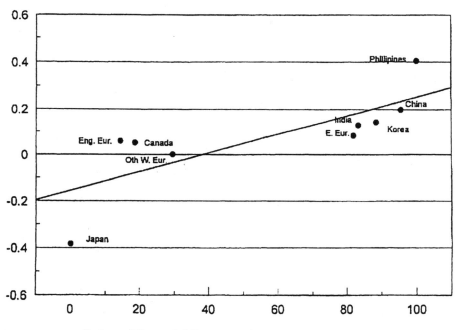

FIGURE 1
Relative Propensity of Wife Working Versus Husband's Potential Return to U.S. Investment: 1985–1990 Cohort

United States for each group. Our measure of permanence was simply 100 minus the percent of each cohort who stay in the United States for ten years, as measured by the difference in the number of immigrant men in each age/country cohort as counted by the 1980 and 1990 censuses.[13] The group with the highest emigration rate by far is the Japanese, whereas Filipinos have the lowest emigration rate by far.

Figure 2 graphs the relationship between the group marginal effects on wives working versus the husbands' potential return to U.S. investment for the cohort who entered the United States between 1985 and 1990. The left side simply repeats the graph shown in Figure 1. On the right side, the x axis is the expected gain from U.S. investment, where the potential gains to investment are weighted by the expected permanence of each group.[14]

The left-side graph appears to be made up of two clusters of points around

FIGURE 2
Relative Propensity of Wife Working Versus Husband's Potential Return to U.S. Investment Adjusted for Expected Performance: 1985–1990 Cohort

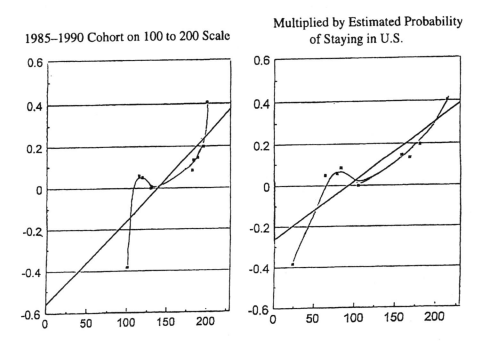

two almost vertical lines or, connecting all the points, as a single sine curve hugging the nearly diagonal straight line that has been fitted by ordinary least squares to these points. This is because the Japanese point (the left-most point) is very low, and the Filipino point (the right-most point) is very high, given the positions of the other groups.

Incorporating permanence into the analysis, all the points suggest a single, nearly linear, relationship—rather than two separate clusters of points. The transformation suggests that the very large Filipino effect on women's labor force participation is explained not only by the high potential return to their husbands' investment in U.S.-specific skills, but by the high probability of receiving that return, as indicated by their very high relative level of permanence. The very small Japanese effect is explained not only by the low potential return to financing their husbands' investment in U.S.-specific skills, but by the high probability of receiving that return.

In summary, based on analyses of the 1980 and 1990 census data, we find a clear relationship between the propensity of married immigrant women to work and the return to investment in U.S.-specific human capital by the husband, adjusting for factors generally included in female labor force participation models as well as variables measuring an immigrant woman's level of U.S.-specific skills. The pattern suggests a family investment strategy in which wives are more likely to work, ceteris paribus, the higher the return from their working in terms of the husband's investment in U.S.-specific human capital that their work finances.

Directions for Further Research

In what has become known as the Family Investment Model, several scholars have pursued the hypothesis that financing investment in host-country skills by immigrant husbands is a factor affecting the labor force decisions, human capital investment, and wages of immigrant married women. In this paper, I have formalized the family investment hypothesis and embedded it in a traditional model of a woman's decision to work. The paper also reviews empirical evidence from one stream of research on this topic by Duleep and Sanders (1993) and Duleep, Regets, and Sanders (1998). Both studies find a positive correlation across immigrant groups between variations in the unexplained propensity of immigrant women to work and the expected return to host-country human capital investment by immigrant men.

A logical extension of this research is to examine whether the relationship found across immigrant groups holds when Hispanic groups are included in the analysis.

Another issue for further research is what happens to variations in the propensity to work and wages across immigrant groups and between immigrant and native-born women as we follow the same groups over time, and how do these patterns relate to the family investment model?

Focusing solely on the effect on the labor force behavior of immigrant women of the return to host-country human capital investment by the husband, two theoretical outcomes are expected. One, we would expect that the greater relative propensity to work of immigrant women married to men who face relatively high returns to investment in host-country human capital would decrease with time in the host country: as immigrant husbands lacking host country skills acquire them, the return to financing their further investment decreases. Two, we would expect the wage profiles of immigrant women married to men facing a high return to investment in host-country human capital to be flatter than the wage profiles of native women or of immigrant women married to men who face a lower return to investment in host country human capital: so as to finance their husbands' investment in host-country skills, immigrant women in the former group would forego investment in their own skills by pursuing work options that are initially higher paying, but offer less opportunity for career investment.

While recent studies have confirmed that at a given point in time there is a positive correlation across groups between variations in the unexplained propensity of immigrant women to work and the expected return to human capital investment by immigrant men, analyses following cohorts over time have not consistently found hours and wage assimilation profiles conforming to the above expectations of the family investment model as currently conceived. Consistent with these expectations, Long (1980) and Beach and Worswick (1993) found that the adjusted earnings of immigrant women were initially greater than those of native-born women, and that this difference decreases as immigrant women spent time in the host country. (Duleep and Sanders, 1993, and Baker and Benjamin, 1997, tested this relationship in a more direct manner by explicitly linking the work behavior of immigrant women to the years since migration of their husbands.) Previous studies have also found a flatter wage profile of immigrant versus native-born women and a flatter wage profile of immigrant women married to men who face a high return to investment in host-country skills (Beach and Worswick, 1993 and Baker and Benjamin, 1997). Yet, following cohorts of immigrant women, Worswick (1996) and Duleep, Regets, and Sanders (1998) do not find that the propensity to work and the hours worked differential among groups decreases with time in the host country. They also fail to find flatter wage profiles of immigrant women in groups where the return to investment in host-country skills is highest for immigrant men.[15] Elucidating the reasons for the variety of results is a topic for future research.

One possible explanation for why there may not be a decreasing propensity to work as a function of a decreasing family investment return is persistence. Using 1980 census data to create a longitudinal panel,[16] Duleep and Sanders (1994) find—as has been found in studies focused on native-born women—that persistence is a key component in the labor force patterns of immigrant women.[17] If women who start to work in response to the family investment return continue to work, then we would expect that intergroup differences that arose because of differences in the family investment return would persist.

From a family investment perspective, the finding by Worswick (1996) and Duleep, Regets, and Sanders (1998) of a high investment wage profile for immigrant women in groups where the return to investment in host-country human capital is high for immigrant men is surprising if one thinks of the impact of the family investment model on the type of work a woman pursues in isolation, apart from her decision to work and ignoring the effect on the present value of lifetime family income of investment in her own human capital. A more gestalt view suggests that a family investment strategy need not lead to the wife pursuing a low investment job path.

Rather than considering in isolation the wife's decision as to whether she pursues a low or high investment job strategy, a more realistic approach may be to think of the family investment strategy as a sequence of steps that the wife takes in order to help finance the career path of her husband and her own career path so as to maximize the net present value of family lifetime earnings. These steps would be: (a) the decision to work, (b) hours of work, and (c) what type of job to take (to invest or not to invest). Lifetime family income optimization dictates that the wife will take steps to finance her husband's investment in U.S.-specific capital until the marginal cost of pursuing this strategy equals the marginal benefit. We assume that there are decreasing returns to investment in the husband's U.S.-specific capital. The cost to pursuing a job path that helps to finance the husband's investment includes the lower present value of the family income that would result from the wife pursuing a low investment job.

Given that a wife works and works a certain number of hours, the additional increase in the family's present value income via the husband's investment that could occur by the wife taking a low investment job may be less than the increased present value income that would occur if the wife invests. The higher the return to investment to the wife, the more likely that the husband's investment would be financed by the wife working and working longer hours, but pursuing a job line with investment. This model is consistent with what Duleep, Regets, and Sanders (1998) find: Asian immigrant women are more likely to work than their West European and Canadian counterparts, and they tend to have lower initial wages and higher wage growth. The lower the wife's own return to investment in U.S.-specific human capital relative to the return of investing in her husband's U.S.-specific human capital, the more likely we would see a high initial wage/low-growth wage profile. These thoughts require more formal and rigorous exploration.

More generally, although the family investment model is discussed in this paper in terms of its relevance to immigrant families, there is nothing that inherently limits its application to immigrant families. Furthermore, the formulation and testing of the model should be extended to include husbands financing the investment of their wives.

Finally, the discussions in this paper reflect a purely human capital theoretical framework. Institutional and cultural constraints that immigrant families face is another avenue for researchers to pursue. Rather than financing investment in host-country human capital by one member of the family working more than would otherwise be the case, some groups may be in a better position than others to borrow money in order to finance investment in host-country human capital. Discrimination is another constraint that may affect intergroup variations in the propensity to work, types of jobs pursued, investment decisions, and wage profiles of immigrant women and men.

These and other yet to be explored issues make the family investment hypothesis a very rich area for future research on immigrant women.

Notes

The author gratefully acknowledges useful comments by seminar participants of the Center on Population, Gender, and Social Inequality of the University of Maryland and participants of the conference "Immigrants and Their Transition to a New Labor Market" at Tel Aviv University.

1. For information on studies of women immigrants from various perspectives refer to the following articles and collections, and references cited therein: Kahn and Whittington (1996), Duleep and Sanders (1993), Boyd (1992), Simon and Brettell (1986), "Women in Migration" (1984), "Situation and Role of Migrant Women: Specific Adaptation and Integration Problems" (1981), and Mortimer and Bryce-Laporte (1981).

2. Long did not explicitly test this hypothesis by linking a woman's labor force participation to her husband's time in the United States. To the extent that husbands' investment decisions influence wives' labor force participation, one would expect the husband's years since migration to be inversely associated with the wife's labor force participation, since the return to investment would decline with years in the United States. Consistent with this expectation, Duleep and Sanders (1993), using U.S. data, and Baker and Benjamin (1997), using Canadian data, find an inverse relationship between a husband's years since migration and the wife's labor force participation, controlling for her own years since migration and other relevant variables.

3. The results shown here from Duleep and Sanders (1993) are based on analysis of the 5 percent "A" Public Use Sample from the 1980 Census of Population. The results from Duleep, Regets, and Sanders (1998) were estimated using the 1990 Census 5 percent Public Use Sample. Technical documentation may be found for these data sets in Bureau of the Census (1983, 1992).

4. For a given level of source-country human capital, the lower the skill transferability to the host country, the greater the propensity to invest. Refer to Duleep and Regets (1997a) for a description of a model of immigrant investment in human capital and empirical evidence. Further empirical evidence can be found in Duleep and Regets (1997b).

5. Hypothetically, a woman who migrated prior to marriage would be expected to have higher U.S.-specific skills and hence a higher market wage and higher propensity to work than a woman who migrated with her husband. We found, however, the reverse. This finding only makes sense from a family investment perspective (Duleep, Regets, and Sanders, 1998).

6. The geographic controls, which we included to capture general demand conditions that would affect the market wage, may also control for the availability, sine cost, of finding work: the characteristics of certain areas may facilitate immigrant women finding work, particularly women lacking U.S.-specific skills.

7. Insights on these cross-group variations in the estimated return to investment in U.S.-specific human capital are given in Duleep, Regets, and Sanders (1998).

8. The marginal effects are simply computed as $\beta p(1-p)$ where β is the estimated logit coeffi-

cient on each group variable. Since group membership is a categorical variable, it would be preferable to evaluate its effect by evaluating the probability at a given set of variables setting the dichotomous explanatory variable to 1 in one calculation, and to 0 in another calculation.

9. Details on the estimation of the husband's full potential earnings are given in Duleep, Regets, and Sanders (1998).

10. It could be argued that the measure of the husband's potential return to investment in U.S.-human capital in the 1980 analysis is preferable to the measure used in the 1990 analysis since the former allows for the possibility that the earnings of immigrant men in each group are affected by discrimination and other unmeasured variables that are specific to each ethnic group. A similar argument could be made for using the earnings of *native-born* men in each group. (Thus the potential earnings of Filipino immigrant men, if vested with U.S.-specific skills, would be the earnings of statistically similar U.S.-born Filipino men.)

Yet, other arguments suggest that the measure used in the 1990 analysis is preferable to either of these other measures. Given changes over time in immigrant cohorts, it is difficult to make the case that the effect of unmeasured variables is the same for recent immigrant cohorts in a particular group as for earlier immigrant cohorts in the same group, or for the native descendants of earlier immigrant cohorts in the same group. For instance, the Asian immigrants who entered the United States immediately after the demise of anti-Asian immigration provisions were much less likely to enter the United States via the kinship admission criteria than has been true of more recent immigrants. One could also argue that there is little in common between recent Asian immigrants and the U.S.-born descendants of early immigrants from Asia who entered the United States in the early 20th century and before as laborers. Using the earnings of native-born whites or native-born men in the general population as the measure of potential earnings has the important advantage of providing a common benchmark for all groups—we needn't wonder to what degree across-group differences in our estimated potential return to investment reflect intergroup differences in the current earnings of immigrants as opposed to differences in the group-specific benchmarks.

11. We standardized the husband's return to investment to a 0 to 100 scale by adding the lowest value of the average returns shown in Table 3 to each value, dividing each value by the highest value, and multiplying by 100.

12. The other cohort results are graphed in Duleep, Regets, and Sanders (1998).

13. A more sophisticated analysis and computation of source-country emigration rates can be found in Ahmed and Robinson (1994).

14. We converted our 0 to 100 scale to a 100 to 200 scale by adding 100 to each value in the previously used 0 to 100 scale so that the lowest value, otherwise zero, could be influenced by the emigration rate.

15. Worswick (1996) examines all Canadian immigrant women versus Canadian-born women while Duleep, Regets, and Sanders (1998) examine variations across immigrant groups.

16. To determine whether immigrant women's work decisions are as heavily influenced by persistence as is true for U.S.-born women, we exploited a little used feature of decennial census data that permits following the work behavior of individuals over time. In particular, a woman is defined as currently working (working in time period t) if, in the 1980 census, she reported working in the 1980 census week. She is defined as working last year (time period t–1) if she reported working in 1979. Finally, she is defined as working in time period t–5 if she reported working in 1975. More details on this are given in Duleep and Sanders (1994).

17. For studies of the general population, see in particular Nakamura and Nakamura (1985, 1992), Shapiro and Mott (1994), and Shaw (1994). Goldin (1977) also points to the role of persistence across generations to explain the historically high labor force participation of black women, and Reimers (1985) suggests that cultural persistence in work behavior underlies intergroup differences in women's work behavior.

References

Ahmed, Bashir and Gregory Robinson. 1994. "Estimates of Emigration of the Foreign-born Population: 1980–1990." *Population Estimates and Projections Technical Working Paper Series, no. 9.* Washington D.C.: U.S. Bureau of the Census (December).

Baker, Michael and Dwayne Benjamin. 1997. "The Role of the Family in Immigrants' Labor Market Activity: An Evaluation of Alternative Explanations." *American Economic Review* 87 (4), Sept.: 705–27.

Beach, Charles M. and Christopher Worswick. 1993. "Is There a Double-Negative Effect on the Earnings of Immigrant Women?" *Canadian Public Policy* 19 (1): 36–53.

Boyd, Monica. 1992. "Gender Issues in Immigration and Language Fluency." In *Immigration, Language and Ethnic Issues: Canada and the United States*, ed. Barry Chiswick. Washington, D.C.: American Enterprise Institute: 305–72.

Bureau of the Census. 1992. *Census of Population and Housing 1990: Public Use Microdata Sample, U.S. Technical Documentation.* Washington, D.C.: U.S. Bureau of the Census.

―――. 1983. *Census of Population and Housing, 1980: Public Use Microdata Samples, Technical Documentation.* Washington, D.C.: Bureau of the Census.

Duleep, Harriet Orcutt and Mark C. Regets. 1997a. "Are Lower Immigrant Earnings at Entry Associated with Faster Growth? A Review." Program for Research on Immigration Policy, Discussion Paper PRIP-UI-44, Washington, D.C.: The Urban Institute.

―――. 1997b. "Measuring Immigrant Wage Growth Using Matched CPS Files." *Demography* 34 (2) May: 239–49.

Duleep, Harriet Orcutt, Mark C. Regets, and Seth Sanders. 1998, forthcoming. *A New Look at Human Capital Investment: A Study of Asian Immigrants and Their Family Ties.* Kalamazoo, MI: Upjohn Institute of Employment Research.

Duleep, Harriet Orcutt and Seth Sanders. 1993. "The Decision to Work by Married Immigrant Women." *Industrial & Labor Relations Review* 46 (4) July: 677–90. (An earlier version was presented at the 1988 Annual Meeting of the American Economic Association.)

―――. 1994. "Empirical Regularities Across Cultures: The Effect of Children on Women's Work." *Journal of Human Resources* 29 (2) Spring: 328–47.

Goldin, Claudia. 1977. "Female Labor Force Participation: The Origin of Black and White Differences, 1870 and 1880." *Journal of Economic History* (March): 87–108.

Kahn, Joan R. and Leslie A. Whittington. 1996. "The Labor Supply of Latinas in the USA: Comparing Labor Force Participation, Wages, and Hours Worked with Anglo and Black Women." *Population, Research and Policy Review* 15 (February): 45–73.

Long, John. 1980. "The Effect of Americanization on Earnings: Some Evidence for Women." *Journal of Political Economy* 88 (3): 620–29.

Mortimer, Delores M. and Roy S. Bryce-Laporte, eds. 1981. *Female Immigrants to the United States; Caribbean, Latin American and African Experiences.* Research Institution on Immigration and Ethnic Studies. Occasional Papers, no. 2. Washington, D.C.: Smithsonian Institution.

Nakamura, Alice and Masao Nakamura. 1985. *The Second Paycheck: A Socioeconomic Analysis of Earnings.* Orlando: Academic Press.

―――. 1992. "The Econometrics of Female Labor Supply and Children." *Econometric Reviews* 11 (1): 1–71.

Ngo, Hang-Yue. 1994. "The Economic Role of Immigrant Wives in Hong Kong." *International Migration* 32 (3): 403–23.

Reimers, Cordelia. 1985. "Cultural Differences in Labor Force Participation Among Married Women." *American Economic Review, Papers and Proceedings*, (May): pp. 251–55.

Shapiro, David and Frank L. Mott. 1994. "Long-Term Employment and Earnings of Women in Relation to Employment Behavior Surrounding the First Birth." *Journal of Human Resources* 29 (2) Spring: 248–76.

Shaw, Kathryn. 1994. "The Persistence of Female Labor Supply: Empirical Evidence and Implications." *Journal of Human Resources* 29 (2) Spring: 348–78.

Simon, Rita James and Caroline Brettell, eds. 1986. *International Migration: The Female Experience.* Totowa, NJ: Rowman and Allanheld.

"Situation and the Role of Migrant women: Specific Adaptation and Integration Problems." 1981. *International Migration*, Special Issue. No. 1/2: 1–292.

"Women in Migration." 1981. *International Migration Review*, Special Issue, 18 (Winter 1984): 881–1382.

Worswick, Christopher. 1996. "Immigrant Families in the Canadian Labour Market." *Canadian Public Policy* 22 (4): 378–96.

5

*Gender, Refugee Status, and Permanent Settlement**

Monica Boyd

Abstract: This article examines how gender is implicated in the stages of defining a refugee, the refugee determination process, and the act of final settlement. After a general overview, specific details are presented for Canada. Canada admits refugees for the purpose of permanent settlement, and it has been the first on the international scene to develop gender-sensitive guidelines and to participate in the process of resettling women at risk of harm. However, data show that women are under-represented in the humanitarian-based flows to Canada. When they enter Canada, they are more likely than men to be married and to enter as spouses rather than as principal applicants.

Introduction

During the closing quarter of the twentieth century, the size of the world's refugee population has grown considerably as a result of social, economic, and political instabilities associated with such factors as the formation of new-nation states in the aftermath of colonial rule, the end of the Cold War (UNHCR, 1997c), and the legacies of earlier military action and foreign policies of industrial nations. Scholars note that in many cases, women outnumber men in these populations experiencing forced displacement (Martin, 1991; Keely, 1992). In its 1997 inventory of UNHCR-assisted refugee populations, the Office of the United Nations

High Commissioner for Refugees (hereafter UNHCR) enumerates 118 women (age 18 and older) for every 100 men. For the UNHCR-assisted refugee population in camps or centers, the counts are 126 women for every 100 men (UNHCR, 1997b).

Yet, the over-representation of women in refugee flows reverses to under-representation in claims and/or settlement in industrial countries such as Australia, Canada, the Netherlands, France, Sweden, Switzerland, and the United States (Boyd, 1995; Hovy, 1997; United Nations Secretariat, 1995; UNHRC, 1997b). During the 1980s and early 1990s, women constituted four out of ten adults admitted under specific refugee and asylum adjustment legislation in the United States and Canada (Boyd, 1995). Women also are under-represented as asylum claimants, generally defined as those who make their way to a country and claim refugee status there. Dispositions of asylum applications in 1992 and 1993 show that females filed three out of ten applications in the United States and in Canada (Gordon and Boyd, 1994).

These sex-selective outcomes in settlement reflect the fact that gender is deeply embedded in the processes generating refugee flows and providing humanitarian assistance. When permanent settlement occurs, particularly in an industrial country, it occurs within frameworks that are not gender neutral, although they may appear to be so. What constitutes persecution and what criteria are necessary to determine eligibility for settlement invoke images of behaviors and characteristics that draw selectively from gender identities, gender roles, gender power relations, and systems of gender stratification.

This article demonstrates how gender is implicated both in "becoming a refugee" and in permanent settlement opportunities. The analysis begins by reviewing both the gendered nature of the refugee process and recent initiatives to lessen gender bias. This general overview provides a context for the examination of sex-selective humanitarian-based settlement in Canada. The analysis of unpublished data confirms the under-representation of women in admissions for permanent settlement. But, reflecting the growing awareness that gender biases can exist under the guise of gender neutrality, Canada has been the leader in two areas: a) in proposing gender guidelines for claimants within her borders; and b) in adopting the "Women at Risk" program. Both initiatives represent important conceptual modifications to approaches in refugee determination and permanent settlement processes. However, although such approaches are important, they are not likely to substantially alter the under-representation of women in first-world countries of settlement.

Refugees and Permanent Settlement

Movement into a final country of residence is highly codified in refugee law, in bilateral and multilateral agreements between countries, and in procedures used by agencies such as the Office of the United Nations High Commissioner for Refugees to provide assistance to those in flight. Discussions of those in flight include a myriad of terms not always mutually exclusive or exhaustive, since those in flight can experience diverse and changing statuses (UNHCR, 1997c). However, in this article, the internally displaced and those outside their countries of origins are useful distinctions. The term "internally displaced" refers to those persons who have fled their homes but remain within the borders of their countries. Others will have left their countries of origin. Where protection cannot be assured by the country of refuge or where voluntary repatriation or local integration is not possible, some who have left their countries will obtain permanent resident status in another "third" country.

Permanent settlement in industrial countries in North America, Europe, and Oceania can be initiated in two ways. The first is when individuals or groups are residing outside potential first-world countries of settlement, but are identified by organizations such as the UNHCR or by national governments as in need of permanent settlement in another country. The second occurs when individuals or groups travel to an industrial country and present themselves as in need of sanctuary and thus settlement. In both cases, countries usually demand that persons establish that they are refugees as defined by international law. Until such statuses are granted, usually through interviews, hearings, or adjudications, such persons are called "asylum seekers" or "refugee claimants." Permanent settlement from abroad or petitions for settlement by individuals already within the borders of a potential host thus demands that persons are able to establish that they are refugees by undergoing the process of refugee determination. However, considerable inter-country variability exists in the refugee determination process, which usually is outlined in domestic laws and regulations. Intra-country variations also exist since procedures followed in the refugee status determination process can vary depending on whether persons are processed abroad or within a given country's borders. A final variation arises from the fact that countries of potential permanent settlement often define additional groups in need of protection and settlement in addition to those groups meeting the refugee definition employed by the UNHCR (see below).

Although seemingly gender neutral, gender permeates definitions, the process of refugee determination, selection for permanent settlement, and ultimately the sex composition of those who are settled. The term "gender" rather than "sex" is deliberate here. "Gender" explicitly rejects biological explanations for hierarchies of inequality and power that privilege men and disadvantage women. Rather than being a fixed trait, invariant over time, gender is constructed through social and cultural ideals, practices, and displays of masculinity and femininity (Scott, 1986; Hondagneu-Sotelo, 1994). Embodied in gender roles, relations, and hierarchies, gender is a core organizing principle of social relations and opportunities. The influence of gender becomes especially evident when discussing the situation of women in flight and their chances for permanent settlement in industrial countries.

Who is a Refugee?

According to Article 1 of the 1951 United Nations Convention Relating to the Status of Refugees, a refugee is a person who " . . . owing to well founded fear of being persecuted for reasons of race, religion, nationality, membership of a particular social group or political opinion, is outside the country of his nationality and is unable, or owing to such fear, is unwilling to avail himself of the protection of that country. . . . " Originally intended to deal with the aftermath of World War II, expiration deadlines and geographical restrictions embedded in the 1951 Convention were removed by the 1967 Protocol Relating to the Status of Refugees. For full reproduction of the 1951 and 1967 documents, see Loescher and Loescher (1994).

Signatories to the UN Convention and to the 1967 Protocol agreed to extend protection to those found to be refugees under the UN definition. As of May 1998, 136 governments had signed the Convention or the Protocol. In addition to those covered by the 1951 definition of refugees, other populations are of concern to UNHCR, including those who are displaced internally in their country of origin and those who are outside their country of origin and in a refugee-like situation but not officially recognized as such (UNHCR, 1997b).

The definition of a refugee found in the 1951 Convention and the 1967 Protocol is individualistic in focus. It emphasizes that the determination of refugee status reflects an incompatibility between the applicant and his/her state or country of origin (Spijkerboer, 1994; Connors, 1997). In some situations, violations are committed directly by the state or state-like authorities against the applicant. In other cases, non-state agents of persecution may exist, but the state may be unable or unwilling to offer protection from persecution.

The UN Convention definition of a refugee emerged in the aftermath of World War II and the Cold War, and as such it drew attention to violations committed directly by the state against individuals (Connors, 1997). Critics observe that the focus on the actions of the state and the violation of civil and political rights

Gender, Refugee Status, and Permanent Settlement

privileges the public side of the public/private divide. Such foci, it is argued, mean that the UN Convention definition of a refugee fails to acknowledge forms of persecution that occur within private settings, which represent violations of human rights, and/or where the state indirectly fails to protect individuals from harm.

Such failures especially affect women. In most societies gender roles and gender stratification prescribe that men are the key participants in the public arena, whereas women are found in the private sphere. As a result, the definition of a refugee found in UNHCR documents is held to be gender blind and thus gender insensitive at best, and based on a male prototype at worst. With either charge, the central concern voiced in feminist writings is that the UN Convention definition privileges the recognition of refugee status for men compared to women. Embedded in this concern are two core themes. First, forms of persecution experienced by women in more private settings are less likely to be recognized as grounds for persecution. Second, the indirect roles of the state in generating and/or sustaining harmful acts are not likely to be acknowledged. From a status of women perspective, additional related points are that the emphasis on the violation of civil and political rights both deflects attention away from the affirmative duty of the state to ensure rights, and ignores the existence of societal-wide discrimination against women (Connors, 1997).

The first core theme refers to the denial of human rights to women through rape, dowry-related burnings, sati or widow burnings, forced marriages, compulsory abortions or sterilizations, female genital mutilation, and domestic violence (Foote, 1995). In some situations, the state may be the agent denying basic human rights, or it may fail to offer protection even though such protection is within its capacity. The second theme is operative when women experience acts of harm either because of their association with others and/or because the state does not protect them. Thus, because of their relationship to others who are explicit targets of persecution, women may be forced to witness killings or acts of brutality, or they may be tortured, often through sexual violence inflicted by the military or by police. They may experience abduction, sexual slavery, forced pregnancy, and HIV infection (Spijkerboer, 1994; UNHCR, Executive Committee, 1997). These women may find it difficult to argue that their victimization was based on one or more grounds found in the refugee definition (persecution based on political views, religion, etc.). Rather than their assaults and inflictions being viewed as violation of human rights, they may be perceived by the courts as private acts inflicted by other individuals (Spijkerboer, 1994; Connors, 1997; UNHCR, 1997a).

The common thread running through both concerns is that persecution takes different forms according to the gender of the person and that persecution is experienced differently by men and by women. The discourse over who is a refugee and how best to take women's experiences into account has had several consequences. First, it has flagged violence against women, particularly sexual violence, to be of major concern (UNHCR, 1995). Second, discussion has broadened to include other forms of gender-based persecution, such as harsh or inhuman treatment as a result of the transgression of social mores for which the sanction is death; harmful practices such as female genital mutilation; coercive population management policies, often involving forced abortions or sterilization; and domestic violence for which there is no community or legal state protection (UNHCR. Executive Committee, 1997). Third, it has stimulated discussions on changing the grounds for persecution which are found in the 1951 Convention definition of a refugee.

Two models for change exist within the realm of refugee law (Spijkerboer, 1994). The basic distinction between these two models rests on whether women are persecuted *as* women or *because* they are women. In the former case, the 1951 Convention grounds still hold, although gender may explain why a woman is persecuted, the forms that the persecution takes, and the extent to which women may be at risk (Macklin, 1995). This approach assumes that the refugee definition is not male biased, although it concedes that the public/private divide makes women's experiences less easily recognized as being grounds for persecution. The solution then, is to blur the public/private dichotomy (Greatbatch, 1989; Spijkerboer, 1994), partly by emphasizing the gender-specific ways in which persecution may be manifest. Vehicles for the increase of awareness of how persecution is mediated by gender include guidelines, staff training manuals, and briefing sessions for persons adjudicating refugee status claims and/or providing services to such populations. The second approach argues that refugee law is indeed gendered and, in its current form, cannot adequately recognize the persecution of women in the private sphere. A different definition of refugee is required that either includes gender as a ground for persecution, or interprets the persecution grounds of social group as including gender (Spijkerboer, 1994). This approach assumes a causal connection between gender and persecution: women are persecuted because of their gender (Macklin, 1995). This model emphasizes the pernicious effects of gender discrimination and the complicity of the state in denying women their fundamental human rights.

In actuality, the line between these two alternative approaches for change is blurred. Macklin (1995) observes that in real life one can be persecuted as a woman (raped) for reasons not related to gender, such as membership in a particular ethnic group. Alternatively, one may be persecuted not as a woman (flogged), but because of gender (refusal to conform to gender proscriptions of dress and demeanor). One also may be persecuted as a woman and because of gender (genital mutilation).

Although much discussion and many court decisions exist around whether or not gender is a social group (Connors, 1997; UNHCR, 1997), most legal experts advocate remaining within the confines of the grounds stipulated in the 1951 Convention, while recognizing that the forms of persecution are gendered, and that in some circumstances the grounds of membership in a social group may adequately describe the situation of a woman seeking refugee status (see Connors, 1997; Macklin, 1995; Spijkerboer, 1994). The reluctance to make membership in the social group "women" grounds for persecution partly rests on the following legal considerations: a) what constitutes a social group; b) the tautology created when persecution defines a social group and membership in a social group becomes the grounds for claiming persecution; and c) the fact that the suffering of a particular group sometimes is indistinguishable from that experienced throughout the country of origin (Macklin, 1995; Connors, 1997; UNHCR, 1997). At a global level, however, pragmatic considerations also exist. It is highly unlikely that many nations would agree to change the 1951 UN Convention that specifies gender as a social group. To date, whether women are persecuted because of their gender is decided in the courts on a case-by-case basis, with varying results (UNHCR, 1997a). The case of Kasinga, who argued that she would have to undergo female circumcision if she returned to her country, is perhaps the most widely known case to date in the United States (Malone and Wood, 1997).

Attaining Refugee Status

Feminist-based discourse during the past two decades has unquestionably enhanced awareness of gender-based persecution. This latter phrase refers to the forms of harm that are regularly experienced by women and girls and are directed at them because of their sex (United Nations, Division for the Advancement of Women, 1997). The emphasis on gender-based persecution draws attention to the different forms that persecution can take, depending on the sex of the person. It also recognizes that persecution of women may occur because of the violation of social customs and mores which are gender proscriptive, and that states may fail to provide protection from harm, or may be implicated in the denial of fundamental human rights to women.

Because it broadens the range of experiences that are linked to persecution grounds, awareness of gender-based persecution is a necessary ingredient when considering who is a refugee (Spijkerboer, 1994). But other obstacles to attaining refugee status remain for women. One obstacle is that refugee determination procedures frequently reproduce existing gender hierarchies where men are considered heads of households and women are viewed as dependents. When women flee in the company of male relatives (spouses, fathers, brothers), they may not be asked about their experiences except to corroborate those of male family members (Martin, 1991; Hinshelwood, 1997). In such circumstances, the fates of women who might, on their own terms, meet the definition of a refugee are fused with those of their male relatives. The practice of linking women to men also exists when issuing documents. In countries of asylum, documents such as identification cards, or even papers granting the right to remain, may be issued to men but not to women family members. If men die, are absent, or are subsequently considered not eligible to remain, women may not be able to prove they are legally in the country of asylum (Martin, 1991).

If gender stratification determines where attention is focused and who receives documentation, it also permeates procedures whereby persecution is established. Assessing accounts of harmful acts involves an understanding of the conditions of the country or state from which the person has fled and an understanding of the consequences should the person return. Yet, country descriptions usually emphasize the public sphere. Country-specific information may be genderless, or—as feminist historians note—a "his-story," rather than one that illuminates gender inequalities. Also, few refugee documentation centers have information about the condition of women in any given country (Kelley, 1989).

Gender roles also condition the refugee determination process in two ways. First, shame and negative sanctions can make women extremely reluctant to discuss rape and other forms of sexual violence, particularly in front of male interviewers, in the presence of family members, or when interpreters—who may be known to others in the community—are used (Kelley, 1989; Martin, 1991; UNHCR, 1995). Special efforts often are required to elicit accounts of harm. Such efforts range from culturally sensitive approaches when dealing with sexual violence, to the use of female interviewers. To date, few countries have female staff involved in the refugee determination process (Kelley, 1989; UNHCR, 1995).

By affecting social interaction styles in interviews, gender roles also influence the refugee determination process. Deference or nervousness in situations of authority, hesitation in speech, reticence, or aversion of direct eye contact may be behaviors deemed appropriate for women in some societies. Yet they may be interpreted by interviewers as indicating deceit, shiftiness, or uncertainty. Trauma-induced styles also compound these difficulties (Agger, 1994). Because of a need to control the despair, terror, and anger over rape, torture, and other abuses, survivors may appear relatively emotionless and detached. Such actions may be viewed as suspicious, contrived, or rehearsed, with the result that a woman's story is not evaluated as credible (Hinshelwood, 1997; UNHCR, Division of International Protection, 1997).

Permanent Settlement

Three outcomes exist for persons who are refugees or in refugee-like situations. Once conditions in the country or area of origin become safe, return (repatriation) may be possible. For others, local settlement and integration in the country of first asylum may occur. The third option is final settlement, involving the transfer of refugees from the country where they sought refuge to another that has agreed to accept them on a permanent basis. Under UNHCR auspices, the third outcome is relatively infrequent, occurring only when the life, liberty, safety, health, or human rights of refugees are at risk in the country in which they originally sought refuge.

In order for the third outcome to exist, a person usually must be defined as a refugee and thus have his/her claims of persecution validated through the refugee determination process. However, industrial countries which agree to resettle refugees often add admissibility criteria to the basic eligibility criteria. These additions derive from concerns that resettled refugees do not pose health or security threats to the host population, and that they will not require extensive and long-term social assistance. In these circumstances, eligibility is necessary, but not sufficient. Criteria of admissibility, which usually include assessments of education, job skills, and income potentials, also must be met.

Even when women are able to establish gender-related persecution and are accorded refugee status, they may experience difficulties in becoming accepted for permanent settlement in an industrial country because of admissibility criteria. Gender stratification in refugee camps can result in refugee men occupying important mediating positions that, in turn, increase their chances of selection for settlement elsewhere (Martin, 1992). Gender stratification in most societies, particularly less industrialized ones, also means that women often have less education than men, and exhibit different or non-existent labor market skills and experiences. Such characteristics suggest women are likely to experience greater difficulty in meeting the self-sufficiency criteria invoked by an industrial country for admission. As well, many women have children and other dependents for whom they show responsibility. This fuels concern that women refugees will take longer than men, particularly single men, to acquire self-sufficiency. Gender inequalities in earnings in the host country also contribute to potential economic difficulties faced by women. As a result of all these concerns over self-sufficiency, selection procedures favor the permanent settlement of men (Kelley, 1989).

Cumulative Impacts: The Canadian Case

The preceding overview shows that gender is deeply embedded in the elements that link refugees and permanent settlement. Who is a refugee, the structure of the refugee determination process, and admissibility criteria associated with settlement selection practices of industrial nations can assume a male-public sphere prototype. In such settings, women may face difficulties in attaining refugee status either because of the persecution grounds that are part of the definition of a refugee or because the social interaction of the refugee determination process reflects gender roles and gender hierarchies. Even if refugee status is attained, admissibility criteria may pose additional obstacles for the permanent settlement of women in another country. The likely cumulative impact is that refugee settlement in industrial nations is sex selective. Men, not women, predominate.

Unpublished Canadian data illustrate the predominance of men in refugee admissions. Between 1985 and 1994, approximately 40,000 women were admitted to Canada, having established their eligibility by meeting the UN Convention definition of a refugee (Table 1, column 3). In contrast, close to 66,000 men, age fifteen and older, were admitted as Convention refugees during the same period. The Canadian Immigration Act, of 1976, and amendments introduced in Bill C-86 (December, 1992), also provide for the admission of other groups on humanitarian grounds. "Designated classes" is a term used to capture a variety of " . . . 'refugee like' situations such as mass outflow (Vietnam), disproportionate punishment for violation of strict exit controls (self-exiles) and the internally displaced, including political prisoners" (Employment and Immigration. Refugee Affairs Immigration Policy Group, 1993). During the ten-year period, many more men entered Canada in this category than did women (Table 1, column 4).

In addition to numerical counts, sex ratios also reveal the under-representation of women in humanitarian-based flows to Canada. The "immigrant" category in Table 1 refers to those migrants who enter for purposes of family reunion or on the basis of economic contributions. For every 100 men in this group, 118 women entered Canada, reflecting in part the movement of wives to join husbands already present in Canada. In contrast, for every 100 men admitted in the UN Convention refugee category, 61 women were admitted. A similar ratio describes the situation for admission in the "designated" classes.

Women are particularly under-represented in humanitarian-based admissions if they are single. For every 100 men who were single and admitted as UN Convention refugees, only 40 women were admitted between 1985–1994. They were also substantially under-represented among those who were the principal applicants for

TABLE 1
Sex Ratios (Females per 100 Males) by Category of Admission for Persons Age 15 and Older, Canada, 1985–1994

	Total (1)	Immigrants (2)	Convention Refugees (3)	Designated Class (4)
Numbers				
Women	770,929	677,300	40,392	53,237
Men	725,304	573,349	65,720	86,235
Sex Ratios (F/M)				
Total	106	118	61	62
Marital Status				
Single	86	100	40	45
Married	109	116	82	72
Other	349	398	201	140
Applicant Entry Status				
Principal Applicant	74	87	36	29
Spouse	722	671	1045	1256
Dependents	89	89	87	85

Source: Special tabulations purchased by the author from Citizenship and Immigration Canada.

admission. "Principal applicants" is a term referring to those persons who file applications for admission, are evaluated for admission, and are issued the primary visa for entry. Conversely, among those admitted as spouses, women far outnumber men (Table 1).

These data confirm that entry into Canada is gendered in two ways for refugees and persons considered by Canada to be in need of asylum. First, men substantially outnumber women in the Convention refugee and designated classes. Second, when men enter Canada on the basis of humanitarian criteria, their profile elicits images of autonomous migrants, whereas the profile for women is suggestive of tied-movers, or dependents. Of those admitted to Canada as UN Convention refugees, over half of the men are single. Conversely, slightly over half of all women admitted as UN Convention refugees are married. Only 2 percent of men admitted as UN Convention refugees enter as spouses of the principal applicant, whereas over one-third of women do (Table 2). Over 90 percent of all men admitted as UN Convention refugees are principal applicants, rather than spouses or dependents.

Gender differences also exist in the mode of entry into Canada. Between 1985 and 1994, slightly over one-half of the men were granted admission after they

TABLE 2
Marital Status and Applicant Entry Status for Persons Age 15 and Older by Sex and Category of Admission, Canada 1985–1994

	Immigrants		Convention Refugees		Designated Persons	
	Women (1)	Men (2)	Women (3)	Men (4)	Women (5)	Men (6)
Marital Status	100.0	100.0	100.0	100.0	100.0	100.0
Single	33.2	39.1	36.3	56.0	32.9	45.4
Married	57.0	58.0	55.4	41.4	59.9	51.4
Other	9.8	2.9	8.4	2.6	7.2	3.2
Applicant Entry Status	100.0	100.0	100.0	100.0	100.0	100.0
Principal Applicant	54.4	73.7	53.7	91.2	42.5	90.4
Spouse	29.8	5.2	37.0	2.2	47.6	2.3
Dependents	15.8	21.0	9.3	6.6	9.9	7.2

Source: Special tabulations purchased by the author from Citizenship and Immigration Canada.

had traveled to Canada and sought asylum, compared to less than half of the women entering in the UN Convention category (Table 3, column 2). The pattern persists for those entering the designated classes categories although most in this group are processed abroad. Membership in a designated class is usually determined by ministerial orders, and by definition involves the identification of groups outside Canada. This favors a higher rate of processing of cases outside Canada.

Why are women admitted for permanent settlement on the basis of humanitarian principles less likely than men to be processed within the country? Immigration officials attribute the lower representation of women in the within-Canada admissions to the fact that compared to men, women may be less likely to undertake or be successful at making long, often clandestine, journeys to reach Canada. Compared to men, women may lack the same level of economic resources and networks to undertake such journeys. Gender roles may dampen or preclude their reliance on male traffickers to negotiate border crossings. Rape and other forms of sexual violence while making such trips are real risks as well.

Earlier discussion noted the difficulties that women may have in proving their refugee status claims. The fact that a higher percentage of women than men are likely to be processed outside Canada does not disprove the existence of such difficulties. In both types of settlement processes, women who are admitted for humanitarian reasons are under-represented relative to men, suggesting a sex-selective process at work. This under-presentation occurs in every year throughout the

TABLE 3
Within Canada and Outside of Canada Place of Processing for Persons Age 15 and Older, by Admission Categories, Canada 1985–1994

	Immigrants (1)	Convention Refugees (2)	Designated Class (3)
Percentages			
Women	100.0	100.0 1	00.0
In Canada	21.5	46.5	22.7
Abroad	78.5	53.5	77.3
Men		100.0	100.0
100.0			
In Canada	17.2	51.9	28.6
Abroad	82.8	48.1	71.4
Sex Ratios			
In Canada	148	55	49
Abroad	112	68	67

Source: Special tabulations purchased by the author from Citizenship and Immigration Canada.

ten-year period under review. However, yearly statistics indicate increases over time in the overall percentages of women in the permanently settled adult refugee population (Canada. Citizenship and Immigration Canada. International Refugee and Migration Policy Branch, 1994).

Gender Sensitivity: New Initiatives

As a country, Canada has a lengthy history of accepting newcomers, as well as of attentiveness to gender equality issues. This latter attentiveness has generated considerable attention to the situation of immigrant women. It also has elicited proactivity regarding the three elements of the refugee-permanent settlement link (definition, refugee determination procedures, and admissibility criteria) that can depress the numbers of refugee women admitted to Canada.

On International Women's Day in 1993, the chairperson of the Immigration and Refugee Board of Canada (IRB) released guidelines for women refugee claimants fearing gender-related persecution (Immigration and Refugee Board of Canada, 1993; Mawani, 1993). Mandated by Canada's Immigration Act of 1976, and Bill C-86, which amends the act to adjudicate the claims of those seeking asylum, the IRB consists of three divisions: the Convention Refugee Determination

Division, the Immigration Appeal Division, and the Adjudication Division. The chairperson is authorized to issue guidelines to assist members of these divisions in carrying out their duties.

The guidelines were the first to be drafted by any country to specifically address the issue of gender-related persecution. Since then, guidelines have been adopted by the United States (U.S. Department of Justice, Immigration and Naturalization Service, 1995; Scialabba, 1997) and Australia (Anonymous, 1997). Despite their similarities and differences (Macklin, 1998, forthcoming), all of these guidelines focus on the need to be gender sensitive when considering the grounds for persecution and to take special efforts where possible in the refugee determination process (such as having female interviewers). All stop short of declaring gender to be a social group and, thus, explicit grounds for persecution.

With respect to the Canadian guidelines, Macklin (1995) correctly notes that the guidelines supply gender-sensitive advice to statutory interpretations. The definition of a refugee found in the 1951 UN Convention remains unaltered. However, the guidelines highlight the fact that women refugee claimants fall into four broad categories: 1) those who fear persecution on the same Convention grounds and in similar circumstances as men such that the risk factor is not their sexual status per se, but their identity (national, ethnic, religion); 2) those who fear persecution solely for reasons of kinship, that is because of the status, activities, or views of their spouses, parents, siblings, or other family members; 3) women who fear persecution resulting from certain circumstance of severe discrimination on grounds of gender, acts of violence either by public authorities, or at the hands of private citizens; and 4) women who fear persecution as the consequence of failure to conform to or transgression of certain gender-discriminating religious customs, laws, and practices in their country of origin. The 1993 guidelines also provide examples of how Convention grounds of race, religion, nationality, and political opinion could be mediated by gender to produce situations in which women would be at risk of persecution. The document suggests that in some circumstances the family might be considered as a particular social group insofar as kinship may constitute the risk factor. This suggestion seeks to address the cases wherein women were persecuted because of the activities of other family members. The 1993 guidelines also discuss the possibility that gender might be considered a social group.

In 1996, revised guidelines were issued. Slightly modified from the original version, these included more discussion of women as a social group who are persecuted as a result of their membership in that group. Decision makers are urged to refer to a 1993 Supreme Court decision, *Canada (Attorney General) v. Ward*, that occurred shortly after the original 1993 guidelines were issued, which outlined the categories defining a social group (Tranter, 1993; Adjin-Tettey, 1997). At the same time, the revised guidelines stop short of declaring gender a social group, and thus a basis for fearing persecution. Despite ongoing discussion of whether or not women form a particular social group (Foote, 1994; Adjin-Tettey, 1997), one reason for the stance taken by the 1993 and 1996 guidelines is that the IRB lacks the jurisdiction to add gender, as this can be accomplished only through parliamentary legislation (Macklin, 1995). The 1996 guidelines also repeat the admonitions found in the 1993 guidelines that refugee status is an individual remedy and that a claim based on social group membership may not be sufficient to elicit refugee status. A female claimant would need to show that she has genuine fear of harm, that the harm would be sufficiently serious to constitute persecution, that there would be a reasonable possibility such persecution would occur if she were to return to her country, and that she would have no reasonable expectation of adequate protection. Under such stipulations, for example, stating that one disagrees with laws and practices that subordinate women to men in the country of origin would not be sufficient to establish persecution on the grounds that one is a woman.

The Canadian guidelines have been hailed as a watershed for gender-related persecution issues. However, they are not without critics. For some, the guidelines go too far, either because they (erroneously) are viewed as opening the gates to a flood of bogus claimants (MacMillan, 1993b), or because they evoke Western values in the refugee-determining process by suggesting that some cultural practices may cause women to be at risk of persecution. Others argue that the guidelines do not go far enough. They remain as guidelines rather than as changes in regulations, and they fail to stipulate that gender is a social group (MacMillan, 1993b; Macklin, 1995). Critics also charge that the guidelines place women in enormous difficulty when domestic violence exists. A woman hypothetically could claim domestic violence as grounds for persecution, but under normal IRB practices, refugee claims of spouses tend to be heard jointly. Macklin (1995) notes that a woman is not likely to give the necessary evidence when the perpetrator of her persecution is also part of the case in which refugee status is sought.

A final objection is that the guidelines have jurisdiction only for refugee claimant cases heard within Canada, where IRB members must demonstrate compliance with the issued guidelines for gender-related persecution. Canadian officials overseas are not held accountable to these guidelines (Foote, 1995). A divide is thus created between women who present themselves in need of asylum inside Canada and those who do so outside. The former have their cases heard by adjudicators who must report if gender-related persecution was an issue in the case, and how it was decided. If their refugee claims are successful, the former also do not have to satisfy admissibility criteria to settle in Canada. In contrast, women who experience gender-related persecution and who are outside of Canada may or may not be successful in attaining refugee status. If they do attain such status, they may not be admissible because of poor prospects for settlement.

Have the Canadian guidelines been successful? Yes, if one considers that they stood as a model for subsequent action in Australia and in the United States (U.S. Department of Justice, Immigration and Naturalization Service, 1995). However, it is difficult to show that the guidelines improve the chances for women to be deemed Convention refugees given the variability that exists across IRB adjudication boards in classifying cases as gender-related persecution. Available evidence indicates that in 1994, 64 percent of the finalized gender-related claims handled by the IRB resulted in the applicant obtaining refugee status (Foote, 1995). Case analysis also illustrates the circumstances in which claims of gender-related persecution are rejected or accepted (MacMillan, 1993a; Macklin, 1998).

Women at Risk

The Canadian guidelines for women fearing gender-related persecution are directed at the definition of a refugee and the manner in which the refugee determination process occurs. The geographical domain is limited to those who apply for refugee status from within Canada. A second initiative exists that reverses the focus. It targets women who qualify for refugee status and who are living outside Canada. This initiative is called the "Women at Risk" program.

Although the focus of this article is on the permanent settlement of refugee women in industrial countries, most women (and men) who are in flight do not experience this outcome. Much of the literature about refugee women emphasizes the extreme vulnerability of refugee women to violence and abuse that occur in flight and in temporary settlement areas, including camps in areas near the countries of origin. Women who are single heads of family or whose adult male relatives are unable to support them are at risk of expulsion, *refoulement* (forcible return), sexual harassment, rape, torture, prostitution, and other forms of exploitation. Added to these risks are the difficulties associated with uprootedness, deprivation of a normal family life, and an absence of community or family ties (UNHCR, Division of International Protection, 1997). Such vulnerability frequently co-exists with low chances for permanent settlement, since these women also are likely to be assessed by potential settlement countries as requiring a great deal of assistance due to trauma, number of children, and generally low levels of education.

Starting in 1987, the UNHCR requested assistance in offering protection by way of permanent settlement to these vulnerable women. Canada's program started in 1987, with admissions first occurring in 1988 (Spencer-Nimmons, 1994). Since then, programs have been established by Australia and New Zealand. The Canadian "Women at Risk" program targets two groups of females who either meet the UN Convention refugee definition or are considered members of designated groups:

> a) "Women at Risk" will be in precarious situations where the local authorities cannot ensure their safety. This includes women who are experiencing significant difficulties in refugee camps, such as harassment by local authorities or by members of their own communities. Urgent protection cases, such as women in physical danger, or in danger of refoulement are to be accorded first priority.
>
> b) "Women at Risk" also may be applicants who are not in immediate peril but who are existing in permanently unstable circumstances which allow for no other remedy. Because of a low level of skills, or because they are accompanied by small children, or other factors, they may be women who have been passed over by Canada or by other resettlement countries in the past. At the same time they should show potential for eventual successful establishment in Canada.... (Immigration Manual, 3:13, No 2, June, 1990).

Critics of this program note that although the program is intended to handle hardship cases where women are at extreme risk and cannot remain in their place of residence, admissibility criteria are invoked. In fact, "relaxed" criteria of admissibility are applied. However, it is not clear what these are, leading to concerns that the subjectivity of visa officers plays too great a role in selecting women for settlement in Canada (Foote, 1995). Other concerns focus on the scarce resources available for administering the program in the field, the deleterious effects of overseas staff having to deal with different government departments, each with potentially different goals, and the lack of awareness by visa and protection officers of female-specific needs and experiences (Spencer-Nimmons, 1994). Administratively, perhaps the greatest criticism focuses on the delays in removing women (and their dependents) from situations of extreme danger. In recent years, the waiting time for the necessary processing has crept upwards from the three months considered to be an absolute maximum. One result of the delays is that field personnel who seek to remove women from dangerous situations are not bringing these to the attention of Canadian officials, since resolutions appear so long term. This is partly responsible for the declining admissions to Canada in the mid-1990s. In April 1998, an international workshop was hosted by Citizenship and Immigration

Canada on the Women at Risk program worldwide (known as Assistance to Women at Risk or AWR), where this problem was discussed along with others. An overview UNHCR report on the worldwide AWR programs is in preparation. The Canadian response includes efforts at reducing the time delays in processing cases.

A final criticism is that the numbers admitted are small, particularly in the face of needs and other settlement mechanisms. Table 4 shows the number of cases and persons (women and dependents) admitted to Canada between 1988 and 1997 in the Women at Risk program. The net addition of 1,026 persons through this program represents less than 1 percent of all Convention refugees admitted during this period. This partly reflects the high expenditures associated with the program. But the numbers are small when compared with the large refugee populations in which women and children predominate.

Conclusion

Increasingly, studies of migrant women ask how gender is implicated in the process of international migration (Hondagneu-Sotelo, 1994; Lim, 1995; Ellis, Conway and Bailey, 1996; Grieco and Boyd, 1998). This article shows that gender is an integral part of the refugee experience. Gender influences the answering of "who is a refugee?" Gender can affect procedures used in the refugee determination process, and through admissibility criteria it produces a sex-selective settlement process in which men are more likely to be resettled than are women.

The importance of gender is shown both in the general review of the refugee-settlement link and with reference to one specific country, Canada. Canada has adopted gender-sensitive guidelines for use in refugee claimant cases, and has also implemented a process of resettling women who are at risk outside Canada. Yet, relative to men, women remain quite under-represented in the humanitarian-based flows to Canada.

Will such trends change in the direction of gender parity? Certainly the last decade has been one of world-wide emphasis on women refugees and on having their experiences captured by a gender-sensitive model of refugee determination. However, with respect to humanitarian-based settlement patterns in industrial nations, the under-representation of women is likely to persist for some time for at least two reasons. First, current demographic trends carry with them the seeds of the future. In Canada, for example, men predominate in the humanitarian-based flows, and they are less likely than women to be married. The higher percentages of single men in the Convention refugee and designated group categories imply a reduction in the possible later migration of women. Once a refugee is given perma-

TABLE 4
Admissions under the Women at Risk Program, Canada, 1988–1997

Years	Number of Cases (Families)	Total Number of Persons
1988	40	97
1989	30	87
1990	28	67
1991	65	140
1992	36	111
1993	51	153
1994	21	85
1995	26	78
1996	17	54
1997	44	154
Total	358	1026

Source: Unpublished tabulations, Citizenship and Immigration, Canada.

nent resident status he or she can sponsor close relatives, provided the sponsor is considered able to assume the required financial and social responsibilities (Boyd, 1989). However, if such men are single, there presumably are no wives to subsequently sponsor.

Second, gender stratification means that in many areas of the world, women have less education and less experience in the labor market or in the formal economy. Related gender roles ensure marriage and childbearing at relatively early ages. In many countries, particularly those subject to political and military strife that generate populations in flight, gender equality will not be quickly attained. In turn, admissibility criteria invoked by countries of potential settlement mitigate against the admission of these women, even if they are eligible for permanent settlement. Taken together, such obstacles do not bode well for gender parity in future refugee settlement flows to industrial countries.

Note

* The author thanks Bela Hovy of the UNHCR, Geneva, and Janet Dench, Canadian Council for Refugees, for helpful comments on earlier drafts. Mr. Hovy also provided invaluable information on the world's refugee population and on the settlement activities of the UNHCR. The article also benefited from discussions with several persons at Citizenship and Immigration Canada. The author takes full responsibility for all imperfections in the text.

Bibliography

Adjin-Tettey, Elizabeth, 1997. Defining a Particular Social Group Based on Gender. *Refuge 16* (October): 22–25.

Agger, Inger. 1994. *The Blue Room: Trauma and Testimony Among Refugee Women—A Psycho-Social Exploration*. London: Zed Books.

Anonymous. 1997. Australia: Department of Immigration and Multicultural Affairs. Refugee and Humanitarian Visa Applicants Guidelines on Gender Issues for Decision Makers, July 1996. *International Journal of Refugees 9* (Autumn, special issue supplement): 195–212.

Boyd, Monica. 1989. *Migrant Women in Canada: Profiles and Policies*. Ottawa: Employment and Immigration Canada. Public Affairs Inquiries and Distribution.

———. 1995. Migration Regulations and Sex Selective Outcomes in Developed Countries. Pp. 83–98 in United Nations Department for Economic and Social Information and Policy Analysis, Population Division, *International Migration Policies and the Status of Female Migrants*. New York: United Nations.

Citizenship and Immigration Canada. International Refugee and Migration Policy Branch.1994. *Refugee Claims in Canada and Resettlement from Abroad*. Statistical Digest. November. Ottawa, Canada.

Connors, Jane. 1997. Legal Aspects of Women as a Particular Social Group. *International Journal of Refugees 9* (Autumn, special issue supplement): 114–128.

Ellis, Mark, Dennis Conway and Adrian J. Bailey. 1996. The Circular Migration of Puerto Rican Women: Towards a Gendered Explanation. *International Migration 34:*31–64.

Employment and Immigration Canada. Refugee Affairs Immigration Policy Group. 1993. *Canada's Resettlement Programs: New Directions*. Ottawa: Employment and Immigration Canada. January.

Foote, Victoria. 1994. Refugee Women as a Particular Social Group: A Reconsideration. *Refuge 14* (December): 8–12.

———. 1995. *Refugee Women and Canadian Policy: Gaining Ground?* North York, Ontario: York University, Centre for Refugee Studies.

Gordon, Linda W. and Monica Boyd. 1994. Refugees to North America: Gender Issues and Implications. Paper presented at the annual meeting of the Population Association of America. Miami, May.

Greatbatch, Jacqueline. 1989. The Gender Difference: Feminist Critiques of Refugee Discourse. *International Journal of Refugees 1* (October): 518–527.

Grieco, Elizabeth and Monica Boyd. 1998. *Women and Migration: Incorporating Gender into International Migration Theory*. Working Paper Series 98–139, Florida State University, Center for the Study of Population. Tallahassee.

Hinshelwood, Gill. 1997. Interviewing Female Asylum Seekers. *International Journal of Refugees 9* (Autumn, special issue supplement): 159–164.

Hondagneu-Sotelo, Pierrette. 1992. Overcoming Patriarchal Constraints: The Reconstruction of Gender Relations among Mexican Immigrant Women and Men. *Gender and Society 6:*393–415.

Hovy, Bela. 1997. The Sex and Age Distribution of Refugees and Others of Concern to UNHCR: Statistical Evidence. Presented at the annual meeting of the Population Association of America, Washington, D.C., March.

Immigration and Refugee Board of Canada. 1994. Guidelines Issued by the Chairperson Pursuant to Section 65(3) of the Immigration Act: Women Refugee Claimants Fearing Gender Related Persecution. March 9. Ottawa: IRB.

———. 1996. Guidelines Issued by the Chairperson Pursuant to Section 65(3) of the Immigration Act. Guideline 4: Women Refugee Claimants Fearing Gender Related Persecution: UPDATE. November 25. Ottawa: IRB.

Keely, Charles B. 1992. The Resettlement of Women and Children Refugees. *Migration World 20*(4): 14–18.

Kelley, Ninette. 1989. *Working with Refugee Women: A Practice Guide*. Geneva: International NGO Working Group on Refugee Women.

Lim, Lin Lean. 1995. The Status of Women and International Migration. Pp. 29–55 in United Nations Department for Economic and Social Information and Policy Analysis, Population Division, *International Migration Policies and the Status of Female Migrants*. New York: United Nations.

Loescher, Gil and Ann Dull Loescher. 1994. *The Global Refugee Crisis: A Reference Handbook*. Santa Barbara, CA: ABC-CLIO Inc.

Macklin, Audrey. 1998. (forthcoming) Comparative Approaches to Gender Based Persecution: Canada, US and Australia. In Doreen Indra (ed.), *Engendering Forced Migration*. Providence: Berghahn Books.

———. 1995. Refugee Women and the Imperative of Categories. *Human Rights Quarterly 17* (May): 213–277.

MacMillan, Leanne. 1993a. Gender Case Analysis: A Look at Recent IRB Decisions. *Refuge 13* (July-August): 11–15.

———. 1993b. Reflections on the Gender Guidelines. *Refuge 13* (July—August): 2–3.

Malone, Linda A. and Gillian Wood. 1997. *In re Kasinga*, Interim Decision 3278. 1996 Westlaw 379836, 35 ILM 1145 (1996) Board of Immigration Appeals, 1996. *The American Journal of International Law 91* (January): 140–147.

Martin, Susan Forbes. 1991. *Refugee Women*. London: ZED Books Ltd.

Mawani, Nurjehan. 1993. Introduction to the Immigration and Refugee Board Guidelines on Gender Related Persecution. *International Journal of Refugee Law* 5(2)240–247.

Scialabba, Lori L. 1997. The Immigration and Naturalization Service Considerations for Asylum Officers Adjudicating Asylum Claims from Women. *International Journal of Refugees 9* (Autumn, special issue supplement): 174–181.

Scott, Joan. 1986. Gender: A Useful Category of Historical Analysis. *American Historical Review* 91:1053–1075.

Spencer-Nimmons, Noreen. 1994. Canada's Response to the Issue of Refugee Women: the Women at Risk Program. *Refuge 14* (December):13–18.

Spijkerboer, Thomas. 1994. *Women and Refugee Status: Beyond the Public/Private Distinction*. Hague, Netherlands: Emancipation Council.

Tranter, Linda. 1993. A Step Forward in Protecting Human Rights: *Canada v. Ward*. *Refuge 13* (July-August): 16–18.

UNHCR. 1995. *Sexual Violence Against Refugees: Guidelines on Prevention and Response*. Geneva.

———. 1997a. Gender-Related Persecution: an Analysis of Recent Trends. *International Journal of Refugees 9* (Autumn, special issue supplement): 79–113.

———. 1997b. *Refugees and Others of Concern to UNHCR. 1997 Statistical Overview*. Geneva.

———. 1997c. *The State of the World's Refugees: A Humanitarian Agenda*. Oxford: Oxford University Press.

United Nations. Division for the Advancement of Women. 1997. Gender-Based Persecution: Report of the Expert Group Meeting. EGM/GBP/1997/Report. New York: United Nations.

UNHCR. Division of International Protection. 1997. *Resettlement Handbook*. Geneva.

UNHCR. Executive Committee of the High Commissioner's Programme. 1997. Progress Report on Refugee Women and UNHCR's Framework for Implementation of the Beijing Platform for Action. Standing committee 9th meeting August 15. EC/47/SC/CRP.47.

United Nations Secretariat. 1995. Measuring the Extent of Female International Migration. Pp. 56–79 in United Nations. Department for Economic and Social Information and Policy Analysis, Population Division, *International Migration Policies and the Status of Female Migrants*. New York: United Nations.

United States. Department of Justice. Immigration and Naturalization Service. 1995. Memorandum: Considerations for Asylum Officers Adjudicating Asylum Claims from Women (From: Phyllis Coven) May 26. Washington, D.C.

6

Gender in Language and Life: A Dutch American Example

Suzanne M. Sinke

> Abstract: This case study of language shift among turn-of-the-century Dutch Protestant immigrants highlights how language operates to create and reinforce social systems of meaning. The author describes how gender variations in language acquisition relate to social and economic positions of the migrants and their age at arrival. At the individual, familial, and ethnic group level, language acquisition was gendered. Men and women had different reasons for learning or preserving their language, with women occupying the extremes of both innovation and retention. Using sociolinguists' interviews, immigrant letters, literary works, and a variety of other sources, the author argues that the relative absence of gender and class distinctions in English grammar reinforced a particular vision of America that also included freedom from these elements.

Change language, change perception. Sociolinguists and linguistic anthropologists have chronicled such shifts extensively, and at times have sought to describe the meaning of such shifts in terms of changing social relations within the minority-language or bilingual communities, including gender dynamics.[1] Others have explored gender roles and their relations to language in a wide variety of settings.[2] However, their most common methods, participant observation and questionnaire, are not available for past populations. Among historians, the interest in language and the creation of meaning through language in recent historical scholarship on gender has less often addressed language shift among immigrant populations.[3] We seek in this article to describe the shifts in perception related to language shift for one historical ethnic group, and in the process add to our understanding of how ethnicity and gender interact in situations of changing language.

Learning a foreign language effectively requires utilizing the patterns of thought that the language embodies.[4] Whether one agrees with the patterns is another matter, but to become fluent, one must recognize them. As historians of immigration, we have sought to chronicle the move from one culture to another, and in particular, how perceptions of gender and class change in that process. (I came to study language in that context.) Language shift in an immigrant population takes place at different levels: individual, family, and ethnic community, to name the most prominent.[5] Within those categories, people have different access to language acquisition, different levels of incentive and compulsion to shift, and different evaluations of language shift. At each level, the difference is gendered, but other factors, most notably age, also affect who shifts and why.[6] Crossing a linguistic boundary, in other words, can have very different meanings.

To describe that process, we conducted a case study of Dutch Protestant immigrants in the United States. My focus was on the turn of the century, the period in which much of this ethnic group made the linguistic shift from Dutch to English, or in sociolinguistic terms, English became the socially dominant language. Nonetheless, Dutch language use continued fairly extensively until World War II, and only after that time underwent a decline indicating imminent language death.[7] One of our major sources for information on language was a collection of interviews with nearly 300 people, carried out under the aegis of the P.J. Meertens Institute in the 1960s. Since these impressions were filtered through the lens of age, however, we sought out contemporary sources as well. We utilized several hundred "America" letters (from the U.S. to the Netherlands), church and philanthropic organization records, and Dutch American newspapers, to name a few.[8]

The Dutch came to the United States in three separate waves of migration: colonial, mid-nineteenth to early twentieth century, and post-World War II. The first, which began in the early colonial era, had largely assimilated into an American identity, and conversely, American identity had incorporated aspects of Dutch American life to a point that words, names, and aspects of ethnic culture were no longer foreign by the time the second wave began arriving in the mid-nineteenth century.[9] The descendants of the colonial group still included a few Dutch speakers, and in general, members of the American branch of the Dutch Reformed Church provided help for their co-religionists. The second wave of migrants began in the 1840s with several congregations of seceders from the Reformed Church, the quasi-state church of the Netherlands. These pietists, led by their dominies (ministers), founded the major Dutch American colonies of the era and had an impact far beyond their numbers. A second religious movement in the Netherlands in the 1880s spurred another group of religious conservatives to migrate in disproportionately large numbers.[10] While the majority of the immigrants from the Netherlands in this period came for economic and familial reasons, the role of religion in founding and maintaining the Dutch settlements had important influences on language and on ideas of gender. All studies of Dutch language use in the United States noted the close relationship between Dutch language retention and Calvinist religious activity.[11]

Language use, both in terms of knowing standard language and in terms of fluency in a second language, related to education patterns. Immigrants from the Netherlands at the turn of the century generally were literate. School attendance in the Netherlands ran around 90 percent for children of elementary school age in 1900, when the Dutch parliament passed a mandatory school attendance law.[12] Most Dutch elementary schools were co-educational, but with gender-specific curricula. For girls, the emphasis was on household skills in addition to basic literacy, whereas boys took additional academic subjects.[13] Schoolbooks of the period sought to maintain the social system; hence they stressed the differences of the *standen* or social castes. Orthodox Calvinist schools, which constituted about one third of elementary schools in this time period and after 1889 enjoyed public subsidies, used the Bible and catechetical texts as their main sources for instruction.[14]

Dutch immigrants in the U.S. reflected the literacy rates and the attention to education which characterized their homeland. In the 1910 Public Use Sample, about 96 percent of Dutch immigrants as a whole and 94 percent of Dutch women above the age of fifteen were listed as being able to read.[15] The immigrants transferred the *schoolstrijd* or school controversy that had raged in the Netherlands over whether to grant public funding to Christian schools. Those who affiliated with the Reformed Church generally sought to work within the public school system, influencing the schools in their areas to adopt their preferred curricula and hire teachers from within the ethnic group. The more conservative Christian Reformed often set up their own "independent" schools. These Christian schools nearly all included Dutch as part of the curriculum because catechetical texts were read and taught in Dutch.[16] Even in this group, however, the interest was in bilingualism. They still wanted the children to learn English.

The educational background of most Dutch immigrants, which included basic literacy but not much beyond that, meant that most had only limited competency in standard Dutch. In the Netherlands, a dialect of Dutch was the most common mother tongue for residents of rural areas, including the main regions of emigration. There were a wide variety of local dialects. Linguists grouped them into five or six families of dialects, plus Frisian, which gained the status of a separate language (with its own dialects) in the mid-twentieth century.[17] One of the early linguistic developments in Dutch American communities was a convergence toward standard Dutch, a process that Caroline Smits chronicled as taking place in the period up to World War I, concurrent with learning English for many. The dialects spoken by most immigrants resembled one another and standard Dutch relatively closely, which assisted in this process.[18]

In general, Dutch and Dutch dialects also resembled English in many ways. Like English, they developed out of the West Germanic family of languages, and Dutch, in most instances, had an intermediate position between standard German and English. For speakers of Dutch and its dialects, English was a relatively easy language to learn. Yet standard Dutch differed from English in a number of ways, some of which were important to perceptions. In Dutch, all nouns had a gender: masculine, feminine, or neuter. The articles combined masculine and feminine in one form (*de*) and had neuter as a separate category (*het*), but to choose a pronoun or decline an adjective, one had to know the word's gender. References to people in various occupations or activities grammatically required specifying the sex of the individual (*schrijver* = male writer; *schrijvster* = female writer). As in German, plurals referring to people would be in feminine plural form only if all members of the group were women. If one or more men were included, regardless of the number of women, the plural form was "generic"—male. Dutch people used titles or lack thereof to indicate *stand* or caste/class much more extensively than was typical in American English. This applied not only to members of the nobility, but also to the distinction between employers and employees, bourgeiosie, and working class. These distinctions also appeared in which form of address was used by whom. Two levels of formality existed grammatically: a formal you (*u, gij* [old fashioned or dialect]), and an informal you (*jij*). Dutch immigrants to the United States generally came from the class of people who were the informal "you"s in many social settings in the Netherlands.

For the Dutch, English embodied a new world. English was the language of freedom—free from conventions, free from many aspects of gender, free from levels of formality that could imbue class distinctions.[19] We do not argue that this was so automatically. There are many other ways besides grammar for a language to impose class and gender differences.[20] New speakers of a language, however, were less likely to notice those distinctions, particularly if they were used to much more overt ones. Further, the social circumstances in which the Dutch lived reinforced the freedoms they experienced in grammar.[21] What, in their eyes, was a society with relatively few class divisions and offered women and men many more opportunities than in the Netherlands, was reflected in the grammatical changes they encountered.

A key to this shift was the Dutch status in an American ethnic and racial hierarchy. The Dutch enjoyed the privileges of race and ethnicity in a society that increasingly stressed such characteristics. When the Dillingham Commission published its monumental study of immigrants in 1911 as a prelude to immigration restrictions, the Dutch came out in the text as one of the "good" groups.[22] In a number of ways, the Dutch were similar to those from various other nations coming in the same period. They generally were from very modest economic circumstances, often farm hands or domestics, or from situations where conditions were deteriorating, as with skill or job obsolescence due to technology, or farms which became too small to support the family. But the Dutch differed from many immigrants of the period in that they came more often in families and went disproportionately to rural areas at a time when industrialization enticed most immigrants to cities and favored single young men. The assistance of Dutch-descended individuals in the U.S. further privileged this group of immigrants.[23] None of this exempted the Dutch from some elements of discrimination. They faced legislation banning foreign languages in public schools and then in public in the Midwest, and during World War I, found themselves the target of attacks by those who often confused or saw little difference between Dutch and Deutsch (German). The degree to which Dutch Americans felt betrayed and upset by such acts underscored their evaluation of their own ethnic group's status.[24] In all, their privileged ethnic and racial status meant that they faced few barriers to economic and social mobility in the "new world" of freedom.

The perception of freedom and of new opportunity was partially a function of migration. While the immigrants' knowledge of what they left behind was not totally static, increasingly they missed the new developments of the "old" world. So, just as Herbert Brinks illustrated that there was a specific demographic component to calling one's homeland the "old world"—many of the people to whom immigrants wrote were literally older—so too did immigrants often not hear about new trends from their homeland.[25] This reinforced the association between innovative behavior and "America." Trends that took place concurrently or with limited time lapse in urban areas of the Netherlands and the U.S., immigrants read about and experienced in their new setting. Considering that the turn of the century was a period in the Netherlands in which earlier class patterns were breaking down as industrialization reached more rural areas, and one in which the women's movement began to make rapid progress, especially in opening up occupations for women and improving working conditions for some female employees (not to mention in gaining suffrage), the impression immigrants had of their homeland became outdated rapidly.[26] That did not make the perception any less real to them.

"American" had the association of new and innovative. In some cases, this was figurative. Advertisers who wanted to introduce new products would use phrases or even entire advertisements in English in otherwise Dutch-language publications. They also would adopt the conversational style typical of American advertising in this period: "Drink a glass of Ezinga's milk at bedtime. You'll sleep better...."[27] Conversely, even after Dutch American publications switched to English, they would use older images of the Netherlands, such as a woman in a traditional costume, to create nostalgia for Dutch products such as Droste cocoa or Frou-Frou wafers.[28] English was also literally part of the association with newness due to a pattern of loan words for new inventions creeping into the letters of immigrants (threshing machine, picture show, telephone, automobile).[29]

In terms of gender roles, nearly all Dutch and Dutch American commentators agreed that they were different in America, and the biggest differences applied to women. In America women had much more freedom and a wider variety of opportunities than women in the Netherlands, and both Dutch immigrants and visitors from the Netherlands provided ample evidence to support this assumption. Whether in terms of more job opportunities or better wages, a more elaborate institutional life, greater roles in churches and philanthropy, legal rights, or even physical mobility, Dutch immigrants were astounded at what American women could do. Their evaluations of American women's gender roles, however, varied substantially. Men, almost without exception, disapproved of various apects of women's gender roles, particularly the freedom and "leisure" they perceived among American women. Women tended to have more mixed feelings. Young immigrant women often embraced American opportunities and the language that provided them, while women who arrived as married adults were some of the least likely to learn English and the strongest opponents of linguistic shift. On the spectrum of language conservators and language innovators, women occupied the extremes.

In our research for a book on Dutch immigrant women, the women who most challenged Dutch gender roles all switched to English relatively quickly after migration and lived most of their adult years primarily among English speakers, in some cases almost abandoning their Dutch ethnic contacts. For example, Cornelia de Groot studied English even before coming to the United States. She joined her sister, who was married to an American, in San Francisco. Unlike the vast majority of Dutch immigrant women, she never married.[30] Family members recalled her advocacy of women's suffrage, which also went against the grain. De Groot worked as a freelance journalist, writing for the San Francisco *Chronicle* and other English-language journals. She published a book about her childhood in the Netherlands as part of a series on "Children of Other Lands" in 1917. In *When I was a Girl in Holland*, De Groot described the limited educational and occupational op-

Gender in Language and Life 131

portunities available to her there, and cast her migration story as one of emancipation.[31]

Anna Kuijt offered another example of a woman who used English as a vehicle for challenging gender roles. Kuijt moved to Chicago in 1907, joining two siblings. She worked as a domestic servant, sometimes for Dutch Americans, but once her English skills improved mainly for AngloAmericans, who paid better wages. Unlike domestics in the Netherlands who were tied to year-long contracts, she changed jobs frequently, far too frequently according to her brother. In numerous cases, her siblings tried to control and advise her, but she refused. When her chronic leg ailment left her in their care for an extended stay, Kuijt's siblings tried to get her to return to the Netherlands. She refused. When she had recovered, Kuijt took a job cleaning in a hotel, which allowed her to have evenings and two days a week free. Much to her relatives' dismay, she lived in a rented room and ate out at a restaurant. In 1918, Kuijt, already in her late thirties, wrote to her brother in the Netherlands that she had married Dudley Bates, a "Yankee" (generic white American), after a short courtship. Her brother in Chicago wrote angrily that Kuijt had not informed the family members in the area ahead of time. Kuijt's last surviving letter indicated her nephews should try to write to "Uncle Dudley" in English because he could not understand any Dutch.[32] Like many young immigrant women, Kuijt took advantages of job opportunities and the singles culture of the city.[33] English language use was crucial to these activities, and eventually helped her to marry someone from outside her ethnic background.

A third example was Cornelia De Bey (de Beij), who attended non-Dutch programs of higher education, becoming first a teacher and then a doctor. She later worked with Hull House reformers and was elected to the Chicago school board. De Bey further defied convention by wearing "male" clothing and sharing her home with an AngloAmerican woman. She was quite active in the suffrage movement, and notably, gained information about the Dutch suffrage movement from an American contact, Anna Howard Shaw, head of the National American Woman Suffrage Association.[34] De Bey's commitment to the English language reflected that of other rebels. A children's book based on her childhood described language use in her family when she was young: "Though Dutch was spoken in the family, and familiarly among the people of the parish, Cornelia was thoroughly, nay, almost aggressively, American. She spoke English, and a great deal of it, among her companions. . . . "[35] The pattern of women consciously choosing to leave behind the language *and* some of the gender role conventions was consistent for women who pushed linguistic innovation.

These women formed one extreme. That they all lived in urban areas was not surprising. The kind of challenges they posed would have been more difficult to achieve in the small and insular Dutch American settlements in more rural areas. In those regions, young women were more likely to make moderate demands for change, and less likely to achieve them due to communal pressure. For the more rebellious in rural areas, the more likely option was to leave town. English was also related to that possibility. Further, the "rebels" illustrated a pattern noted on both sides of the Atlantic for young single women to switch more quickly than male peers into the dominant language, whether standard Dutch as opposed to dialect in the Netherlands, or English as opposed to Dutch in the United States.[36]

An essential part of the age difference was the access young women had to the private life of people outside their ethnic group. Serving as a domestic was one of the few possibilities for learning nursery rhymes and patterns of child socialization, names for household items, cooking and other aspects of food preparation specific to American ways, and customs of American household organization. Adult women, unlike adult men, did not have access to the American version of their workplace. Only very close friendship with Americans might have provided this. The idea of a division between private and public spheres in American life meant that men were more likely than women to have access to (public) male roles in English at later stages in life. Young women, on the other hand, had the greatest access possible to American life.

At the other end of the spectrum were the women who opposed shifting language. Sociolinguists generally view European women from the kind of background that produced most Dutch emigration as conservators of language. Women trained young children in basic language skills. They passed on their household knowledge with terminology as well as training and equipment. They used the terms and experiences they knew in order to imbue the next generation with a religious world view, one where the father ruled the home. Certainly this was also the case for many Dutch immigrant women, who used Dutch in their homes. For those who came as adults with children, particularly if they entered rural communities, their chances for learning the new language were minimal. They might learn some English from their children in a generational role reversal, or through a laborious comparison of Dutch and English Bibles. Parents often switched to an English Bible at home at some point after the first or last child began school, trying to maintain religion for the following generation, even if the language was lost.[37] A few immigrant women took opportunities related to Americanization programs. But official statistics reaffirmed the inability of older Dutch immigrant women to speak English. In the Dillingham Commission reports of 1911 focusing on employees, Dutch women who arrived before age fourteen were listed as English speaking over

99 percent of the time, as opposed to just over 34 percent of those who were above age fourteen at migration. In contrast, over 80 percent of Dutch men in the older at migration category were listed as knowing English.[38] For those not in the paid work force, most household tasks did not require English-language skills. Only in purchasing was it a major issue, and that might be handled by the father or a child. The standard comment in women's letters, that men's needs always came first in terms of farm equipment, household items, and other purchases, had a basis not only in familial power, but also in differential access to consumption due to language skills.

Information about women who sought to maintain Dutch was less forthcoming than that about the rebels, for the latter group attracted and sometimes demanded attention, whereas the more conservative group was occupied with raising children, keeping households and running farms, and less likely to voice their sentiments in public settings. For some women, as with men, Dutch was strongly related to religion. One woman reminisced about a discussion in her Holland, Michigan, church women's group at the time when some younger women wanted to form an English language group. "And one of the ladies in the Dutch group said, but in heaven they will have to speak Dutch."[39] While the sentiment was religious, it also heralded the trend of older women losing their status as advisors to younger ones in one of their main social outlets.

Women were most likely to enforce language retention in the home. One author quoted her mother as scolding: "'This is a Dutch household, and you will speak Dutch here.'"[40] The mother, "Betje" Moerkerk, was also the driving force in sending her children to Dutch catechism classes and trying to keep them out of contact with American life, which she frequently labeled as immoral. The inability of Moerkerk to communicate with American doctors concerning several major health problems that persisted despite treatment only contributed to her lack of confidence in their abilities.[41] This was a sentiment shared by many Dutch immigrants, and a reasonably well-founded one based on the development of medical science in the Netherlands compared to the United States in the late nineteenth century.[42] For women, who generally handled informal care of the ill, Dutch was the language of "proper" medicine, just as it was for "proper" religion.

Dingena T. van Beek Berkhout's reminiscences typified the slow shift out of Dutch and into English that commitment to the mother tongue promoted. Van Beek Berkhout was born in the province of Zeeland in 1893 and migrated to the United States with her parents in 1908. The family settled in Grand Rapids, Michigan, a heavily Dutch American community. She worked in the family bakery, where they did business in both Dutch and English, and she attended church services in both languages. In reminiscing about her linguistic background, Van Beek Berkhout stressed that it was her mother who ingrained in her an appreciation for her native tongue, so that nearly sixty years later, she was still fluent in Dutch and proudly recited the Dutch poem:

> I was raised in the Netherlands
> I learned to speak in the Netherlands
> I will continue to promote the same
> kind of love for the language
> Not that I revile the foreign
> Everything has its worth
> But I say, for me, Dutch
> is the most beautiful language on earth.[43]

The interest of such women in maintaining their Dutch and passing it on to the next generation did not preclude learning English, but it did slow language death. That many older women, especially those who came as married adults, tried to maintain Dutch in their homes and communities was not simply a matter of access to learning English. Their (limited) roles of authority, status, and power were often linked to Dutch.

Dutch was also the language needed to maintain ties to the Netherlands. There was an irony in the English word "family" for Dutch speakers. In Dutch, *gezin* referred to nuclear family, while *familie* indicated extended family. It was extended family contacts that were harder to maintain after migration. The shift toward English pushed people toward more reliance on those in the U.S., and generally toward more reliance on nuclear families. Because men were more likely to migrate and to have greater decision-making power over whoever would follow, be it a sibling, a spouse, or a parent, the overall pattern was one in which men were somewhat more likely to be able to recreate an extended family in their new setting. In the oral tradition of one Wisconsin family, the decision to migrate was specifically one of duties to nuclear family versus extended family. The daughter retold the poignant story of her mother, whose husband decided to leave for America. The father knew it would be a difficult decision for his wife to make, but posed it in terms of "'I am going to America ... will you come along?'"[44] The wife agreed, much to the chagrin of her parents. Among their reasons for opposition to the move was the fact that she was the only daughter, and hence the prime candidate to care for them in old age. On the docks, the grandfather held his grandson in his arms: "my father walked up to him and took that child and went onto the boat."[45]

Retaining Dutch could be a way for a woman to maintain contact with the

Gender in Language and Life 135

extended family she left behind. Further, women's familial roles were more closely tied to extended family, whether caring for the elderly, offering moral and housekeeping support during and after the birth of a baby, providing advice on household tasks, or simply socializing over coffee. One of the ways in which women frequently evaluated America was in terms of how many family members were there. As one woman from Pella, Iowa, reminisced:

> Mother? ... oh, she missed Holland heaps at first, oh yes. She had one brother here, that was all, and my father had more brothers and sisters. That helped, but it was still like she could not break away from her house, from her family as easily.[46]

Men also faced these problems, but not to the same degree, both because of the greater ability to bring in their relatives and the difference in gender roles. Men had a variety of roles apart from the family; married women had few. Women may have conserved the mother tongue more often than men, but I would argue that this was as much a matter of pragmatism as conservatism. Whereas young women saw opportunities opening to them through English, older women saw more lost than gained.

For men, a similar but narrower spectrum of language shift existed. The degree to which a man could move into an English-language world and succeed was epitomized by Edward Bok, editor of the *Ladies Home Journal* from 1889 to 1919. Bok's parents moved to Brooklyn when he was young, and thereafter, the family had little to do with other Dutch immigrants. Bok entered public schools with no training in English. As he described it (in the third person): " ... with a change of vowel here and there the English language was not so difficult of [*sic*] conquest. At all events, he set out to master it."[47] Later in his autobiography, he chided the public school system as generally inadequate in teaching English, and a major barrier to Americanization.[48] In any case, Bok obtained an elementary education, but then had to train himself beyond that.

Bok took over as editor at the *Ladies Home Journal* after establishing a reputation with other publishing firms. A few years later, he married the daughter of the publisher (who was not of Dutch descent). Historians in recent years have disagreed on the impact of his editorship on the content of the journal and on the meaning of that content for journal readers.[49] In editorials and in choosing columns, Bok often took relatively conservative positions, opposing woman suffrage and highlighting mothers, wives, and daughters of famous men, for example. These were positions that fit with an idea of women as parts of families rather than individuals, a position widely held among Dutch immigrants as well as many others. Yet the journal still focused on women, encouraged individual consumption, and brought up controversial issues that raised readers' awareness. It also created a Anglo-bourgeois image of women, one many immigrants challenged.[50]

Bok's autobiography, *The Americanization of Edward Bok: The Autobiography of a Dutch Boy Fifty Years After,* was a rags-to-riches story with little ethnic content, despite the title. It followed the form of autobiographies of the day, and won a Pulitzer Prize. It included a clearly fictional account of some of his ancestors and an inaccurate, at best, rendition of why the family came to America. The book did not sell well among Dutch immigrants, who generally did not read the *Ladies Home Journal* anyway, nor did it do as well as hoped in Dutch translation, perhaps due to the perception in the Netherlands that autobiographical writing was pompous. Others suggested that some of the "Dutch virtues" that Bok delineated were not Dutch at all. Bok lived in an English-language world, but he still used and promoted his Dutch ancestry under certain circumstances. After retirement, he took various positions promoting better relations between the United States and the Netherlands, making numerous trips across the Atlantic and illustrating that he had not lost his Dutch language skills.[51] For all that, Bok was exceptional. Elements of his language use were not.

Young immigrant men, while wanting some of the economic opportunities provided by America, generally were less happy about the shifting gender roles. Aart Plaisier typified this position. Plaisier, a cabinetmaker who made his way into the furniture industry around Grand Rapids, Michigan, noted gender role differences from the outset.

> Often you can see children, that is boys or girls . . . fly through the city in large autos . . . Also, women are often seen driving horses and wagons. And women also ride with the horses between their leg. . . . There are also many lovely girls here, but you must be careful. If you try to stop and say hello to such a girl, she calls a police agent, and then you go to jail or pay $18.00. Yes, the stinkers do, in fact, have such a law here. Sometimes the girls walk along the streets and show off like peacocks ··· [52]

Later that year, he wrote that young "Dutch" women would not or could not speak Dutch. In the same letter, he reported he was in English-language class three evenings a week.[53] The propensity of men to go back to the Netherlands to find a spouse rather than marry a second-generation woman, or to complain about young women who had been in the United States too long, was related to a general idea of changing gender roles. As Plaisier wrote: "I think that I will go back to the Netherlands to look before I marry, maybe I can turn up a helpmate. It is sad here regarding the females."[54] His brother seconded the opinion:

> Now they say that there are no girls in America, but I can tell you that there are more girls than boys here in Grand Rapids, but they don't want to speak Dutch and they have a lot of say in things.[55] . . . the girls are nice enough, but they are the boss.[56]

Aart Plaisier eventually did marry a woman of the second generation, though one from a rural area, and the couple took charge of a farm from her family and went into raising and marketing crops.

The most common pattern in language usage among Dutch immigrant men was the practical approach that associated learning English with economic opportunities and success: "This year there were a lot of farmers shipping their cattle . . . By this time I can speak English just as well as Dutch so that I can help myself very well on these trips."[57] The author, Ulbe Eringa, had come to the United States in his twenties, and lived with an American family for a period in order to learn the language. He had been in the U.S. almost thirteen years when he wrote about this fluency, but he, like others, reported being able to function in English within months of arrival. Further, one of the reasons he reported for wanting to learn English was to stem the shift of children away from older ideals, so he could teach Sunday school.[58]

Immigrant ministers were often leading proponents of the shift to English for this reason as well, seeking to insure that the next generation would remain in the church. Shifting from teaching and preaching in Dutch to English could be difficult, though most managed this relatively well due to better educational possibilities and background. Given that churches held three (different) services each Sunday, switching one service to English provided a way to ease the congregation into the language. But even those who advocated the shift found aspects of American religious practice creeping in with the language: "Many women as well as the men pray publicly."[59] The common practice in the Netherlands was for women to be silent in mixed settings. Likewise, one dominie who opposed switching a service to English explained that he felt those interested in the switch actually were less interested in the language than in the "more informal" style of service.[60] The minister of a Christian Reformed Church in Holland, Michigan, reported in a denominational publication about leading the "Young Ladies' Mission Circle" in studies of Biblical women and in writing essays critical of the Campfire Girls, Y.W.C.A., and W.C.T.U. The article made the purpose clear:

> There is a tendency especially among our English-speaking churches, to conform to the church life as it evinces itself in the broad American church world. Our young people in general, even of our Dutch congregations, show that tendency. All are afraid to be called narrow and bigoted. . . . the Reformed truth

is as broad as the universe ... Our young people must be indoctrinated, thoroughly indoctrinated.[61]

Whether he knew it or not, he was following the advice that had appeared a decade earlier in another denominational publication. In a 1908 news story on the woman's suffrage movement in *De Gereformeerde Amerikaan*, the author first argued forcefully that giving women the vote would be to overturn God's order. He went on: "And be on the lookout for all organizations, which, directly or indirectly, contribute to this movement."[62] In any case, many ministers sought to use English in order to preserve religion.

Preserving religion and patriarchy went hand in hand. To maintain the father-dominated homes that many orthodox Protestants sought to create and replicate, fathers had to keep control of language. Thus, the need for fathers to learn English rapidly enough to stem dissension among the younger generation was also more acute than for mothers. For all that, "Yankee" society assumed women were the primary force in the home, Dutch American households generally still followed a more patriarchal pattern in which the father's role in the home was predominant. It was the father who led in reading the Bible and who made the decisions (sometimes in consultation with a spouse, but not necessarily) about when the language in the family would shift. It was primarily the father's decision whether the children would attend religious education programs featuring Dutch language, or whether they would attend public schools. Thus, in familial roles as in economic roles, men who were or intended to be fathers required skills in English.

Thus, older Dutch immigrant men faced similar circumstances of generational shift that occurred for their female counterparts. A major difference, however, was the degree to which they *could* learn English and, thus, maintain their position in the new as well as the old language. A minority of women who migrated as adults would have the opportunity to learn English, particularly to reach a level of fluency. While older men might not learn it as quickly or as well as their children, most did learn English because of their economic roles, which put them in regular contact with English speakers. Women, often primarily occupied in the home, did not have this option. This made for different perceptions of language shift.

Thus far, our comments have dealt largely with a range of individual and familial responses. Next, we turn to the ethnic group as a larger unit. Within Dutch Protestant America, language itself was changing in this period. Migration had begun on a large scale in the late 1840s and, hence, a second and even a third generation existed in some of the older settlements. Newer migrants sometimes joined these communities, and in most cases had ties to them. On the one hand, they were learning Standard Dutch in order to speak to those of different provincial backgrounds. This operated as an important aspect of ethnic group cohesion. On the other hand, communities began to use English on more formal levels: a church service here, advertisements and then articles in the paper there, a form of language on the street which some called "Yankee Dutch." In linguistic terms, English became the language of choice in more domains of activity.[63]

The move to standard Dutch helped build ethnic group cohesion. Whereas the early arrivals named their communities and described themselves in local or provincial terms, the process of mixing created a more generic Dutch identity. For new immigrants, intermarriage as a concept meant crossing provincial boundaries. As the group switched to English, the idea of "marrying out" increasingly meant outside the broader Dutch or Dutch-descended population. Even later, beyond the period of study, it went a step further to mean religious mixing.

In the process of switching from Dutch to English, the ethnic group was moving away from a language with formal gender to one without. For obvious reasons, it was easier to do more things in America if one knew English. Thus, people associated speaking English with activity, particularly new activity. This had important psychological implications.

> And mother said, Nel is a born American, she wants a bit of everything, she does a bit of everything, and mother got pleasure out of that, that I did all those things. Well, then I was a Sunday School teacher and that was in English and I belonged to various organizations. ...[64]

The association, sometimes found in interviews such as this, replicated the sense that language allowed the young to challenge the normal generational hierarchy and, particularly for women, prescribed gender roles, at least in terms of economic endeavors and certain opportunities outside the home. It also illustrated that in some cases mothers supported their daughters in these efforts.[65] Male community leaders, from ministers to fathers, sought to control the meanings of English language life in this context. They made compromises, allowing women a more public voice, the possibility to teach Sunday school, opportunities to go to denominational colleges and to become missionaries. Increasingly they endorsed a new vision of womanhood, not the "New Woman" by any means, but a vision which allowed for greater individual ambitions. As the leaders of the next generation went on for education, learning Dutch in high school or college was a common phenomenon for the young men. Because the language was primarily associated with the study of theology, the absence of women, who were barred from such training, was not surprising. Women who crossed the boundary into English were not likely to go back.

More importantly, crossing the boundary into English brought a shift from a more class-based world into one in which, despite economic distance between migrants, there was greater adherence to one common (bourgeois) standard of language. In nineteenth-century Dutch, titles were used to create class distinctions. A domestic servant, even one from roughly the same economic background as her employer, referred to her employer as *mevrouw*, whereas the servant was called by her first name.[66] The same was true for both male and female farmhands. In English, the class element largely disappeared. In the Midwest and the Plains states, where most Dutch immigrants settled, jobs of this sort were on a much more egalitarian basis. Dutch American domestics and farmhands described their employers by their first names, or sometimes by title and last name, but not by a title only, which was seen in the letters of Dutch domestics to the United States. Their employers called them by their first names and "you," which sounded like the Dutch formal you [*u*]. This combination was the kind that two adult family members might use in the Netherlands in talking to one another.

In addition to servants and hired hands, the other group of people consistently referred to by the informal "you" in Dutch were children. Within the family, addressing one's parents and siblings with the formal "you" could be a sign of respect, or it could be a sign of putting distance between one another. Around 1900, at least among the bourgeoisie, Dutch parents in the Netherlands began allowing children to call them *jij* (informal "you"). After World War I, this went a step further, so that parents would allow their children to call them by their first names.[67] Among the immigrant letter writers, a formal "you" (*u*) continued to predominate, though the more old-fashioned *gij* [thou] began to fade by 1920. Young people, those writing late in the period of study, and those who frequently spoke English were more likely to use the informal "you." The switch reinforced a lack of hierarchy in America, and the association of English language usage with an innovation in Dutch language use as well.

The lack of standards of formality interspersed immigrant letters in other ways. H. Koopman, born in the town of Borger, in the province of Drenthe, described his status in 1894 thus:

> If your children were here, they would be far better off because those who start out as laborers in Borger remain laborers. Better possibilities are available here. But I don't want to urge anyone to come here because the surroundings are entirely different. But I have an American spirit and I like it much better than in the Netherlands. In the city I can enter a tavern and sit next to a lawyer to drink beer and smoke a cigar. We walk down the same streets. And at a public meeting I can go in and sit down with any gentleman and wear clothes that are as good and fine as his—including starched collars and fashions of that sort.[68]

"Gentleman" in this case is a translation of *Mijnheer*. Koopman sent his relatives in the Netherlands some books in English. He did this in a period when he had been in the United States for only a couple of years, himself.

Much of the Dutch American community tried to adopt middle-class norms in referring to men and women in English. This meant a standard "Mr." for most men, with other common titles for ministers (dominie), doctors, and professors. The titles of professional status were basically identical. Again, the major shifts came in referring to women. In church consistory minutes, obituaries, and newspaper stories, women went from birth names followed by marriage information (Minke de Vries, married Brouwer) or first name and married name followed by birth name (Minke Brouwer, née De Vries), to simply title and husband's name (Mrs. Gerrit Brouwer).[69] The best example of this shift we encountered was in an entry to the minutes of the Holland Home board meeting. This group, which ran a major nonprofit home for the elderly in Grand Rapids, Michigan, kept minutes in Dutch until the 1930s, but English words and phrases kept creeping in. At one meeting, board member Emma Stoel Heyboer was listed as "Mrs. Joh," then the "Mrs. Joh" was crossed out and "Emma" written over it, followed by "Heyboer."[70] Single women became "Miss." Shifts in names showed, once again, a growing acceptance of American middle-class standards. While linguists may regard women as the ones most likely to choose a more standard/bourgeois form, in almost all these cases it was men who did the writing. As titles changed, two continued to hold on in Dutch: *dominie* (minister), and *juffrouw* (minister's wife or teacher). The first was already formally adopted into English, and the second no longer had the marital or class status components it originally held in Dutch. Both, notably, were titles of respect.

Translating gendered job titles into English also required a new way of thinking. Given that many Dutch immigrants settled in rural areas, titles referring to farming were some of the most common. Men often adopted "farmer" rather than *boer* to describe their activities. In the Netherlands, a *boer/boerin* had a relatively high class status, whereas many of the emigrants had been farm laborers. But without the class system and without so many servile servants, the *boer* and *boerin* could not exist in America. While "farmer" reasonably accurately described what a man did, "farmer's wife" in the American connotation did not describe Dutch immigrant women and their more extensive activities on farms. Thus, when Cornelia De Groot, herself the daughter of a *boer* and *boerin*, wrote about women working on farms, she labeled them "farmerettes."[71] The term did not catch on, but the distinction of women's activities in rural areas continued.[72]

Clearly, anglicization meant adopting different class ideals. Long before Dutch American publications switched to English, they began to use "ladies" as a loan word to refer to women. This borrowing signified a shift toward a bourgeois American ideal, a move into the middle class ideologically, if not economically.[73] Dutch Americans rarely used the Dutch equivalent for ladies, *dames*, because in migrant circles it continued to have a somewhat negative (aristocratic, snobby) connotation, one associated with the caste-like *standen* of the Netherlands.[74] Women's church groups followed this pattern as well. Those adopting Dutch titles used some form of *vrouwen*, the generic term for women/wives, not *dames*. Yet, even those groups that used Dutch exclusively in their meetings frequently took the title "Ladies' Aid."[75] Like most linguistic borrowing, it referred to a group for which there was no precedent in Dutch. In an editorial for *The Banner*, the author explained their origin:

> The present-day societies are noble successors to the organizations started about a century ago by Elizabeth Fry, Florence Nightingale, the German Frauen Verein of 1813, and the women's associations which arose in our country during the Civil War and the decade following it.[76]

The ethnic group as a whole viewed such women's organizations as American.

Many of the women's activities that Dutch-language religious newspapers reported originally appeared elsewhere in English. *De Heidenwereld* [Heathen World], for example, regularly carried reports from the Women's Executive Committee of the Reformed Church, a group dominated by colonial-descended Dutch. They also carried reports from English speaking missionaries, including some by Dutch descended men and women who went into the mission field. These, as well as articles from English-language publications such as *Mission Field*, helped reinforce the association of activity, especially for women, and English. The ministers who edited church-related (and often general) magazines, found their clientele expanding as women's missionary societies took root rapidly in Dutch American communities.

Reaching out to this new clientele, however, entailed a different tradition of reporting on women, one that was unfamiliar and made some editors uneasy. The editor of *The Banner*, for example, wrote that he was pleased with much of the work of the Ladies' Aid or Dorcas societies, but these groups sent in far too much information for the paper about their activities, particularly about how many clothing or bedding items they produced. He also warned that such groups could become "Talking Clubs," a common fate of "American" women's church groups.[77] The editorial, as a whole, hinted at a problem these women faced, and at why they have since received so little attention. Much of what the papers published dealt with theology, sometimes in excruciating detail. Women were not supposed to delve into this subject, certainly not for a mixed audience. Yet, what women did in their groups aside from discussion of religious topics was questionable as "news."

A similar change in the evaluation of women's activities took place in redefining the *koffie* [literally "coffee," but colloquially "coffee break"]. As men increasingly took to American work standards without coffee breaks, the once honorable and mandatory pause turned into a women's "gossip" session. It was part of a larger process that eliminated not just the word *gezellig* [German *gemütlich*], but also the concept. For those who remembered the mixture of sociability, pleasant surroundings, coziness, and fun that it embodied, it was a major loss. This shift in thinking became the subject of one of many cultural commentaries by "Yankee Dutch" writer Dirk Nieland: "Wat is er toch alletaim 'n gehossel en 'n gehurrie in deze wereld. 't Is toebed, want het maakt de piepel niet seddelsfaider." [What is there all the time a hussle and hurry in this world. It is too bad, because it doesn't make the people satisfider.] [78]

"Yankee Dutch" was generally a mixture of English words, written with a Dutch accent, anglicized Dutch words, English words altered to fit Dutch grammar, and other variations on a combination of the two languages.[79] It mimicked the everyday speech of many Dutch Americans who mixed the languages, sometimes without knowing it. As a literary genre, however, it mainly served as in-group humor and social commentary. Dirk Nieland published several works in this "language" in the 1920s and beyond. In "Nog Wurser Femmelie Troebels" [Even Worse Family Troubles], the author presented the main character's son-in-law as someone with little courage: " . . . a good kid, oh sure, you bet! And a good cabinet maker, too! . . . But I mean, to use his brains with women."[80] As the main character, Lou Verlak, and his wife, Lena, arrived to visit their daughter, who had just come home from the hospital with a new baby, they were aghast to find their son-in-law washing diapers. Lena explained "that was a shame that a man had to do housework after his job."[81] The division of household labor appeared frequently in other parts of the book, as in descriptions of spring cleaning, when the main character Lou disappeared.

Nieland paid attention in his writings to cultural shifts, such as women's fashions. In "De Sonnieschoel Pikkenik" [The Sunday School Picnic], he described how the fastest woman runner lost the race when she tripped on her old-fashioned long skirts.[82] He also noted changing ideals about women's body size: "The world is funny. But maybe eating is going out of fashion. I have heard that lately women have started to just eat a tiny little bit, because they want to be skinny, because that is the fashion."[83] Just as his writing took an intermediate position between English and Dutch, so too did his evaluation of shifts in women's roles. The same was true for his evaluation of gender and language. "Zwaantje spreekt geen Hollandsch meer" [Zwaantje No Longer Speaks Dutch] poked fun at Zwaantje, who after only two years in the United States refused to speak Dutch. She ran into problems in a store ordering shirt baize fabric—*baai* in Dutch—getting instead a red-headed boy. What was even more telling, however, was Zwaantje's interaction with her mother: "And if she has to talk with her mother/Who does not even understand "yes" or "no,"/—Whether it be in a streetcar or in a store—/Then she avails herself of whispering."[84] At the end of the poem, however, Zwaantje had to speak Dutch after all in order to be understood. Language shift was, in this case, both the subject and the vehicle for social commentary.

For those Dutch Americans who shifted to writing in English, gendered standards also applied, and those standards differed according to the audience. The autobiographies of Edward Bok and Cornelia De Groot, mentioned earlier, were aimed at a non-Dutch descended audience more than at those of the same background. While Bok's fit the ideal for a contemporary American autobiography, De Groot's was a children's book, a typical genre for women writers. In both cases, they blended into an American white identity, yet could still refer to their ethnic background. Those writing for the Dutch American group in English had different limitations. Arnold Mulder, for example, wrote novels that, at times, ridiculed the strict orthodoxy of many Dutch immigrants.[85] While he encountered some resistance, he continued to live in Holland, Michigan, and find an audience among the ethnic group throughout his life. The same was not true of Cobie de Lespinasse. Though from a prominent family in Orange City, Iowa, de Lespinasse did not remain there, but moved to a non-Dutch setting on the West Coast. Her novel, *The Bells of Helmus,* clearly based on her own youth in Orange City, also challenged religious othodoxy, particularly as it had an impact on gender roles. The exchange between the minister's wife and a man who disagreed with his wife's religious views was typical:

> "*Juffrouw*, you mean well and I honor you for it. But the wife must obey the man. He is the head of the house and she must obey. The Bible teaches this."
> "And if Lena will not obey, Kees?"
> "Then I shall strap her. The man is the head and the wife must obey."[86]

The novel was published by a non-Dutch American press and gained scathing comments from commentators within the community who read it.[87] Yet, the novel had difficulty attracting a broader audience, for it was too heavily interlaced with disputes and jargon only those in the group could appreciate. In the literary culture of Dutch Americans, religion and gender were both important themes, but how far one could challenge them before losing the audience on grounds of apostacy was a fine line. Just as Dutch America generally had more difficulties with women than men taking an active role in determining religious policy, so too the community had less tolerance for a woman writer attacking either religion or gender. The offshoot was a very limited range of acceptable genres for Dutch American women wanting to write for the group. Further, there was the somewhat accurate perception that there were no Dutch American women writers—rather there were American women writers of Dutch descent.

Language shifts also affected literature in other ways. The switch to English generally accelerated the loss of archaic language. While some replaced their Dutch Bibles with the King James version in English, the rough equivalent to the old *Statenbijbel* authorized by the Synod of Dordt and published in 1637, many adopted a more modern version. The desire for sermons, devotional literature, and other materials geared for the Dutch American audience, but no longer available in Dutch, helped support the foundations of three major religious publishers which exist to this day: Zondervan, Baker Book House, and Eerdmans. These became the publishers of Christian school materials, for example.

For the most part, Dutch American children learned to function in English with their parents' and churches' active support. As much as Dutch American communities wanted to maintain a degree of isolation from the rest of the world, they also wanted to function economically in a broader American context. That required skills in English. Religion, rather than language, was generally considered the crucial part of group identity and, hence, one could shift supposedly without giving up the core. Yet, language shift did help create a different world, one in which women could do more (even in the church) and in which class distinctions faded in importance for both men and women. The lack of gender and (easily discernible) class distinctions in English did not create those patterns in America, but the language reinforced what people saw and helped them create a mental world in which neither gender nor hierarchy had the same meaning as it had before. In the time of transition, before the patterns of words as symbols of class and gender systems had ingrained themselves into peoples' lives, when they still remembered a different way of thinking, language assisted in changing life.

Notes

I would like to thank Caroline Smits, Walter Kamphoefner, Donna Gabaccia, David Gerber, Hasia Diner, and Nancy Green for comments on earlier versions of this material. I also wish to acknowledge the assistance of staff members at the P.J. Meertens Institute, Rijksarchief Leeuwarden, Heritage Hall at Calvin College, and Joint Archives of Holland (Michigan). Research for the essay was made possible by several fellowships which I acknowledge here: U.S. Foreign Language and Area Studies, Dutch Ministry of Education, and McMillen Dissertation Grant (University of Minnesota).

   1. See, for example, Susan Gal, *Language Shift* (New York: Academic Press, 1979); Pauline Burton, Ketaki Kushari Dyson, and Shirley Ardener, eds., *Bilingual Women* (Oxford: Berg, 1994); Don Kulick, *Language Shift and Cultural Reproduction* (New York: Cambridge University Press, 1992). For U.S. immigrants, one of the key works is Joshua Fishman et al., *Language Loyalty in the United States* (The Hague: Mouton, 1966), though gender is not a major component of this work.
   2. See Kira Hall and Mary Bucholtz, eds. *Gender Articulated: Language and the Socially Constructed Self* (London: Routledge, 1995); Micaela di Leonardo, ed., *Gender at the Crossroads of Knowledge* (Berkeley: University of California Press, 1991).
   3. For some insight on language study related to gender and history, see Joan W. Scott, "On Language, Gender, and Working-Class History," *International Labor and Working-Class History* 31 (Spring 1987): 1–13. Some historians have combined research on personal correspondence and U.S. ethnic perceptions effectively and, in these studies, issues of language figure heavily. For an overview of this material, see David A. Gerber, "The Immigrant Letter between Positivism and Populism: The Uses of Immigrant Personal Correspondence in Twentieth-Century American Scholarship," *Journal of American Ethnic History* 16 (Summer 1997): 3–34. Among historians combining the study of language and gender, there are at least two main theoretical directions. Virginia Yans McLaughlin exemplifies one, using anthropological techniques in combining gender and ethnic studies, focusing on oral histories: "Metaphors of Self in History: Subjectivity, Oral Narrative, and Immigration Studies," in *Immigration Reconsidered* (New York: Oxford, 1990), pp. 254–290. A second approach derives from linguistics. Betty Bergland, for example, utilizes study of discourse to evaluate immigrant women's autobiographies: "Ideology, Ethnicity, and the Gendered Subject: Reading Immigrant Women's Autobiographies," in *Seeking Common Ground*, ed. Donna Gabaccia (Westport: Greenwood Press, 1992), pp. 101–121.
   4. On this, see Cliff Goddard and Anna Wierzbicka. "Discourse and Culture," in *Discourse as Social Interaction*, ed. Teun A. van Dijk (London: Sage Publications, 1997), p. 232. They adopt Dell Hymes's phrase "communicative competence" to describe the ways in which a speaker must not only use appropriate grammar and vocabulary, but also a style that fits the language and the setting. Dell Hymes, "The Ethnography of Speaking," reprinted in *Readings in the Sociology of Language*, ed. Joshua Fishman (The Hague: Mouton, 1968), pp. 99–138.
   5. This contrasts somewhat with the more elaborate model of "domains" of speech that Fishman and others utilize.
   6. Goddard and Wierzbicka note age and gender are "near-universal" in requiring different discourse styles. Other factors which can determine speech categories they describe as being much more culturally bound, including things such as kinship, clan, ethnicity, caste, or rank. Goddard and Wierzbecka, "Discourse and Culture."
   7. There are several studies of Dutch language use in the U.S. in the twentieth century. See especially, Caroline Smits, *Disintegration of Inflection: The Case of Iowa Dutch* (Proefschrift, Vrije Universiteit te Amsterdam, 1996); Philip Webber, *Pella Dutch: The Portrait of a Language and its Use in One of Iowa's Ethnic Communities* (Ames: Iowa State University Press, 1988); and Jo Daan, *Is was te bissie . . . Nederlanders en hun taal in de Verenigde Staten* (Zutphen: Walburg Pers, 1987).
   8. Many of the sources are related to my book project on Dutch immigrant women, *Home is Where You Build It: Dutch Immigrant Women in the U.S., 1880–1920* (Urbana: University of Illinois Press, forthcoming).
   9. For an overview of the three waves, see Suzanne M. Sinke, "Dutch," in *A Nation of Peoples: A Sourcebook on America's Multicultural Heritage*, ed. Elliott Barkan (Westport: Greenwood, forthcoming 1999).
   10. The most complete study of Dutch immigration in this period remains Jacob van Hinte, *Netherlanders in America*, 2 vols. (Grand Rapids: Baker Book House, 1985 [Reprint and translation of 1928 edition]).
   11. See, for example, Smits, *Disintegration of Inflection*, p. 6.

12. The law passed by one vote. According to its provisions, children had to attend school for six years and to pass all classes up to the age of thirteen. Further, they needed to attend school "regularly." Hans Knippenberg, *Deelname aan het lager onderwijs in Nederland gedurende de negentiende eeuw. Een analyse van de landelijke ontwikkeling en van de regionale verschillen* (Amsterdam: Koninklijk Nederlands Aardrijkskundig Genootschap, 1986), p. 53. See also Fr. de Jong, "Vermenigvuldiging en deling: De groei van he Nederlandse Onderwijs," in *Honderdvijfentwintig Jaren Arbeid op het Onderwijsterrein 1836–1961*, ed. I.J. Brugmans (Groningen: J.B. Wolters, 1961), p. 112.

13. The Dutch school law of 1878 required that instructors teach girls handwork. Knippenberg, *Deelname aan het lager onderwijs*, pp. 51–52. See also Corstius and Hollema, *De Kunst van het Moederschap*, pp. 54–55.

14. P. Th. F. M. Boekhout and E. P. de Booy, *Geschiedenis van de school in Nederland* (Assen: Van Gorcum, 1987), p. 156.

15. I calculated these data using SPSS on a subfile of Dutch-born immigrants from the 1910 Public Use Sample, created at the University of Minnesota. The sample included 170 Dutch-born women, and 271 Dutch-born men. For comparison, the 1910 U.S. census listed a little over 120,000 persons born in the Netherlands. See Appendix 2 in Stephan Thernstrom, *Harvard Encyclopedia of American Ethnic Groups* (Cambridge: Harvard University Press, 1980), p. 1059.

16. See Philip Webber, *Pella Dutch*, pp. 64–65.

17. O.Vandeputte, P. Vincent, T. Hermans, *Dutch* (Lauwe: Stichting Ons Erfdeel, 1986), pp. 55–56. See also Vakgroep Neerlandistiek, Universiteit Wenen, "Dialecten," <http://www.ned.univie.ac.at/ publicaties/taalgeschiedenis/nl/dialecten.htm>, 14 May 1998.

18. Smits, *Disintegration of Inflection*, p. 15–17.

19. This, I would argue, helps answer David A. Gerber's question about what one German immigrant woman gained by experimenting with English, "'You See I Speak Wery Well Englisch': Literacy and the Transformed Self as Reflected in Immigrant Personal Correspondence," *Journal of American Ethnic History 12* (Winter 1993): 62.

20. Studies of linguistic differentiation of African American servants from their employers, for example, illustrated how some Americans sought to impose these distinctions. Likewise, British English managed to incorporate class into vocabulary, accent, and linguistic mannerism. See Judith Rollins, *Between Women: Domestics and their Employers* (Philadelphia: Temple University Press, 1985), chapter 5; and Peter Burke, "Introduction," in *The Social History of Language*, eds. Peter Burke and Roy Porter (Cambridge: Cambridge University Press, 1987), pp. 1–20.

21. This is a crucial point. See Joan W. Scott's "On Language, Gender, and Working-Class History," *International Labor and Working-Class History* 31 (Spring 1987): 1–13, in which she critiques Gareth Stedman Jones on specifically this point. Compare Gareth Stedman Jones, *Languages of Class: Studies in English Working Class History, 1832–1982* (Cambridge: Cambridge University Press, 1983).

22. [William P. Dillingham et al.], *Reports of the Immigration Commission*, 42 vols. (Washington: U.S. Government Printing Office, 1911).

23. On this topic, see Sucheng Chan, "European and Asian Immigration to the United States in Comparative Perspective, 1820s to 1920s," in *Immigration Reconsidered*, pp. 37–75.

24. The burning of a church and school in Iowa was the most violent of these. Van Hinte, *Netherlanders in America*, p. 1015.

25. Herbert J. Brinks, "Impressions of the 'Old' World 1840–1948," in *The Dutch in North America*, eds. Rob Kroes and Henk-Otto Neuschäfer (Amsterdam: VU University Press, 1991), pp. 34–47.

26. For an overview of Dutch women's activities, see W.H. Posthums-van der Goot, ed., *Van Moeder op Dochter* (Leiden: E.J. Brill, 1948); Selma Leydesdorff, *Verborgen arbeid, vergeten arbeid* (Assen: Van Gorcum, 1977).

27. Reprinted in Suzanne Sinke, "Home Builders: Meat, Bread, and (sometimes) Oranges!,"

Origins 14 (1996), p. 4. On advertising and the "American bluff" of arguing all things American as better, see Anderw R. Heinze, *Adapting to Abundance: Jewish Immigrants, Mass Consumption, and the Search for American Identity* (New York: Columbia University Press, 1990), ch. 10.

28. For these images see Sinke, "Home Builders," pp. 2–8.

29. On this, see, for example, Rob Kroes, *The Persistence of Ethnicity: Dutch Calvinist Pioneers in Amsterdam, Montana* (Urbana: University of Illinois, 1992), pp. 90–93.

30. In the 1910 Public Use Sample, the percentage of Dutch immigrant women who were never married at age 45 was 1.2 percent. In the Netherlands, figures for never married women over age 30 were close to 20 percent. See Suzanne M. Sinke, "I Don't Do Windows: Gender Roles in International Perspective, A Turn-of-the-Century Dutch Example," *Journal of American Ethnic History* 17 (Winter 1998): 4–5.

31. Cornelia de Groot, *When I was a Girl in Holland* (Boston: Northrop, Lee & Shepard, 1917). The work was reissued privately in 1991 by Cor Bakker, who included a supplement of some of her writings and family stories about her. On her life, see Annemieke Galema and Suzanne Sinke, "Paradijs der Vrouwen? Overzeese migratie naar de Verenigde Staten van Friese vrouwen rond de eeuwwisseling," in *Vrouwen in den Vreemde*, eds. Annelies Dassen, Christine van Eerd, and Karin Oppelland (Zutphen: Walburg Pers, 1993), pp. 30–46.

32. Kuijt's letters appear in translation in *Dutch American Voices*, ed. Herbert J. Brinks (Ithaca: Cornell University Press, 1995), pp. 443–450. The rest of the Kuijt family letters are in the Heritage Hall Collection, Calvin College.

33. Various scholars have written about this phenomenon. See, for example, Elizabeth Ewen, *Immigrant Women in the Land of Dollars* (New York: Monthly Review Press, 1985).

34. On De Bey, see Mary Pieroni Schiltz and Suzanne M. Sinke, "De Bey, Cornelia Bernarda," in *Historical Encyclopedia of Chicago Women*, eds. Adele Hast and Rima Lunin Schultz (forthcoming).

35. Lucy Fitch Perkins, *Cornelia: The Story of a Benevolent Despot* (Boston: Houghton Mifflin, 1919), p. 2. The author based the story on tales recounted to her by an adult Cornelia De Bey.

36. For an overview of this work, see Susan Gal, "Language, Gender, and Power," in *Gender Articulated*, pp. 172–173.

37. Jo Daan, "Problems of Code Switching: Dialect Loss of Immigrants of Dutch Descent," in *Papers from the Third Interdisciplinary Conference on Netherlandic Studies*, ed. Ton J. Broos (Boston: University Press, 1988), p. 151.

38. *Reports of the Immigration Commission: Abstracts of Reports of the Immigration Commission*, vol. 1, Senate Document 747, 61st Congress, 3rd session, 1911. "Per cent of foreign-born employees who speak English, by sex, age at time of coming to the United States, and race," p. 481, and "Per cent of foreign-born employees who speak English by sex and race," p. 474.

39. Petronella M. de Boer van Pernis migrated from Rotterdam to Holland, Michigan, in 1908 at the age of 22. Tape 1004, P.J. Meertens Institute.

40. Lini de Vries, *Up From the Cellar* (Minneapolis: Vanilla Press, 1979), p. 9.

41. De Vries, *Up From the Cellar*, passim. De Vries is acid at best and scathingly critical in most sections in describing her mother. The title comes from a common punishment her mother advocated, sending the child to the cellar. De Vries was born in 1905 in New Jersey, where her family lived in two major Dutch American settlements, Paterson and Prospect Park.

42. Medical education was generally considered better in Europe until the twentieth century. See Robert P. Hudson, "Abraham Flexner in Perspective: American Medical Education, 1865–1910," in Judith Walzer Leavitt and Ronald L. Numbers, eds., *Sickness and Health in America* (Madison: University of Wisconsin Press, 1985), pp. 153–154.

43. Translation of:
In Nederland ben ik opgevoed
In Nederland leerde 'k spreken

> Ik zal voor die taal steeds in 't gemoed
> dezelfde liefde kweken
> Niet dat ik op 't vreemde smaal
> Ik let alles in z'n waarde
> Maar ik zeg, voor mij is hollands taal,
> de schoonste taal op aarde

Tape 1035, woman born in Ooltgensplaat in 1893, emigrated with parents [and seven siblings and an aunt] in 1908 and settled in Grand Rapids, Michigan, P.J. Meertens Institute.

44. The family migrated in 1904. Tape 1053, P.J. Meertens Institute.

45. Ibid.

46. Tape 1097/1101, woman born in 1912 in Pella, Iowa, P.J. Meertens Institute.

47. Edward Bok, *The Americanization of Edward Bok: The Autobiography of A Dutch Boy Fifty Years After* (New York: Charles Scribner's Sons, 1922), p. 4.

48. Ibid., pp. 438–439.

49. On this see Johannes L. Krabbendam, *The Model Man: A Life of Edward W. Bok, 1863–1930* (Proefschrijft, Rijksuniversiteit Leiden, 1995), Introduction.

50. This distinction related particularly to women's roles in rural areas. See Jon Gjerde, *The Mind of the West* (Chapel Hill: University of North Carolina, 1997).

51. On Bok's relations to Dutch Americans and to the Netherlands, see Krabbendam, *The Model Man*, chapter 6.

52. Aart Plaisier to Cornelius van der Waal, 1 May 1910, reproduced and translated in Brinks, *Dutch Immigrant Voices*, pp. 323–324.

53. Letter from 24 November 1910, in Brinks, *Dutch American Voices*, p. 326.

54. Aart Plaisier to Cousin, Grant, Michigan, 6 January 1915, Heritage Hall Collection.

55. Gerrit Plaisier to Cousin, Grand Rapids, Michigan, 27 March 1911, Heritage Hall Collection.

56. Gerrit Plaisier to Cousin, Grand Rapids, Michigan, 18 May 1911, Heritage Hall Collection.

57. Ulbe Eringa to Minne and Jikke Sjaarda, Running Water, South Dakota, to Oosterend, Friesland, September 13, 1905, reprinted and translated in Brinks, *Dutch American Voices*, p. 195.

58. For information on this individual, see also Brian W. Beltman, *Dutch Farmer in the Missouri Valley: The Life and Letters of Ulbe Eringa, 1866–1950* (Urbana: University of Illinois Press, 1996).

59. Bernardus de Beij to Pieter A. Lanting, 1 April 1870, Chicago, to Winsum, Groningen. Heritage Hall Collection.

60. Van Hinte, *Netherlanders in America*, p. 1009.

61. "Holland Notes," *The Banner* (25 January 1917), p. 64.

62. "Op 's Werelds Tooneel: De Beweging om den Vrouwen vol Stemrecht," *De Gereformeerde Amerikaan* (September 1908), p. 504.

63. On domains, see Joshua Fishman, *Language Loyalty in the United States* (The Hague: Mouton, 1966).

64. Tape 1004, woman born in Rotterdam in 1886, migrated with parents in 1908 and settled in Holland, Michigan, P.J. Meertens Institute.

65. This parallels several aspects of Sydney Stahl Weinberg's findings on Jewish immigrant women in *The World of Our Mothers* (New York: Schocken, 1988).

66. For example, a domestic in Kralingen wrote to her sister in Beaverdam, Michigan: "Here everything goes on as always. *Mijnheer* [master, male equivalent for *mevrouw*] has been at home for some time.... *Mevrouw* still suffers from nerves ... they both send their greetings." Lucie to Sister [Susan D. Langreis], Kralingen, 1 June 1895, Heritage Hall Collection [my translation].

67. W.H. Posthumus-Van der Goot and Anna de Waal, *Van Moeder op Dochter: De maatschappelijke positie van de vrouw in Nederland vanaf de franse tijd* (Nijmegen: SUN, 1977 [1948]), p. 221.

68. H. Koopman (probably to Brother; Chicago to Borger—1894 fragment), reproduced in *Dutch American Voices*, p. 431.

69. To confirm my impression of this shift, I specifically examined obituaries from *De Hope. Weekblad in het Belang can Maatschappij, School en Kerk* from 1880, 1898, and 1919. This newspaper, published from Hope College in Holland, Michigan, enjoyed a circulation not only in the area, but also among Reformed Church members in various parts of the country. On the paper, see Van Hinte, *Netherlanders in America*, p. 456.

70. Holland Union Benevolent Association, Board Meeting Minutes book 1896–1900, 1 September 1898, p. 209.

71. Cornelia De Groot, "Nine Farmerettes—They Prove Woman is not Weak," article from unknown journal, date estimated at 1906. Reproduced in *When I Was a Girl in Holland*, supplement.

72. See also Gjerde, *The Minds of the West*, part 3.

73. This is a form of passing according to some studies, compare Mary Bucholtz, "From Mulatta to Mestiza: Passing, and the Linguistic Reshaping of Ethnic Identity," in *Gender Articulated*, pp. 354–361.

74. The exception was in speeches, where *"Dames en Heren"* remained a standard form of greeting.

75. A classic example was the Ladies' Aid society associated with the Holland Home, which included representatives from various women's church auxiliaries in the Grand Rapids, Michigan area. Despite its name, the group kept minutes in Dutch for almost forty years. Holland Home Archives.

76. "Advertising our Women's Societies," *The Banner*, 29 April 1915, p. 264.

77. Ibid., p. 264.

78. Nieland, *'n fonnie bisnis* (Grand Rapids: Wm. B. Eerdmans, n.d. [1929?]), p. 71.

79. Academics disagree as to what exactly should be included as "Yankee Dutch." In popular parlance, any mixture of Dutch and English qualifies, and I use that definition here. Only a speaker of Dutch and English could get the full effect. On the phenomenon see Walter Lagerwey, ed., *Neen Nederland, 'k vergeet u niet: Een beeld van het immigrantenleven in Amerika tussen 1846 en 1945 in verhalen, schetsen en gedichten* (Baarn: Bosch & Keuning, 1982), p. 121 ff.

80. *'n fonnie bisnis*, p. 97. "'n goed kid, o sjoer, joebet! En 'n goed kebbenetmeeker, hoor! . . . Maar ik meen om zijn breens te joezen bij de woemens."

81. *'n fonnie bisnis*, pp. 97–98. "dat 't 'n sjeem was dat 'n man efter zijn jaap nog houswerk doen moest. . ."

82. *'n fonnie bisnis*, p. 51.

83. *'n fonnie bisnis*, p. 117. "'t is fonnie in de wereld. Maar mebbie komt 't eten nog wel uit de fesjen. Ik heb gehoord dat latse woemens al gestaart zijn met een heel luddel bit te eten, omdat ze schinnie willen zijn, want dat is in de fesjen."

84. Van Hinte, *Netherlanders in America*, p. 952.

85. See Van Hinte, *Netherlanders in America*, pp. 948–950.

86. Cobie de Lespinasse, *The Bells of Helmus*. Portland: Metropolitan Press, 1934, pp. 71–72.

87. See Nella Kennedy, "The Man from Helmus: Dr. A.F.H. de l'Espinasse," in *A Century of Midwestern Dutch-American Manners and Mores—and More* (Orange City: Northwestern College, 1995), pp. 1–9.

7

A Dynamic View of Mexican Migration to the United States

Katharine M. Donato

Introduction

For most of the twentieth century, the principal mechanism that has connected Mexico with the United States has been immigration northward. The idea of going north for opportunity has resulted in the arrival of many Mexicans without legal papers authorizing them to work.[1] It has also created a migration process that, by most accounts, is dynamic (Massey et al., 1994; Escobar Latapí et al., 1998). Therefore, as the determinants and consequences of migration have shifted over time, migration to the United States from Mexico has ebbed and flowed.

During the same period, women's presence in international migration has changed and scholarship on gender and migration has improved (see *International Migration Review*, vol. 18, 1984; Simon and Brettell 1986; Gabaccia 1989, 1992; Pedraza 1991; Donato 1993; Kanaiaupuni 1998). Despite improvements, however, many questions remain about differences in the migration process of women and men from particular countries to the United States. This is especially true for Mexico, a nation that is the largest source of U.S. migration (Passel and Woodrow, 1987; Warren and Passel, 1987; U.S. Department of Justice, 1996), and has a long history of sending many more men than women to the United States (Donato, 1992).

In this article, we examine the extent to which patterns of migration vary by legal status and community of origin over time, and emphasize how gender differentiates the processes of legal and undocumented migration. Throughout, the article speculates about specific contextual conditions, such as immigration policies or economic trends, that may explain the dynamic process of women's and men's migration and the differences in their chances of migrating by legal status, gender, and community of origin. On the whole, taking legal status into account reveals more diversity in migration patterns than suggested by Massey et al. (1994), who examined the prevalence of migration from Mexico to the United States and developed a theory of cumulative migration.

We set the context for our analysis of migration as a dynamic process by reviewing community studies that show how the factors that motivate Mexico-U.S. migration have changed over time. We then describe the data and methods used to estimate the chances that women and men will migrate on a first U.S. trip, with and without documents, since 1942. Examination of the probabilities reveals three key findings. First, there is considerable variation in the chances of migrating by age forty by community of origin. Second, across all communities, by the mid-1990s, the overall chance of migrating rose sharply from the level set in 1990. Third, gender differentiates migration trends especially by legal status. These insights led us to consider their implications in the final section of the article.

Factors Motivating Migration from Mexico: A Dynamic View

We begin by analyzing findings from prior studies to determine what factors were considered to be most important in initiating and sustaining Mexico-U.S. migration, and how these have changed. The studies are summarized in Table 1 from oldest (top) to newest (bottom), and the major factor motivating migration runs from demand (on the left) to supply and network ties (on the right). In general, they illustrate how a migration process that began largely as demand-pull recruitment has evolved into a more complex migration relationship in which supply-push and network factors play ever larger roles (Escobar Lapatí et al., 1998).

First Wave Studies. The earliest studies of emigration communities emphasized how U.S. government-approved recruitment of Mexican workers and large wage gaps between border areas and northern states motivated Mexican migrants to search for employment before 1930 (Taylor, 1929, 1931, 1932, 1933). After a decade that witnessed severe economic depression, large-scale deportation of many Mexicans from the United States, and World War II, labor recruitment between the two nations once again emerged as a strategy to increase agricultural labor.[2] Hancock (1959) found that Mexicans migrated because of very high wage ratios between places in the United States and Mexico. They were also attracted to migration because of the basic freedoms it insured: justice that was more impartially administered than in Mexico, including treating ordinary citizens with respect (1959).

By the 1960s and 1970s, studies revealed that economic factors still played a strong role in motivating and sustaining migration. Wiest (1973) emphasized the

TABLE 1
Case Study Grid
Factors Initiating and Sustaining Mexican Migration to the United States

Year of Study	Factors Influencing the Initial Decision to Migrate		
	Demand-Pull	Supply-Push	Network/Other
First Wave Studies Prior to 1960s			
Taylor (1929, 1930, 1931, 1932, 1933)	Bracero recruitment	Low wages in Mexico	
Hancock (1959)			
Second Wave Studies (1960s–1970s)			
Weist (1973)	Bracero recruitment	Low wages in Mexico	
Cornelius (1976a, 1976b)	Bracero recruitment		
Reichert (1979, 1981, 1982)	U.S. agricultural employment		
Reichert and Massey (1979, 1980)			Family Reunification
Roberts (1982)	U.S. agricultural employment		
Mines (1981, 1984) and			
Mines and de Janvry (1982)	U.S. agricultural employment		
Mines and Massey (1985)	Bracero recruitment		
Dinerman (1982)	Bracero recruitment		
Third Wave Studies (post 1980)			
Taylor (1987, 1992) and			
Stark and Taylor (1991)	Bracero recruitment	Low wages in Mexico	
Massey et al. (1987)	Specific U.S. employment		
Goldring (1990)			
Massey (1987)			
			Social connections to other migrants
Donato et al. (1992)			Wage/job information
Lindstrom (1991)			Family reunification
Donato (1993)			Family reunification
Kanaiaupuni (1998)		Landlessness and personal attributes	Family reunification
Massey (1987)			

Factors Sustaining Migration

Year of Study	Demand-Pull	Supply-Push	Network/Other
Factors Sustaining Migration			
First Wave Studies Prior to 1960s			
Taylor (1929, 1930, 1931, 1932, 1933)		Low wages in Mexico	
Hancock (1959)		Low wages in Mexico	
Second Wave Studies (1960s–1970s)			
Weist (1973)		Low wages in Mexico	
Cornelius (1976a, 1976b)	U.S. agricultural employment		
Reichert (1979, 1981, 1982)	U.S. agricultural employment		
Reichert and Massey (1979, 1980)	Family Reunification		
Roberts (1982)	U.S. agricultural employment		Wage/job information
Mines (1981, 1984) and			
Mines and de Janvry (1982)	U.S. agricultural employment		Prior U.S. experience
Mines and Massey (1985)			Wage/job information
Dinerman (1982)		Drought in Mexico	Prior U.S. experience
Lopez (1988)		Owning Mexican land	Prior U.S. experience
Chavez (1988)	U.S. nonfarm employment		Prior U.S. experience
Third Wave Studies (post 1980)			
Golding (1990)			Information about specific U.S. jobs
Taylor (1987, 1992) and			
Stark and Taylor (1991)			Close relatives in U.S.
Massey et al. (1987)			Wage/job information
Massey (1987)			Social connections to other migrants
Donato et al. (1992)			Wage/job information
Lindstrom (1991)			Women migrate if there is an active migrant in family
Donato (1993)			Women migrate if member of household is IRCA amnesty recipient
Kanaiaupuni (1998)			Family reunification
Massey and Espinosa (1996)			Quantity and quality of social ties

economic effects of emigration by describing immigrants in the late 1960s as legal green carders who took advantage of huge income differences between the two nations.[3] Most green card commuters were former Braceros who intended to return to their Mexican village after migration. Other studies also reported many former Braceros had become green card commuters, traveling seasonally from homes in Mexico to U.S. jobs (Cornelius 1976a,b).

A decade later, studies reported that most Mexican migrants were sojourners employed in agriculture, but many had illegally entered the United States. For example, Reichert (1979, 1981) noted that there was about one illegal U.S. migrant for every two legal migrants. By this time, the wage gap between seasonal farm jobs in the two nations had narrowed somewhat,[4] but remittances were not promoting stay-at-home development. As migrants' households in Mexico raised their standards of living, they also became more dependent on recurrent migration as a way to maintain their status (1981).

Other studies also described the evolution of migration in Mexican origins. In a small village in Zacatecas, Mines (1981, 1984) reported that over half of the village's income came from remittances sent home by persons employed in the United States. By 1979, this community had reached a "migratory equilibrium," where the population remained stable because, as many young residents went northward and settled abroad, many workers older than forty illegally shuttled between homes in Mexico and seasonal U.S. farm jobs (Mines and de Janvry, 1982).

Mines and Massey (1985) used migration patterns in two communities to describe how migration networks mature. In both, although Mexico-U.S. migration began in the 1920s, it reemerged in 1942 with U.S. recruitment of Mexican agricultural workers, and along with it, increased numbers of men crossed illegally. The pattern of illegal migration persisted until 1954–55, when the United States cracked down on illegal migrants (called Operation Wetback) and the Bracero program expanded. Thereafter, for a short time, migration shifted back toward legal, but seasonal moves. However, after a severe drought in 1957, illegal immigration increased again. By the 1970s, migration networks had matured and sister communities were established in the United States.

Reichert and Massey (1979, 1980) used these data to separate migration into two phases: pre-1965, and post-1965, when many women and children outmigrated to join ex-Braceros who had become legal U.S. immigrants. Estimates suggest that as many as 80 percent of the 55,000 Mexican immigrants admitted to the United States in 1962 were ex-Braceros who obtained permanent labor certification (U.S. Senate, 1965).[5]

By the end of this first wave of studies, authors had begun to compare findings from one community to another. However, a strong emphasis remained on the economic factors that motivate migration. Using data from farmers in four Mexican states (San Luis Potosí, Guanajuato, Puebla, and Oaxaca), Roberts (1982) concluded that some local farm income was needed to attempt to migrate. He argued that because incomes in Oaxaca were so low, many migrated to Mexican cities where they had contacts (1982). However, from the state of Guanajuato, where farm incomes were considerably higher, a significant number of people migrated across the U.S. border. Dinerman (1982) also found differences in migrants and nonmigrants in two communities in Michoacan, where the "rate and frequency of U.S. migration were much higher" in one community than the other (1982). Although both communities sent Braceros in roughly equal numbers, migrants from one community had, by the early 1970s, shifted to nonfarm U.S. employment, and hired workers in Mexico to tend their plots. In the other community, fewer ex-Braceros owned land, and more ex-Braceros migrated within Mexico, until government support for handicraft activities created local job opportunities.

Second Wave Studies. As the number of studies grew, authors relied on larger data sets that often encompassed multiple communities and permitted them to draw inferences. Perhaps the most cited study is that done by Massey, Alarcón, Durand, and Gonzales in *Return to Aztlan* (1987). This book was built around extensive interviews in four communities using a ethnosurvey instrument. It concluded that the integration of the southwestern United States into the national economy in the late 1800s created a demand for Mexican labor, the restructuring of Mexican agriculture created a supply of workers willing to migrate, and the railroads provided the link between U.S. demand and Mexican supply (1987).

Return to Aztlan makes four points about the process of Mexico-U.S. migration in the twentieth century. First, few Mexicans migrated from these communities before the 1950s and, when they did migrate, they were as likely to move within Mexico as to migrate illegally to the United States. Second, Mexican migration was almost stopped in the 1930s as a result of the Depression and repatriations. Third, Bracero program recruitment began significant U.S.-bound migration after 1942, and this migration continued at roughly Bracero-era levels after U.S.-government approved recruitment was stopped in 1964. Fourth, illegal migrants comprised at least 50 percent of first-time U.S.-bound Mexicans except in the late 1950s, when the Bracero program was at its peak.

In general, Massey et al. (1987) described an upward trend in a migratory process that began over one hundred years ago. The significant blips in an other-

A Dynamic View of Mexican Migration to the United States

wise steadily rising migration flow occurred in the 1930s, when Mexico-U.S. migration slowed or stopped, and in the late 1950s, when many migrants went legally to the U.S. as Braceros. That the volume of migration continues to grow suggests that Mexico-U.S. migration is a dynamic social process with a strong internal momentum fueled by social ties and difficult to stop (Massey et al., 1987). Furthermore, rising probabilities that young men by age forty make a first unauthorized U.S. trip between the mid-1970s and the late 1980s suggested that the Immigration Reform and Control Act (IRCA), designed to reduce illegal migration, had little noticeable impact on stemming the tide of illegal migrants (Donato et al., 1992a).[6]

In their review of past studies, Durand and Massey (1992) argued that Mexico-U.S. migration evolves similarly in each community and that differences in factors motivating and sustaining migration results from the origin community's stage of migration. For example, when communities first participate in migration, they typically send mostly young men who migrate illegally without their families for U.S. farm or other unskilled jobs. Over time, however, migration streams mature and many women and children accompany male family members from a Mexican community.

Therefore, as migration develops and matures in local communities, more immediate family members, wives and children, join their spouses (Reichert and Massey, 1980; Fonseca and Moreno, 1988; Gonzalez and Escobar, 1990; Goldring, 1990; Donato, 1993, 1994; Donato and Kanaiaupuni, 1998). In one study, women were especially likely to make a first U.S. trip by 1990, in some cases joining men who had migrated seasonally for years (Kanaiaupuni, 1998). In another, the chance that women would migrate increased considerably if they had an immediate relative who received temporary amnesty as a result of IRCA (Donato, 1993). And in some communities, social networks have facilitated the chances of making a first trip northward because they promote employment specialities that fit niches in the U.S. economy (Goldring, 1990). Cornelius (1990) too reported that U.S.-bound migrants from four communities had followed well-trodden network paths to a few U.S. destinations.

A recent salient contribution to this literature is Massey and Espinosa (1997). Based on an analysis of data from twenty-five Mexican communities, they found that what motivates Mexico-U.S. migration is much more complex than what is suggested by policy makers or popular media. Neither a wage differential nor peso inflation/devaluation was the major factor explaining illegal or legal migration during the last twenty-five years. What drives Mexican migration to the United States are three key processes: social capital formation, which exists because Mexicans who are related to migrants are more likely to migrate themselves;[7] human capital formation, which is captured by U.S. experience; and market consolidation of U.S. and Mexican economies (1997).

To sum, this section has reviewed the leading studies of Mexican emigration communities to determine what factors initiated and sustained migration to the United States. In general, studies suggest that the factors motivating migration have shifted away from economic and wage differences to a complex set of social and economic mechanisms that make Mexico-U.S. migration a challenge for policy makers to control. In particular, the studies lead to several conclusions:

- Early studies identify the Mexico-U.S. wage differential as well as U.S. recruitment of Mexican workers, especially in the 1942–64 period, as key factors that unleashed immigration from Mexico. For this reason, most early migrants were young men from rural areas coming to work on U.S. farms.
- Immediately after the Bracero program ended in 1965, studies suggest that Mexicans increasingly entered first as legal green card holders. By the late 1960s, however, the studies also document an upward rise in the volume of illegal migration.
- All studies agree that, by the early 1990s, the probability that a young man would make a first trip to the U.S. had risen to very high levels, that more women and children had begun to migrate, and that noneconomic factors, such as the social capital and network ties that Mexicans have to migrants, and experience in the United States, motivated young men and women to migrate.

Prevalence of Mexican Immigration. To understand these and other findings, Massey et al. (1994) developed a theory of cumulative causation and a dynamic way of viewing the process of migration across communities. Using data from nineteen Mexican communities, the authors documented how migration unfolds over time by analyzing trends in the prevalence of migration in origin communities for the 1940–89 period. On the whole, they found that prevalence rose, and that rates of change in migration differed, over time and by community.

Their analysis depicted three patterns of male and female migration in these origin communities. The first was one of rising migration prevalence since 1942, where women's movement lagged behind men's by approximately twenty years. The second pattern was that migration rose early in the 1940s, stagnated and declined in the 1950s and 1960s, and then experienced an upturn by the early 1970s. The third pattern was very slow growth, whereby at the end of the 1980s, migration levels remained low.[8]

A Dynamic View of Mexican Migration to the United States

We build on these findings by developing an alternative method to understand the dynamic process of migration across communities. In general, the method permits an identification of trends in the chances of migrating over time, by legal status and gender. It also allows us to speculate about specific structural conditions (e.g., immigration policies, political conditions, or economic trends) that may explain community differences in the propensity to migrate from Mexico. Before presenting our findings, however, the data and methods are described below.

Data and Methods

Data. For this analysis, we use data from the Mexican Migration Project (MMP, 1995). The MMP data were collected in the 1980s and early 1990s from about 200 households in each of thirty-nine communities in western central Mexico. The communities range in size from small ranchos with populations of approximately 1,000 people, to a section of Guadalajara which had a 1990 population of 2.9 million (Table 2).

In each of the thirty-nine communities, households were randomly selected and interviews were conducted in the winter months of December and January, when sojourner U.S. migrants often return to Mexico. Individual migration histories were compiled for all members of the household, and included detailed information about the year of the first (and subsequent) U.S. trip, duration of stay, occupation, place of destination, and legal status. Interviewers spoke with household heads and obtained information on all children, whether they were present or not, and if absent, whether they were in Mexico or the United States. For household heads, migration histories were compiled for each year after age fifteen, and they included such questions as whether the person migrated to the United States and if so, with or without documents. In addition, interviewers collected data in the summer following the Mexican data collection from about approximately twenty migrant households who had resettled in the United States.

Methods. One strength of the MMP data is that they permit me to separately distinguish between the chances of making an initial (first) or subsequent (two or more) trips to the United States. Together these events determine the overall flow of legal and illegal migrants across the border (Donato et al., 1992). In this report, we examined the chances that male household heads and women migrate on an initial U.S. trip, and for men, the chances that they migrate on a subsequent trip.

For the analysis, we drew on two basic sources of information: the birth date and the date of the first trip to the United States (compiled for all household members), and the history of border crossing (gathered from household heads). Given each subject's date of birth and year of first trip, we first constructed sepa-

TABLE 2
Characteristics of 39 Mexican Communities Sampled for Study of U.S. Migration

Type of Community and Name	State	1990 Population[a]	1940 Population	Mexico Survey Year	Sample Size*	U.S. Sample*
Metropolitan Areas						
Community 24	Jalisco	2,870,000[b]	229,235	1982	200	16
Community 2	Guanajuato	868,000[b]	74,155	1987	200	0
Community 32	S.L.P.	526,000[b]	97,762	1993	200	0
Community 19	Michoacán	493,000[b]	44,304	1991	200	20
Community 15	Guanajuato	363,000[b]	32,377	1991	200	20
Community 29	Michoacán	217,000[b]	20,583	1992	200	13
Community 35	Zacatecas	109,000[b]	26,673	1994	239	10
Community 31	Guerrero	101,000[b]	21,882	1993	100	0
Community 28	Jalisco	74,000[b]	22,170	1992	201	20
Smaller Urban Areas						
Community 1	Guanajuato	52,000	12,015	1987	201	20
Community 38	S.L.P.	42,000	29,556	1994	200	0
Community 26	Guanajuato	34,000	8,341	1992	200	15
Community 9	Michoacán	32,000	5,452	1989	200	20
Community 17	Jalisco	31,000	13,003	1991	200	20
Community 27	Guanajuato	24,000	5,698	1992	200	15
Community 13	Guanajuato	21,000	5,635	1990	200	20
Community 11	Nayarit	20,000	4,720	1990	200	20
Community 4	Guanajuato	17,000	6,159	1988	200	22

rate year-by-year life histories up to the date of the first U.S. trip for both men and women. That is, we built discrete-time person-year files that followed each subject from birth to the date of the survey or to the first U.S. trip, whichever came first. For the recurrent trip analysis, we built a similar discrete-time person-year file but constructed it from year-by-year files that began with the year migrants returned from their first trip up to the year of their next trip.

Because the outcome measure was trichotomous (migrated illegally, legally, or did not migrate), we used multinomial logistic regression to estimate the chance of migrating with and without legal papers versus not migrating at all (the reference category) (Hosmer and Lemeshow, 1989). We began by estimating age-period models and age-period-community models by sex (models available from author

TABLE 2 (Continued)

Type of Community and Name	State	1990 Population[a]	1940 Population	Mexico Survey Year	Mexico Sample Size*	U.S. Sample*
Towns						
Community 36	S.L.P.	13,000	13,923	1995	201	0
Community 23	Jalisco	12,000	5,531	1982	200	20
Community 12	Nayarit	12,000	551	1990	200	20
Community 18	Zacatecas	8,000	2,821	1991	365	20
Community 33	Colima	7,000	6,641	1995	200	20
Community 22	Michoacán	7,000	5,131	1982	200	20
Community 14	Michoacán	7,000	3,046	1990	200	20
Community 8	Michoacán	6,000	2,304	1989	200	20
Community 6	Jalisco	5,000	2,167	1988	200	20
Community 3	Jalisco	4,000	1,257	1988	200	22
Ranchos						
Community 7	Jalisco	3,000	615	1988	200	15
Community 20	Jalisco	3,000	1,900	1982	106	14
Community 21	Jalisco	2,000	1,128	1982	94	6
Community 10	Michoacán	2,000	808	1989	150	20
Community 5	Guanajuato	2,000	1,630	1988	150	10
Community 34	Zacatecas	2,000	30,894	1995	149	0
Community 30	Zacatecas	1,000	384	1991	187	0
Community 16	Guanajuato	1,000	303	1991	100	10
Community 39	S.L.P.	1,000	29,556	1995	100	0
Community 25	Jalisco	1,000	275	1992	100	7
Community 37	S.L.P.	1,000	13,933	1995	102	0

* Sample size refers to number of households in the sample
[a] Rounded to nearest thousand
[b] Population of metropolitan area
Source: Mexican Migration Project (1995).

upon request). From them, we calculated the conditional chances that male household heads (or women) of a given age migrate legally or illegally on an initial U.S. trip. Using these probabilities as a baseline, we built life tables that produced the cumulative chances that men (or women) by age forty would make a legal trip, illegal trip, or not migrate, in a certain year (Shyrock et al., 1976). The probabilities depict the lifetime migration experience in some community and year by age, assuming the probabilities of Mexican out-migration that prevailed up to 1994, and show what would happen if a male household head born into this community were to go through life subject to the probabilities of out-migration prevailing in different years. (See the appendix for more details.)

Migrating on a First and Subsequent U.S. Trip

Let us begin simply. For example, for Community 2, a large metropolitan area in the state of Guanajuato, Table 3 shows that the chance that a young man aged 20–24 would migrate illegally to the United States was just 1 percent in 1994. Applying the year-by-year migration probabilities to all men who were in the sample illustrates that about 16 percent of men will migrate once illegally by age forty.

To better understand trends over time, consider a typical community, say number 11, which in 1990 was a small urban area with a population of 20,000. Table 3 shows that 12 percent of men aged 20–24 in this community took a first illegal trip in 1980. Ten years later, when legal migration associated with IRCA's amnesty program was quite high, approximately the same percentage of young men—11 percent—was likely to take a first unauthorized trip. Just one year later, the chance of making an illegal first trip among young men dropped to 5 percent, but by 1994, it rose to 7 percent. This means 7 of one-hundred young men in community 11 made a first illegal trip to the United States in 1994.

Probabilities for communities 3 and 10, which are more typical of the villages that depend on emigration and remittances to supplement earnings from a mostly agricultural economy, tell similar stories. In general, young men were more likely to make a first illegal U.S. trip in all years up through 1986. In that year, the chance of making a first illegal trip from community 10 was 45 percent, twice as much as making a first legal trip. For community 3, the chance of making an unauthorized trip was 38 percent, more than ten times higher than making a legal trip.

One year later, this pattern had changed. In community 3, young men still faced higher chances of migrating illegally than legally, but the difference between the two narrowed considerably after 1986. For men in community 10, however, the pattern reversed itself. Beginning in 1987, the chance that a young man would migrate legally was higher than migrating illegally. In 1992, sixty of one-hundred young men in community 10 made a first authorized trip, representing the highest legal migration probability recorded since 1980.

The second panel of Table 3 presents cumulative probabilities that a young man would have taken at least one unauthorized or legal trip to the United States by age forty. The probabilities for each community are based on the chances of out-migration that were estimated for each community between 1980 and 1994. Young men enter the pool of potential migrants at birth, and leave at age thirty-nine or by

TABLE 3
Predicted Cumulative Probabilities that a Male Household Head Migrates on a First U.S. Trip, for Selected Communities, 1980-94

Community and Legal Status	1980	1981	1982	1983	1984	1985	1986	1987	1988	1989	1990	1991	1992	1993	1994
Predicted Probabilities at Age 20–24															
With Documents															
Community 2	.00	.01	.00	.00	.01	.00	.00	.01	.02	.01	.02	.01	.02	.01	.01
Community 11	.03	.03	.03	.03	.03	.03	.03	.05	.09	.09	.10	.08	.11	.04	.08
Community 3	.03	.04	.03	.03	.03	.03	.03	.06	.11	.12	.11	.10	.14	.05	.10
Community 10	.23	.25	.23	.23	.23	.21	.21	.37	.52	.57	.51	.53	.60	.34	.51
Without Documents															
Community 2	.01	.01	.01	.01	.02	.02	.02	.01	.01	.01	.01	.01	.01	.00	.01
Community 11	.12	.11	.09	.09	.13	.14	.15	.08	.09	.05	.11	.05	.06	.03	.07
Community 3	.32	.31	.27	.26	.34	.36	.38	.24	.26	.15	.30	.15	.17	.11	.20
Community 10	.38	.37	.33	.33	.40	.43	.45	.25	.22	.13	.25	.14	.13	.13	.18
Cumulative Probabilities by Age 40															
With Documents															
Community 2	.11	.12	.10	.10	.11	.10	.11	.18	.18	.19	.15	.21	.07	.16	.29
Community 11	.18	.20	.20	.21	.18	.15	.15	.35	.55	.41	.50	.58	.31	.46	.52
Community 3	.08	.09	.09	.09	.08	.07	.06	.18	.39	.23	.35	.40	.25	.30	.30
Community 10	.33	.36	.36	.37	.33	.29	.28	.55	.78	.63	.76	.79	.68	.71	.71
Without Documents															
Community 2	.29	.27	.23	.23	.31	.34	.36	.20	.08	.18	.08	.09	.05	.10	.16
Community 11	.81	.79	.77	.76	.81	.84	.85	.63	.35	.56	.37	.36	.33	.44	.47
Community 3	.92	.91	.91	.91	.92	.93	.94	.82	.60	.77	.64	.60	.67	.70	.70
Community 10	.67	.64	.64	.63	.67	.71	.72	.45	.22	.37	.24	.21	.32	.29	.29

death. So the pool of those who could migrate, or the denominator, is all men in the community under age forty who have so far not migrated legally or illegally.

Once again, in community 2, for example, men by age forty had a 29 percent chance of migrating illegally on a first trip in 1980. By the mid-1980s, the chance that a man would make at least one illegal trip rose to 27 percent but then quickly fell. By 1987, the chance dropped to 20 percent, and in 1988 to 8 percent. The decline continued through 1992, when the lifetime chance of making a first unauthorized trip was 5 percent. However, one year later, it had risen to 10 percent.

So far, our results suggest three key findings. First, from some communities, virtually all young men will make an initial U.S. trip by age forty. Second, the chances of migrating illegally and legally vary considerably by origin community—they are lower in larger metropolitan areas than in smaller rural communities. Third, despite declines immediately after 1986, the probability of making an initial undocumented U.S. trip by age forty began to rise again by 1994.

Table 4 presents the same two sets of probabilities calculated for women in the four communities. Like those for men, the patterns reveal that: (1) by age forty, many women will migrate to the United States on a first trip; and (2) the incentives to migrate have changed since 1980. However, unlike those for men, the year-by-year probabilities show that women were more likely to migrate legally than illegally, and that shifts in the chances of migrating legally and illegally were more gradual than those for men. For example, declines in the chances that a woman would migrate illegally occurred in the 1990s rather than immediately after 1986.

Finally, the probabilities presented in Table 5 suggest that recent repeat trips to the United States were more likely made with legal documents rather than without them. In communities 2, 11, and 10, the lifetime chance of making a second trip (after making a first) with legal documents was much higher than making an illegal trip in the mid-1990s. Before 1987, however, the chance of making a second unauthorized trip was much higher than migrating legally.

To better understand migration trends over a longer period of time for all thirty-nine communities, we estimated the probabilities separately for each year beginning in 1943. From these probabilities (available upon request), we derived Figures 1 and 2. Each illustrates trends in the chances that a male household head (or a woman) migrates on a first U.S. trip

On the whole, the data reveal the same difference that we observed earlier between the predicted and cumulative probabilities. The predicted chances that young men migrate on a first illegal or legal trip at age 20–24 were quite low throughout the period, but magnified over forty years, the chances of migrating were considerably higher. Figure 1 documents several interesting trends in the chances of legal and illegal migration since the early 1940s. For example, in the

TABLE 4
Predicted Cumulative Probabilities that a Woman Migrates on a First U.S. Trip, for Selected Communities, 1980–94

Community and Legal Status	1980	1981	1982	1983	1984	1985	1986	1987	1988	1989	1990	1991	1992	1993	1994
Predicted Probabilities at Age 20–24															
With Documents															
Community 2	.01	.01	.01	.01	.01	.01	.01	.01	.01	.01	.02	.02	.02	.03	.04
Community 11	.11	.12	.12	.14	.12	.13	.13	.13	.14	.14	.15	.17	.20	.25	.32
Community 3	.05	.05	.05	.06	.05	.05	.05	.06	.06	.06	.07	.08	.10	.13	.17
Community 10	.19	.19	.20	.23	.21	.21	.21	.22	.23	.23	.26	.29	.32	.40	.47
Without Documents															
Community 2	.01	.01	.01	.01	.01	.01	.01	.01	.01	.01	.01	.01	.01	.02	.01
Community 11	.20	.20	.20	.21	.22	.23	.24	.25	.25	.27	.31	.36	.34	.38	.28
Community 3	.12	.12	.13	.14	.14	.15	.15	.16	.16	.18	.21	.26	.25	.30	.22
Community 10	.15	.15	.15	.16	.16	.17	.18	.18	.19	.20	.23	.26	.24	.26	.18
Cumulative Probabilities by Age 40															
With Documents															
Community 2	.25	.26	.27	.31	.28	.29	.30	.31	.20	.24	.29	.32	.45	.51	.69
Community 11	.53	.53	.54	.56	.53	.52	.51	.52	.51	.50	.49	.54	.57	.70	.70
Community 3	.40	.41	.41	.44	.41	.40	.40	.40	.40	.39	.39	.44	.48	.61	.61
Community 10	.72	.72	.73	.75	.72	.71	.71	.71	.70	.70	.69	.73	.75	.84	.84
Without Documents															
Community 2	.13	.14	.14	.15	.15	.16	.17	.17	.10	.12	.14	.13	.16	.11	.16
Community 11	.47	.47	.46	.44	.47	.48	.49	.48	.49	.50	.51	.46	.43	.30	.30
Community 3	.60	.59	.59	.56	.59	.60	.60	.60	.59	.60	.60	.56	.52	.39	.39
Community 10	.28	.28	.27	.25	.28	.29	.29	.29	.29	.30	.31	.27	.25	.16	.16

TABLE 5
Predicted Cumulative Probabilities that a Man Migrates on a Subsequent U.S. Trip, for Selected Communities, 1980–94*

Community and Legal Status	1980	1981	1982	1983	1984	1985	1986	1987	1988	1989	1990	1991	1992	1993	1994
Predicted Probabilities at Age 20–24															
With Documents															
Community 2	.02	.02	.02	.02	.02	.02	.02	.03	.04	.05	.08	.06	.08	.03	.09
Community 11	.10	.09	.10	.09	.09	.09	.09	.15	.19	.22	.30	.25	.32	.15	.34
Community 3	.06	.05	.06	.05	.06	.06	.05	.10	.12	.16	.21	.17	.23	.10	.24
Community 10	.37	.35	.39	.35	.37	.36	.34	.52	.58	.68	.73	.68	.76	.55	.75
Without Documents															
Community 2	.05	.05	.04	.05	.05	.05	.06	.04	.05	.02	.04	.03	.03	.03	.05
Community 11	.13	.12	.11	.12	.13	.13	.16	.10	.11	.05	.08	.07	.06	.08	.09
Community 3	.34	.33	.31	.33	.34	.34	.39	.27	.30	.16	.24	.22	.20	.24	.27
Community 10	.36	.36	.32	.36	.36	.36	.41	.24	.23	.12	.14	.15	.11	.21	.14
Cumulative Probabilities by Age 40															
With Documents															
Community 2	.22	.21	.24	.21	.22	.21	.20	.35	.43	.53	.46	.57	.30	.57	.63
Community 11	.41	.39	.45	.39	.41	.40	.36	.59	.78	.78	.75	.82	.62	.78	.78
Community 3	.14	.13	.16	.13	.13	.13	.11	.24	.47	.44	.41	.51	.28	.45	.45
Community 10	.49	.48	.53	.47	.49	.48	.44	.66	.84	.83	.81	.86	.71	.83	.83
Without Documents															
Community 2	.61	.60	.56	.60	.60	.61	.68	.47	.21	.29	.28	.24	.33	.30	.34
Community 11	.59	.60	.55	.60	.59	.60	.64	.41	.20	.22	.24	.18	.36	.22	.22
Community 3	.86	.87	.84	.87	.87	.87	.89	.76	.53	.56	.59	.49	.72	.55	.55
Community 10	.51	.52	.47	.53	.51	.52	.56	.34	.16	.17	.19	.14	.29	.17	.17

* Community 2 represents communities 2 and 24.

A Dynamic View of Mexican Migration to the United States 167

beginning of the Bracero period, the chance that young men would migrate on a first U.S. trip with documents was higher than moving without documents. In 1947, the relative position of these chances changed, and male household heads were more likely to migrate illegally. In the early 1950s, and after Operation Wetback in 1954, the situation had reversed itself and legal migration became the norm until the end of the Bracero program.

Beginning in 1964, however, the cumulative probability that young men migrated legally trended downward, while the cumulative probability of a first illegal trip moved up, peaking at 80 percent in these emigration communities in the 1970s and 1980s. Since then, the lifetime probability that a young man would migrate on a first legal trip to the United States has fluctuated, with legal and illegal probabilities following similar year-by-year patterns. They reached an all-time low of approximately 20 percent in 1990, but then jumped to at least 30 percent by 1994.

These trends are consistent with evidence from some past studies, which suggest that stepped-up enforcement and the increased legalization of Braceros in the mid-1950s helped lower the chances of illegal first-time entry. As the number of Braceros was cut in 1959 and then again in 1963, the chances of illegal entry grew. This upward pattern continued until the mid-1980s, when IRCA implemented a series of incentives explicitly designed to reduce illegal entry to the United States. As a consequence, the probability of first-time illegal migration dramatically declined in the late 1980s, intersected with that for legal migration, and in recent years the chances of legal and illegal migration converged.

An examination of these trends by community reveals that the pressures to migrate have changed over time in the four typical communities featured earlier. In community 2, where migration was less established, the chance of illegal migration was on the whole much lower, and less symmetric, than in other communities. In communities 3 and 10, the most established migrant-sending origins from which virtually everyone migrates on a first trip with or without documents, overall trends reveal remarkably high levels of migration and almost perfect symmetry between the two types of cumulative probabilities. In 1971, from community 3, the lifetime chance of migrating illegally was close to 90 percent, whereas the chance of illegal migration dropped to roughly 10 percent. In that same year, the cumulative chance of migrating on a first U.S. trip from community 10 was 62 percent for men without documents and 38 percent for those making legal trips.

The chances of migrating continued at the same high levels through 1986, but with an important distinction—migrating legally replaced migrating illegally in these two villages. During the post-IRCA period, the chance of making a legal trip by age forty grew to a high of approximately 30 percent in community 3, and 80 percent in community 10. In both communities, upward or downward shifts in the

FIGURE 1
Chances that a Male Household Head Migrates on a First U.S. Trip, for 39 Mexican Communities, 1943–94

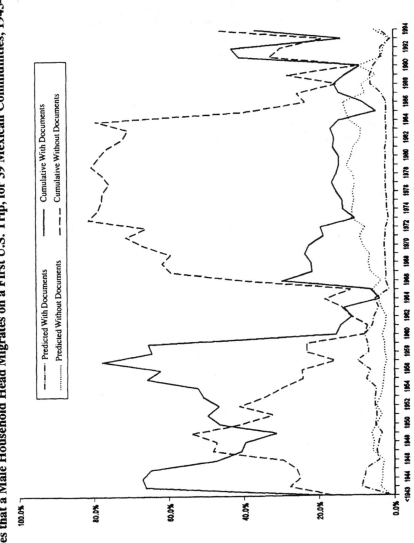

chances of legal and illegal migration essentially mirrored each other—a drop in the chance of illegal migration occurred in the same year that the chance of legal migration increased. Despite the shifts, however, the combined chances of migration suggest that virtually everyone will migrate on a first trip by age forty.

Community 10 illustrated Massey et al.'s (1987) view of how migration has become a self-feeding process. Of the thirty-nine communities in the data set, this community had the longest history of U.S. migration. With a high degree of illegal migration in the past, many residents were in a position to obtain legal papers after the implementation of IRCA's amnesty program. As a result, the probability of migrating on a first legal trip rose remarkably by 1988 and surpassed the chance of making a first unauthorized trip. Later, in the 1990s, with documents themselves, these migrants would then sponsor the legal migration of their dependents, thus facilitating very high levels of legal migration from this community.

In contrast to the patterns outlined above for men, women's chances of migrating on a first legal trip were much higher than for a first unauthorized trip throughout the 1943–94 period.[1] Particularly striking were the two peaks that occurred in the mid-1960s and again in the early 1990s. The first period witnessed the legalization of many Braceros (men), who in turn sponsored their immediate family members (many of them women) for purposes of family unification. The early 1990s was different, however. At that time, a woman's chance of migrating legally by age forty had reached a new high, widening the gap between the probabilities of legal and illegal migration rather than documenting a convergence of the two. This suggests that many women began to legally enter as relatives of IRCA's amnesty recipients.

Interestingly, however, trends in individual communities do not differ much. By 1994, the gap between the chance of migrating with and without documents was consistently wider than it was earlier in the period. In community 3, a woman's chance of making an undocumented U.S. trip approached that for migrating legally until 1989, when legal migration rose again. But in community 10, the gap in the lifetime chances of legal versus illegal migration was consistently larger than that observed for all thirty-nine communities.

Discussion

These data suggest that the majority of men and women will leave west central Mexico on a first U.S. trip by age forty, and that most men will make a subsequent trip. On a year-by-year basis, the major issue is whether Mexicans made their first trips legally or illegally, not whether or not they migrated. Legal status differences were also related to community of origin. From traditional emigration communities, prior high levels of illegal migration have fed on themselves, changing the legal status of newly arriving Mexican migrants without shifting the overall pressures to migrate over the long term. In fact, the present analysis reveals that the chance of migrating on a first trip had begun to rise in the 1990s. For men, the chances of both legal and illegal first-trip migration has increased, whereas for women, only the chance of migrating with legal documents has risen since 1990.

Together with findings from prior studies, the analysis suggests that the pressures to migrate are now as high as ever. Although the legalization program appears related to a rapid rise in the probabilities of legal migration, it is clear that overall pressures to migrate from many communities in west central Mexico remain strong for both men and women. So the question is how to get over the current migration peak or hump (Martin, 1993).

Therefore, the analysis suggests that recent migration from communities with long trajectories of migration has become a self-feeding process (Massey et al., 1987). After 1986, with amnesty and the ability to sponsor their relatives, many more migrants—especially women—have been entering legally. But at the same time that the incentives to migrate legally and illegally have changed, very high levels of male and female migration persist. Thus, controlling the U.S. border through enforcement efforts alone cannot effectively deter Mexicans from migrating because going northward has become a way of life in many communities. The solution lies in a multi-dimensional and dynamic approach to U.S.-Mexico immigration policy. Essential in this approach must be a binational propaganda campaign that is aimed at changing beliefs about migrating to the United States from Mexican communities.

Technical Appendix

The MMP data permit us to separately distinguish between the chances of making an initial (first) or subsequent (two or more) trip to the United States. Together these events determine the overall flow of legal and illegal migrants across the border (Donato et al., 1992). In this report, we examined the chances that male household heads and women will migrate on an initial U.S. trip, and for men, the chances that they will migrate on a subsequent trip.

For the analysis, we drew on two basic sources of information: the birth date and the date of the first trip to the United States (compiled for all household members), and the history of border crossing (gathered from household heads). Given each subject's date of birth and year of first trip, we first constructed separate year-by-year life histories up to the date of the first U.S. trip for both men and women. That is, we built discrete-time person-year files that followed each subject from birth to the date of the survey or to the first U.S. trip, whichever came first. For the recurrent trip analysis, we built a similar discrete-time person year file but constructed it from year-by-year files that began with the year migrants returned from their first trip up to the year of their next trip.

Because the outcome measure was trichotomous (migrated illegally, legally, or did not migrate), we used multinomial logistic regression to estimate the chance of migrating with and without legal papers versus not migrating at all (the reference category) (Hosmer and Lemeshow, 1989). The multinomial logit equation is given below:

$$g_j(x) = \ln \frac{P(Y = j \mid x)}{P(Y = 0 \mid x)}$$
$$= \beta_{j0} + \beta_{j1}x_1 + \beta_{j2}x_2 + \beta_{j3}x_3$$

where j represents legal status of migration on a first (or subsequent) trip and 0 indicates no migration, and where $P(Y = j|x)$ is the probability of migration with legal status j given a set of characteristics represented by the vector x. The effects of the explanatory variables in time t on the log-odds ($g_j(x)$) of migrating with legal status j in t + 1 are; age given by β_{j1}, period given by β_{j2}, and community given by β_{j3}. Note that period and age are time varying, whereas community is a fixed variable.

We began by estimating age-period models and age-period-community models (available upon request). From them, we calculated the conditional chances that male household heads (or women) of a given age migrate, legally or illegally, on an initial U.S. trip using the equation below:

Notes

I gratefully acknowledge support from the U.S. Commission on Immigration Reform, and comments from members of the Binational Study of Migration Between the United States and Mexico. This paper originates from a report written by Philip Martin, Agustin Escobar Lapatí, Gustavo Lopez Castro, and myself for the Binational Study. I also appreciate extensive comments from Marlene Lee, and technical assistance from Kristin E. Espinosa, Brett Hebert, and Rebecca Carter.

1. Of the roughly seven million Mexican-born persons living in the United States in early 1997, four million were Mexican legal immigrants, two million unauthorized immigrants and one million Mexican-born persons who have become naturalized U.S. citizens (INS, 1997).

2. Between 1942 and 1947 alone, some 220,000 Mexican braceros were admitted with U.S. government approval.

3. In 1966–67, Mexicans employed on U.S. farms earned $15 to $25 per day, versus $0.80 to $1.20 in the local day labor market—according to Wiest, "a relatively unskilled temporary job in the United States provides a higher income than jobs . . . in Mexico" (1973).

4. Wages were about $30 per day in the U.S., and $3.80 per day in Mexico at this time (Reichert, 1981).
5. At the time, U.S. policy permitted employers to write letters offering ex-Braceros jobs, enabling many Mexicans to become legal immigrants with the right to unify their families.
6. IRCA did, however, affect the wages and work conditions of Mexican migrants (Donato et al., 1992b; Donato and Massey, 1993; Massey and Philips, forthcoming).
7. As Massey and Espinosa (1997) note, national surveys suggest that approximately half of Mexican adults are related to someone in the United States (Camp, 1993).
8. Using these patterns as a guide, Massey et al. (1994) then classified communities according to their stage in the migration process each year and described how the characteristics of migrants change as prevalence moves from low to high.

References

Arizpe, L. 1982. The Rural Exodus in Mexico and Mexican Migration to the United States. In P.G. Brown and H. Shue (eds.), *Border That Joins*. New Jersey: Rowman and Littlefield.
Arizpe, Lourdes, Fanny Salinas, and Margarita Velásquez. 1989. Efectos de la Crisis Economica 1980–1985 Sobre Las Condiciones de Vida de Las Mujeres Campesinas en Mexico. In *El Ajuste Invisible*. Bogotá, Colombia: UNICEF.
Borjas, George. 1990. *Friends or Strangers: The Impact of Immigrants on the U.S. Economy*. NY: Basic Books, Inc.
Camp, Roderick. 1993. *Politics in Mexico*. New York: Oxford University Press.
Cornelius, Wayne A. 1989. "Impacts of the 1986 U.S. Immigration Law on Emigration from Rural Mexican Sending Communities." *Population and Development Review 15*: 689–705.
———. 1990. "Impacts of the 1986 U.S. Immigration Law on Emigration from Rural Mexican Sending Communities." Pp. 227–50 in Frank D. Bean, Barry Edmonston, and Jeffrey S. Passel, eds., *Undocumented Migration to the United States: IRCA and the Experience of the 1980s*. Washington, D.C.: The Urban Institute.
Dagodag, W. Tim. 1975. "Source Regions and Composition of Illegal Mexican Immigration to California." *International Migration Review 9*: 499–511.
Donato, Katharine M. 1993. "Current Trends and Patterns of Female Migration: Evidence from Mexico." *International Migration Review 27*(Winter): 748–71.
Donato, Katharine M. and Douglas S. Massey. 1993. "Effects of the Immigration Reform and Control Act on the Wages of Mexican Migrants." *Social Science Quarterly 74*(3): 523–41.
Donato, Katharine M., Jorge Durand, and Douglas S. Massey. 1992a. "Stemming the Tide? Assessing the Deterrent Effects of the Immigration Reform and Control Act." *Demography 29*(2): 139–57.
Donato, Katharine M., Jorge Durand, and Douglas S. Massey. 1992b. "Changing Conditions in the U.S. Labor Market: Effects of the Immigration Reform and Control Act of 1986." *Population Research and Policy Review* 11.
———, and S.M. Kanaiaupuni. 1998. Women's Migration from Mexico to the United States. In forthcoming edited volume, Oxford University Press.
Durand, Jorge and Douglas S. Massey. 1992. "Generalizations about Mexico-U.S. Migration: A Critical Review." *Latin American Research Review 27*(2).
Escobar Latapí, Agustín, Philip Martin, Gustavo López Castro, and Katharine Donato. 1998. "Factors that Influence Migration." Pp. 163–250 in *Migration between Mexico and the United States: Binational Study*, vol. 1. Washington, D.C.: U.S. Commission on Immigration Reform.
Galarza, Ernest. 1964. *Merchants of Labor: The Mexican Bracero Story*. Santa Barbara, CA: McNally and Loftin.
Gonzalez de la Rocha, M. 1989. *El Poder de la Ausencia: Mujeres y migración en una comunidad de*

Los Altos, Jalisco. Report prepared for the XI Coloquio de Antropología e História Regionales: las realidades regionales de la crisis nacional.

González de la Rocha, Mercedes and Agustín Escobar Latapí. 1990. *The Impact of IRCA on the Migration Patterns of a Community in Los Altos, Jalisco, Mexico.* Working Paper No. 41, Commission for the Study of International Migration and Cooperative Economic Development.

Grindle, M. 1987. *Searching for Rural Development.* NY: Cornell Press.

Hoffman, Abraham. 1974. *Unwanted Mexican Americans in the Great Depression: Repatriation Pressures 1929–39.* Tucson, AZ: University of Arizona Press.

Hosmer, David W. and Stanley Lemeshow. 1989. *Applied Logistic Regression.* New York, NY: John Wiley & Sons, Inc.

Jasso, Guillermina and Mark R. Rosenzweig. 1990. *The New Chosen People: Immigrants in the United States.* New York: Russell Sage Foundation.

Jones, Richard C. 1988. "Micro Source Regions of Mexican Undocumented Migration." *National Geographic Research* 4:11–22.

Kanaiaupuni, Shawn Malia. 1998. "The Role of Women in the Social Process of Migration: Organizational Strategies of Mexican Households." Unpublished manuscript, University of Wisconsin.

Kiser, G. and M. Kiser. 1979. *Mexican Workers in the U.S.* Albuquerque, NM: University of New Mexico Press.

Lindstrom, David P. 1991. The Differential Role of Family Networks in Individual Migration Decisions. Presented at the annual meeting of the Population Association of America, Washington, D.C.

Lindstrom, David P. 1996. "Economic Opportunity and Return Migration from the United States." *Demography, Vol 33*(3).

Lopez Castro, Gustavo. 1986. *La Casa Dividida: Un estudio sobre la migración a Estado Unidos en un peublo michoacano.* Mexico: Asociación Mexicano de Población, Colegio de Michoacán.

Martin, Philip L. 1993. *Trade and Migration: NAFTA and Agriculture.* Washington, D.C.: Institute for International Economics.

Massey, Douglas S. 1988. "Economic Development and Inernational Migration in Comparative Perspective." *Population and Development Review 14*(3): 383–413.

———, Rafael Alarcón, Jorge Durand, and Humberto González. 1987. *Return to Aztlan: The Social Process of International Migration from Western Mexico.* Berkeley, CA: University of California Press.

Massey, Douglas S. and Kristin E. Espinosa. 1997. "What's Driving Mexico-U.S. Migration? A Theoretical, Empirical, and Policy Analysis." *American Journal of Sociology 102*(4): 939–99.

Massey, Douglas S. and Julie Philips. (1996). "El Nuevo Mercado de Trabajo: Immigrantes en el Norte despues de IRCA." In *Las Relaciones México-Estados Unidos desde la Perspectiva Regional.* San Luis Potosí: Centro de Investigaciones Historicasde San Luis, forthcoming.

Massey, Douglas S., Katharine M. Donato, and Zai Liang. 1990. "Effects of the Immigration Reform and Control Act of 1986: Preliminary Data from Mexico." Pp. 182–210 in Frank D. Bean, Barry Edmonston, and Jeffrey S. Passel, eds., *Undocumented Migration to the United States: IRCA and the Experience of the 1980s.* Washington, D.C.: The Urban Institute.

Massey, Douglas S., Luin Goldring, and Jorge Durand. 1994a. "Continuities in Transnational Migration: An Analysis of 19 Mexican Communities." *American Journal of Sociology 99*(6): 1492– 1533.

Mexican Migration Project. 1995. *Documentation of Data Files.* Philadelphia, PA: Population Studies Center, University of Pennsylvania.

Passel, Jeffrey S. and Karen A. Woodrow. 1987. "Change in the Undocumented Alien Population in the United States, 1979–1983." *International Migration Review 21:* 1304–34.

Reichert, Josh and Douglas S. Massey. 1979. "Patterns of Migration from a Mexican Sending Community: A Comparison of Legal and Illegal Migrants." *International Migration Review 13:* 599–623.

Reichert, Josh and Douglas S. Massey. 1980. "History and Trends in U.S. Bound Migration from a Mexican Town." *International Migration Review 14*(4): 475–91.

Rouse, Richard C. 1992. "Making Sense of Settlement: Class Transformation, cultural struggle and transnationalism among Mexican migrants to the United States." *Annals of the New York Academy of Science, 9645*: 25–52.

Stephens, Lynn. 1990. *Zapotec Women.* TX: University of Texas Press.

Taylor, J. Edward and T.J. Wyatt. 1996. "The Shadow Value of Migrant Remittances, income and Inequality in a Household-farm Economy," *The Journal of Development Studies 32*(6), pp. 899–912.

U.S. Commission for Immigration Reform, 1997. *Binational Study of Migration between the United States and Mexico: A Preliminary Report.* Washington DC: U.S. C.I.R.

U.S. Department of Justice. 1996. *Statistical Yearbook of the Immigration and Naturalization Service.* Washington, D.C.: U.S. Government Printing Office.

Woodrow, Karen A. and Jeffrey S. Passel. 1990. Post-IRCA Undocumented Immigration to the United States: Assessment Based on the June 1988 CPS. In Frank D. Bean, Barry Edmonston, and Jeffrey S. Passel (eds.), *Undocumented Migration to the United States: IRCA and the Experience of the 1980s.*

8

Women and Immigrants: Strangers in a Strange Land

Nina Toren

Abstract: This paper draws an analogy between the fate of women in the labor market and immigrants in the host country by examining the social processes that affect both categories. Immigrants, and women in traditionally male occupations, are usually regarded and treated as strangers, reflected in stereotyping, exclusion, segregation, and assimilation. By conceptualizing gender-based occupational segregation in terms of territory, borders, and migration we attempt to understand this phenomenon and its persistence in a new way and within a wider framework of social distinctions and inequality. These processes are specifically illustrated by two examples: women in a traditionally male occupational sphere, i.e., faculty women in academia, and immigrant scientists.

A stubborn problem that has been recently examined by researchers concerning the changing composition of the labor force is that despite women's increased participation, their entry into male-dominated occupations, and reduction of the "gender gap" in human capital and work experience, gender-based segregation and inequalities in the labor market still persist.

This issue has been investigated within different theoretical frameworks, such as socioeconomic structures and forces (Reskin and Roos, 1990; Rosenfeld and Kalleberg, 1990; England, 1993), organizational arrangements and interpersonal processes (Kanter, 1977; Ridgeway, 1997), family roles and division of labor (Bielby and Bielby, 1988), psychological predispositions and cognition (Deaux, 1985), and so on.

In this article we look at the problem from another angle: we employ metaphors of migration, territory, and borders to conceptualize gender-based segregation and reward inequity in the realm of work. Metaphor is "a way of *thinking* and a way of *seeing*" (Morgan, 1986); using it in research aims to understand something in a new way, enhance the data, and generate new interpretations. We attempt to show that thinking about women in traditionally male occupations as *strangers* in a country that is not their homeland illuminates this development and its persistence and the fate of women who cross the boundaries separating the genders in the sphere of work.

The utility of an approach is its ability to discern the mechanisms producing and maintaining the phenomenon it aims to explain as well as clarify our understanding of more general patterns, which, in the present context, are social categorization, distinction, and differential treatment based on ascriptive attributes, such as race, gender, age, ethnic origin, or nationality.

Sources of Data

The following analysis is based on relevant theoretical and empirical research literatures pertaining to women's position in the labor market and to people migrating from one country to another. The discussion focuses on the general comparable dimensions and largely disregards the variations among women and among immigrants. Obviously, not all women and not all immigrants are alike in respect to personal characteristics and human capital, nor are the social, economic, cultural, and historical circumstances associated with their movement into new territories and work domains. It would be important in future research to examine specific cases within the broad categories addressed in this study.

For original data, we draw mainly on two empirical studies that were conducted in Israel on two specific groups: women scientists in academia, and Russian immigrant scientists. The first study of women in academia began in 1983 with a survey of the entire population of faculty members in the seven institutions of higher education (universities) in Israel. The entire female faculty at that time numbered about 430 women (13.5 percent of the total). Faculty women and men were compared in terms of proportions, promotion, and performance. In many respects, the position of women in academia in Israel resembles that of faculty women in the United States and other western countries; that is, they constitute a minority of the total faculty, are concentrated in the lower ranks of the academic ladder, advance more slowly than their male colleagues, and only a few reach the highest rank of full professor. A sub-sample of fifty women were personally interviewed with a questionnaire concerning their perceptions and attitudes toward their professional careers, family obligations, gender discrimination, etc. (Toren and Kraus, 1987; Toren, 1991).

The second study was mainly concerned with professional integration problems that confront scientists who move from one sociocultural environment to another in spite of the notion that science is culture-free and "the same everywhere." The sample of scientists studied included 207 persons who immigrated from the Soviet Union to Israel in the early 1970s. More than half of these scientists were employed in academic institutions and the others in research and development institutes of government, industry, and the private sector. The second stage of this study was performed following the second large wave of immigration from Russia in the early 1990s and was composed of a sample of 123 scientists who were employed in all institutions of higher education in Israel (Toren, 1988, 1994).

There is *no* overlap between the respondents of the study on immigrant scientists and the study on faculty women.

This article examines the social processes that affect both new immigrants in the host society and women in traditionally male occupations: stereotyping, exclusion, segregation, and assimilation. Both groups are compared in terms of these mechanisms and discern their similar and different manifestations.

Attributed Characteristics of Women and Immigrants

The major stereotypes in a society are those attached to race, ethnic origin, class, and gender. The binary divisions of white and black, high and low, male and female, native and newcomer are basic to the creation and maintenance of social categories that sustain inequality by establishing boundaries of inclusion and exclusion (Bourdieu, 1984; Zerubavel, 1991; Bar-Yosef, 1996).

Both sex and race are physical, personal, primordial, and permanent features, and the boundaries between their categories are (almost) untrespassable. Attributes of a social class or immigrant group are somewhat different; they are not such "simple" and obvious markers that time cannot erase. Immigrant status is usually a transient state, a matter of time, which disappears after a generation or two. Furthermore, one's class can be modified by mobility. Even race or ethnicity may be attenuated to some extent by intermarriage, whereas being female is, so to speak, a "life-long affliction." Gender is more biologically determined and usually more conspicuous. The demarcations between the sexes clearly define membership in one or the other category (with few exceptions). Nonetheless, beyond their biological and ascriptive aspects these categories are to a large extent socially constructed, negotiated, and transformed (Yancey et al., 1976; Epstein, 1988; Bem, 1993; Brekhus, 1994; Nagel, 1994). The "otherness" of outsiders is constructed and nurtured by stereotypes, and their externalization serves to legitimize their differential treatment (Reskin, 1987; Baron and Pfeffer, 1994; Lorber, 1994).

Empirically, these characteristics intersect, such as gender and race (black women), class and gender (middle-class men), and migrant and ethnicity (such as Chinese immigrants in the United States or recent Ethiopian immigrants in Israel). The latter is a good example of social identities and boundaries being constructed and reconstructed rather than "objectively" given. Thus, although Ethiopians are black, they are officially regarded as Jews rather than as a distinct racial group, which shows that sociocultural classifications may supersede biological ones. Similarly, the extreme "one drop rule" or the marking of children of black and white parents as black in the United States illustrates the impact of mental lumping and splitting (Zerubavel, 1996). These categorizations are neither natural nor logical, but are rather the results of social definitions of similarity and difference.

Identities and demarcations are not only imposed from the outside, but also created and adopted by minority group members themselves. Referring to ethnic identity and boundaries, Nagel writes:

> The location and meaning of particular ethnic boundaries are continuously negotiated, revised, and revitalized, both by ethnic group members themselves as well as by outside observers. (Nagel, 1994; see also Yancey et al., 1976).

We have learned from personal experience that immigrants from the former Soviet Union in Israel object to being called "Russians," as is customary, and would rather be identified as "Jews from Russia." This term denotes that they identify themselves as Jews, not Russians, but it also conveys that they set themselves apart from Jewish immigrants from other countries.

Cognitive marking and zoning between groups of people are influenced and shaped by social institutions and prevalent ideologies and are, therefore, in continual flux and open to changing interpretations. For instance, immigration to Israel, the "ingathering of the exiles," and their integration are central values and national goals of the utmost importance in Israeli society as embodied in the Law of Return. By comparison, gender equality—the position of women in society and the labor market—has not been a significant social-political issue and has only recently gained some visibility and interest. The laws pertaining to gender equality of opportunity, employment, pay, and affirmative action are still not prominent, nor are they seriously enforced. Moreover, the traditional emphasis on family and motherhood in Israeli society and Jewish culture hinders both women and men from taking bold steps to change the status quo.

In spite of the fact that men and women enter the academic tenure track at the same level, with identical human capital and credentials (a Ph.D. degree), do the same kind of work of teaching and research, and have "equal opportunity" regarding promotion on a single orderly career line leading to the top, women are generally viewed as having the "wrong" or inappropriate status characteristic of femaleness. This image is portrayed by describing scientists as having stereotypical male, non-female qualities, such as rationality, objectivity, abstract thinking, assertiveness, competitiveness, and the like. This image defines women out, and the few who do enter the gates of science are labeled as less competent than their male colleagues or as exceptions (Zuckerman and Cole, 1975).

These stereotypical perceptions have practical consequences in academia. When recruiting, granting tenure, promoting, and awarding prizes and honors, men are the obvious and favored candidates. Women, on the other hand, are scrutinized more rigorously and stricter criteria are applied in judging their ability and worth. Many doubts accompany the achievements of a woman who performs well according to the accepted requirements (e.g., has published a good number of papers in good journals): Was she just lucky? Does she have some connection to the editor? Is her most recent work of the same quality? Should the credit go to her male co-author? And so on and on. Men's success is easy to accept and they are treated more leniently; they are similar to those who make the decisions, and similarity creates empathy and trust; in short, they are PLU—"people like us" (Baron and Pfeffer, 1994). Women, by comparison, have to convince the committee that they are indeed worthy and overcome the primitive, primordial attitude that they are strangers who do not really belong because they are not suited to do creative work in the realm of science and scholarship. As one woman was told by her advisor: "You do the experiment and leave the theorizing to others!"

The structural outcomes of the operation of gender stereotypes are that faculty women constitute a minority in academia in Israel (and elsewhere), are concentrated in the lower ranks of the academic hierarchy, and advance less rapidly than comparable men. In 1995, women constituted 20.4 percent (up from 16 percent in 1988) of the total faculty ($N = 4,343$) in institutions of higher education. Women compose 7.8 percent of all full professors, 16 percent of all associate professors, 30.8 percent of all senior lecturers, and 34.7 percent of all lecturers.[1]

Women in academia, like immigrants and other minority groups, have a repertoire of identities to choose from and may present one or the other in different situations and for different purposes. They can emphasize their identity as scientists and scholars, or their gender and sexuality (although the latter is usually frowned upon). By playing out a particular identity, people attach themselves to others who share it, and split themselves apart from those who do not. For instance, in this study, we asked female professors in the physical and life sciences why they think they advance more rapidly and farther than women in the humanities and social sciences. A recurrent theme brought up by respondents in this context is represented by the following quote:

> Women in the humanities have lower levels of aspirations, whereas in the natural sciences you have to make a serious decision and be very determined. There is no "half and half" in these fields, no part-time jobs, no intermitting for child care. Women have to devote themselves totally to their work.

Here, women in the sciences differentiate themselves from faculty women in the softer disciplines and in fact argue that they "are like men" in their persistence and total commitment to work. On the other hand, they may draw boundaries between themselves and male scientists and identify with their sisters across scientific disciplines when demanding equality for faculty women in academia or in society in general. Shifting identities and boundary work elucidate other events as well, such as the known phenomenon of "queen beeism," that is, the tendency of successful women to detach themselves from less fortunate ones and to deny that they have been discriminated against in the course of their careers.

Affiliation and Allegiance

Immigrants in the host country and women in non-traditional occupations are regarded as strangers. As Simmel wrote in his seminal essay, *The Stranger*, he is a person whose "position in the group is determined essentially by the fact that he has not belonged to it from the beginning, that he imports qualities into it, which do not and cannot stem from the group itself" (Simmel, 1950). Since they do not belong and are out of place, members of both groups can be told to "go home"— immigrants to their home country and women to their family home.

Strangers are not completely trusted. The allegiance of immigrants to the national community and country, or the work place and career in the case of women, is questioned. For instance, regarding the recent immigrants from the former Soviet Union in Israel, it is claimed that youngsters in this group are reluctant to serve in the army—a prime symbol of patriotism and loyalty—and that many of the older generation, particularly professionals and scientists, look back nostalgically to the country and culture they have left (Gans, 1979). This double and, therefore, doubtful loyalty has a price: suspicion and antagonism surface in stressful situations, such as economic constraints and unemployment, and especially during wars (e.g., attitudes toward Israeli Arabs during eruptions of violence in Israel, or toward Iraqis in America during the Gulf War), and further reinforce immigrants' marginality and distinction from the indigenous and veteran population.

The lesser loyalty and devotion stereotype is also ascribed, mainly by employers and male co-workers, to women in the labor market, particularly those in high positions and demanding jobs. Like new immigrants, women in nontraditional occupations are allegedly less committed; they appear as not totally involved and dedicated to their work compared to male co-workers or colleagues, since their domestic responsibilities are in constant competition with their careers for scarce time, energy, and loyalty. As crudely expressed by a male colleague: "They think more about their children at home than about the mice in the lab!"

Implicitly, this conception also assumes that women are generally less productive, whether publishing scientific papers as academics or getting things done and solving problems as managers. In academic science, these assumptions have served to justify discrimination against women in terms of hiring, salary, tenure, promotion, and inclusion in men's informal collegial networks. Women are punished for their presumed partial commitment and men are rewarded for total commitment. For instance, male professors are reluctant to serve as mentors to women Ph.D. candidates because they think they are unstable workers ("She'll get pregnant and leave"). For similar reasons, women are not welcome in informal information networks, and men prefer to collaborate with male colleagues.

Research evidence, nevertheless, does not support the notion that women devote less effort to outside-the-home work than comparable men. In a study based on two Quality of Employment Surveys in the United States, Bielby and Bielby (1988) conclude that on average, women allocate more effort to work than men with similar family status: " . . . as women add work roles to their family roles, they generate the energy necessary to fulfill their commitments to the two sets of activities." Also Mannheim and Schiffrin (1984), conducting a study on professional women with children in Israel, found that family characteristics, such as number and age of children, did not decrease women's work commitment as measured by work-role centrality (WRC).

Women professors in the sciences are fully aware that theirs is not a nine-to-five job and indeed spend long hours in the lab. A study of the prestigious Weitzman Research Institute in Israel found that a majority of faculty women do not stay away for the entire maternity leave of twelve weeks, but hurry back to work after two or three weeks. Furthermore, in a study of all female full professors, we examined the history of relationships between motherhood and research productivity from the entry rank of lecturer to the highest rank of full professor. The results are in line with the findings of studies in other countries (Astin and Davis, 1985; Zuckerman and Cole, 1987; Kyvic, 1990). Faculty women without children do not publish more than those with children; the most prolific publishers are mothers of two children. Calculating the yearly average number of published articles for a period of twenty years, shows that publication rates increase from zero to two children, and then drop slightly for women who have three or four children. In sum, contrary to expectations, single or childless women are not more, but less productive than mothers (Toren, 1991). The argument that having a family distracts women academics from their work and diminishes their involvement and performance is an unfounded suspicion based on stereotypes attached to strangers, namely people who are regarded as different.

Women's Place, Men's Domain, and Immigrants' Country

Looking at the discourse and imagery associated with women who enter non-traditional occupations, it can be seen that they are often depicted as newcomers in unfamiliar surroundings. A good example is a description of men maneuvering within organizations:

> ... men carry with them a package of invisible, unearned assets that are best described as a weightless knapsack of special provisions, assurances, tools, maps, guides, code books, passports, visas, clothes, compasses, emergency gear, and blank checks. (Peggy McIntosh, quoted in Rosener, 1990).

Women are not equally well equipped; they lack these skills and guiding tools and are hence envisioned as disoriented, wandering in *terra incognita,* an often ruthless, perplexing, and arduous terrain. To use Swidler's (1986) metaphor, women lack the necessary "tool kit" of resources, skills, habits, and styles from which people construct strategies of action.

The territorialization of occupational sex segregation is reflected in other concepts referred to when describing the labor market. Consider for example the notion that certain occupations are "men's domains" or "male dominated." Domain and domination stem from the same root. According to the dictionary, "dominus" means master or owner, and "domain" is the territory over which controlling and ruling are exerted. Even the seemingly neutral word—occupation—has more than one meaning; it means profession, trade, job, business, vocation, etc., but it also means ownership, possession, subjugation, and control (although, this is not the case in other languages). Women who penetrate the occupational spheres occupied by men are viewed as invaders or intruders and their journey is replete with hurdles, obstacles, and barriers (Sonnert and Holton, 1995; Moore and Toren, 1997).

Traditionally, women's proper place, realm, domain, or territory is the home or household, which, since the industrial revolution, has been geographically distanced from the workplace, namely from the male domain. The function of stereotypical traits assigned to women, such as nurturant, caring, emotional, docile, dependent, etc., is to keep them in the home (private sphere) and out of the labor market (public sphere), particularly its primary segments, in which stereotypical male qualities are required, such as rationality, competence, experience, entrepreneurship, autonomy, and assertiveness. Even in predominantly female occupations—nursing, librarianship, teaching, and social work—the genders are separated. The few men (male tokens) who work in these fields are usually concentrated in the better-paying specialties and hold higher administrative positions (Williams, 1995).

The spatial dimension and its significance for women's group formation and political organization were appraised by Simmel over seventy-five years ago, he writes:

> The parallelism in the way of life and the activities of women is of such nature as to effectively prevent the development of associations on the basis of this equality.... because each woman is so totally preoccupied in her own sphere that another, equally situated woman is by the same token totally excluded. (Simmel, 1955).

Like peasants in Marx's conception, women are geographically dispersed and isolated from each other.

Goffman (1977) makes the same point:

> Women as a disadvantaged group are somewhat cut off ecologically from congress with their kind.... women are also separated from one another by the stake they acquire in the very organization which divides them.

Since the 1960s, feminism and the women's movement have contributed a great deal to the awareness of the disadvantaged position of women in the labor market and to legal change enforcing more equity between genders. At present women compose about half of the labor force in most western developed countries, including Israel (up from one-quarter in 1967). They are not, as at the beginning of this century and earlier, confined to their homes, and the boundaries are more permeable than they used to be. The demarcations between the sexes have shifted from those dividing the private and public realms, to within the sphere of paid work itself, as evident in persistent gender-based division of labor. Both developments—the partial detachment of women from their private/domestic niches and their concentration and face-to-face interaction in work settings—have the potential for organization, solidarity, and collective action. However, proximity and increasing numbers are not the only factors in this kind of organization and action. Faculty women in Israeli universities have just recently realized that these developments ("more of the same") are ineffective unless they will be represented in decision-making committees and positions of power at all levels.

Gender boundaries, unlike "real" physical borders between countries which migrants cross, are to a large extent mental-categorical, socially constructed, and bolstered by gender stereotypes; this, however, does not imply that they are not real in their consequences (Epstein, 1988, 1992; Bem, 1993; Brekhus, 1996). Symbolic boundaries are political insofar as they " . . . freeze a particular state of the social struggle, i.e., a given state of the distribution of advantages and obligations" (Bourdieu, 1984). Both kinds of boundaries may shift; however, changing the location of territorial borders between countries is consciously negotiated and declared (though they are frequently disputed), whereas the shift of cultural, cognitive boundaries is a more subtle and developmental process (though here too formal policy and laws can be formulated [e.g., equal employment opportunity, affirmative action]).

An important difference between national or residential territories and occupational areas in the labor market is that the scope of spatial territory is *given,* and the relocation of borders is a zero sum game: one's gain is the other's loss. By comparison, the domain of work may expand or decline; new occupational areas may emerge and old ones may shrink or disappear. It is generally believed that women can more easily enter evolving new fields (such as computer work), new fields in biological research, and new personal and community services than traditionally male-dominated occupations. This means that women enter not only jobs (territories) vacated by men but can create and develop new work areas, such as small businesses, public relations, development of human resources, and the like.

Role Encapsulation, Residential Segregation, and Social Networks

Stereotyping and exclusion of "marked" people and groups are often accompanied by erecting barriers and spatial distancing (e.g., in "total" institutions). Nevertheless, once strangers and minority members, whether immigrants or women, have infiltrated a territory dominated by a majority to which they do not belong, they are usually confined to inferior and marginal lines of work or residential areas, thus forming occupational and geographic enclaves or ghettoes *within* the larger framework.

Geographic, spatial segregation has been extensively discussed in relation to racial, ethnic, and immigrant communities but less so in relation to women in the labor market (Simmel, 1955). As noted earlier, one of the troubling aspects accompanying the dramatic increase in women's labor force participation, particularly in the last twenty-five years, is that it has not significantly changed overall rates of occupational sex segregation/integration. Students of this issue have advanced various explanations (Jacobs, 1989; Reskin and Roos, 1990; England, 1993; Williams, 1995; Ridgeway, 1997). The main reasons for this structural endurance are first, that the majority of women who join the labor force enter traditionally female jobs, the so-called "pink ghettoes," including sales, service, and clerical occupations. Second, even those who enter male occupations, such as management, engineering, and science, are relegated to the less important and rewarding jobs, resulting in sex divisions *within* occupations. Kanter (1977) has termed this process "role encapsulation" or "entrapment," in which token women in work organizations are restricted to specialties considered appropriate to their gender (roughly, health, education, and welfare) and in line with their nurturing, supporting roles. In the legal profession, it was noted that women cluster in specialties, such as child custody, domestic relations, and government; in medicine, most surgeons are men and most general practitioners in public clinics are women, and so on.

The distribution of faculty women among scientific disciplines in Israeli universities in 1996 clearly illustrates these disciplinary and hierarchical divisions. Women are very small minorities in the traditional male sciences—6 percent in mathematics and computer sciences, 8 percent in the physical sciences, 9 percent in engineering. In the "softer" disciplines, they constitute larger minorities—21 percent of the total faculty in the social sciences, and 36 percent in the humanities (Statistical Report, 1997). In all scientific and scholarly fields, women are concentrated in the lower ranks (lecturer and senior lecturer), and only a few reach the highest rank of full professor. Of all female academicians, 27.5 percent are currently in the lecturer rank (the lowest tenure-track rank), 40 percent are senior lecturers (the glass ceiling or bottleneck), 21 percent are associate professors, and 11.4 percent are full professors (Statistical Report, 1997). The gender-based distribution among scientific fields has not changed significantly for many years; the hierarchical divisions have improved slightly in the last decade as noted above.

Changes in the "color" or ethnic composition of residential areas occurs through two related processes. Traditional residents move out and a considerable number of blacks or members of a subordinate ethnic group move in. In turn, this is exacerbated by "white flight." This is precisely what happens in the domain of work. Examining the dynamics of gendered occupational segregation, desegregation, and resegregation, Strober (1984) argues that men in the labor market have first choice of available or new occupations; they choose the jobs most attractive to them. Jobs that men do not want are then offered to women, and then to those next in the queue, e.g., immigrants. When women enter jobs that have been abandoned by men for better opportunities, men in turn continue to move out because they feel "uncomfortable" working with women who would disrupt ("pollute") the certainty and trust built on sameness and familiarity (how will a woman react when told a dirty joke or, more seriously, in a crisis?). Furthermore, men fear that women's presence will adversely affect the income and prestige of their jobs. Other monopolized resources are in danger of usurpation as well, such as control over decisionmaking and networks of informal relationships.

A male occupation may in the course of time change its gender and become female, as for example bank-telling and high-school teaching in the United States (Strober, 1984; Reskin and Roos, 1990). These changes are graphically depicted as a "... process by which women chase men through resegregating jobs or specialties as economic transformations change the availability of qualified male workers for a given job" (Ridgeway, 1997). These transformations do not necessarily lead to occupational gender integration, but rather to resegregation and the retention of the disparities between men and women in the labor market.

Strangers and newcomers are usually excluded from certain kinds of social relations. Women do not participate in the informal male networks and cliques in academic science, nor are they embraced by the macho camaraderie of blue-collar unions who have a distaste for both women and immigrants, or the tightly-knit social groups of the indigenous veteran population (e.g., army buddies) based on shared meanings, collective memory and experience, to which outsiders are not easily accepted (Toren, 1994).

In contrast to women's ghettoization in particular occupations, specialties, and ranks, immigrants' residential segregation is not imposed only from the outside. In particular, those with common racial or ethnic origins frequently choose to live near "their own" people and keep themselves apart from those surrounding them. Recent research shows a distinct tendency of the 1990s Russian immigrants to flock to communities and neighborhoods populated by their countrymen (Damian and Rosenbaum-Tamari, 1996).

Spatial proximity and exclusion from networks of social relations intensify in-group identification and solidarity, distancing from the external environment, and adherence to cultural traditions and internal ties. For instance, the Russian press in Israel often blames the host society:

By summarily rejecting the Russian-speaking intellectual elite, Israeli society itself has greatly contributed to the creation of a self-contained cultural enclave in which a seventh of the country's population now lives. (Wartburg, 1994: Lissak and Leshem, 1995)

Marking and maintaining boundaries serve to strengthen the integration and sense of belonging of *insiders* as well, such as men in male occupations, e.g., the "old boy's network," versus women in "the outer circle" in academia, or friendships among Israeli-born "Zabarim" versus "new immigrants," e.g., the so-called "Russians."

We can thus distinguish among three kinds of segregation—cultural as expressed in stereotypes and symbols, spatial referring to physical location or used as metaphor, and social divisions based on social relations and networks. When these overlap they reinforce each other, resulting in augmented degrees of differentiation, contrast, and inequality.

Culture and Territory

In the social sciences, culture has always been a central concept by which social systems are described, studied, and compared. It is also a concept that has undergone many modifications and acquired different meanings (Swidler, 1986; Nagel, 1994). In anthropological and migration studies, culture and country, society and space, peoples and places, tribes and territory are closely linked. Hence, people who move from one place to another are often seen as "torn loose from their culture" and "uprooted." We usually use such strong terms in regard to refugees who are coerced to leave their homeland, but "voluntary" migration for economic and other reasons has similar effects. It is interesting that the word used for the process of immigrant integration in Hebrew is *Klita*, conventionally translated as "absorption" but literally meaning the taking root of a plant. This botanical metaphor is similar to the "arborescent root metaphor" in the nationalist discourse linking nation to land, people to place (Malkki, 1992).

Traditionally, the prescribed remedy for cultural uprootedness and territorial displacement was the assimilation of newcomers into the host culture and society. This meant first and foremost learning the local language, becoming aware of and familiar with taken-for-granted norms and shared meanings, and behaving according to the sometimes tacit ground rules. One way of thinking about an immigrant as integrated and assimilated is when he/she knows how to circumvent the formal rules and is familiar with the shortcuts, back alleys, and informal ways of doing things.

The concept of *culture* became pertinent to the study of women in nontraditional occupations, such as science, engineering, and management, when it was introduced into the theory and research of organizations in the 1980s (e.g., Schein 1980). "Organizational culture" and "corporate culture," composed of values, beliefs, traditions, myths, and rituals, quickly became indispensable elements of organizational theorizing and discourse. It is widely agreed, not only among feminists, that the dominant culture in work organizations is fundamentally masculine; it has been created, shaped, and maintained by men for men (Kanter, 1977; Epstein, 1988; Acker, 1990). Women, particularly in traditionally male occupations and higher positions in organizations, can accordingly be perceived as persons (e.g., new immigrants) confronting an unfamiliar culture to which they were not socialized and with which they had no previous experience. In the same vein, the traditional occupants (men) encounter newcomers (women) who may think and behave differently and disrupt the *status quo*.

Symons (1986) vividly describes the obstacles and barriers encountered by women who aspire to managerial careers:

> The corporate world of management may be likened to a tribe, with tribal norms and values and specific rules of conduct... The corporate tribe is made up of insiders—like-minded people who look alike, dress alike, act alike, and trust each other implicitly. When new recruits seek entry major questions are asked. Will they fit in? Can they be trusted to keep the secrets of the clan? A screening process is set in motion whereby recruits are tested for worthiness of membership.

Since men are reluctant to let women onto their turf, and women have no experience in positions of authority, "gaining entry into the tribal territory" is deterred.

The problem confronting women in science, another traditionally male domain, is similar to that of their sisters in management. Faculty women are not part of the inner circles in which scientific information is exchanged and academic culture is produced and sustained by male bonding and tacit understandings:

> In science,... and other professions, the men share traditions, styles, and understandings about rules of competing, bartering, and succeeding. They accept one another, support one another, and promote one another. As outsiders to this milieu and its bartered resources, shared influence, and conferred self-confidence, women are shut out of ways and means to participate and perform. (Fox, 1991)

The main factors that have been suggested to account for academic women's lesser achievements in terms of publications and promotion, such as socialization, lack of mentoring and support, marriage and family, restricted mobility, etc. (Rosenfeld, 1991; Long, 1993), can all be reiterated by saying that the culture and the structural arrangements presently dominant in academia are inhospitable to women. Like new immigrants, women in traditionally male occupations, especially on the higher rungs, do not know the rules of the game and do not "read the map."

Acculturation

In principle, there are two distinct approaches and policies concerning newcomers' assimilation, whether women in traditionally male occupations or immigrants in a new country. The first, as noted above, is to change them and make them more like the dominant majority; the second is to let them be different (for instance, the French policy regarding immigrants of *droit à la différence*). Multiculturalism is a compromise between these two perspectives and also " . . . a feeble acknowledgement of the fact that cultures have lost their moorings in definite places and an attempt to subsume this plurality of cultures within the framework of a national identity" (Gupta and Ferguson, 1992).

From their own point of view, newcomers are confronted with the dilemma of whether or not to be like the dominant majority, that is, to give up their identity and accept the prevailing values, norms, and modes of conduct of the new environment, or to preserve, their own cultural traditions and particular identity. Assimilation and integration processes are usually not comprehensive, but rather a matter of degree. First-generation immigrants tend to keep a niche of their original cultural habits, notably speaking their own language at home. Nor is this process unidirectional; large groups of immigrants are not only influenced by but also influence the local culture. For instance, every wave of immigrants to the United States left its imprint, and some of their language, habits, and folklore have been incorporated in the host society and culture.

Israel, too, grappled with the ideas of the "melting pot" versus pluralism and the "multi-cultural/multi-ethnic" society since its establishment as a state in 1948. In the 1950s, the period of the large wave of immigration from Middle Eastern and African countries and from postwar Europe, the reigning ideology and policy were to absorb, integrate, and forge the various strands into one nation and cultural community. Later, it was realized that various groups of immigrants, including those from the former Soviet Union, should be permitted and even encouraged to preserve some of their cultural traditions. At present, there are several daily newspapers published in Russian, and there is a special official holiday celebrated by Moroccan Jews.

An analogous debate concerns women in academic science and other male-dominated professions. Should women in these occupations perform the job like men? Or, should they be given the opportunity to be different and exercise a different style in performing their work role? Even in science, which is presumed to be universal and meritocratic, detached from any personal characteristics (race, gender and the like), similar queries have been raised. Since science is rational, objective, and the same everywhere, and particularistic considerations are proscribed, how is gender involved in doing science? Keller (1988) argues that science is fundamentally genderized and that "... gender imagery ... was so familiar it had become almost invisible." Science is fraught with gendered symbols, metaphors, and images, ranging from definitions of the scientific method to the presentation of scientific "facts" (for example, the different accounts of the functions of egg and sperm in the process of fertilization).

Recently, *Science*, the prestigious publication of the American Association for the Advancement of Science, devoted a special issue to *Women in Science* (March, 1992), and a later issue (April, 1993) to *Gender and the Culture of Science* with the lead article's title—"Is there a 'Female Style' in Science?" The answer is not unequivocal; however, anecdotal testimony suggests that many female scientists feel that they differ from male colleagues in lab management, attitudes to students and colleagues, and choice of research topics, and that "... their style is not as readily accepted in the inner circles of research ... that barriers to their approach must be broken down if they are to achieve fully equal status in the world of science" (Barinaga, 1993).

As in the case of immigrants, the ideology concerning women is moving from more conservative, coercive ideas to more liberal, egalitarian ones, albeit very slowly. More women do not currently try, nor are they necessarily required, to emulate male models of managing, doing science, or practicing law and medicine. Because of the growth of the feminist movement and public awareness, women are less motivated to prove that they do not differ from men. Moreover, some believe that the presence of women in greater numbers can make the culture of work organizations and occupations more humane, cooperative, and self organizing. This resembles the recognition that the adaptation of immigrant groups to the dominant population and culture in the host country involves reciprocal influences.

However, ideologies concerning gender equality or cultural pluralism do not immediately eradicate the strangeness and otherness, both of women in male professions and immigrants in a new country. The growing diversification of the work place in terms of gender is a fact that all parties involved will have to learn to live with and recognize its potential advantages.

Conclusion and Discussion

To paraphrase Levi-Strauss, we have delineated the likeness of unlike social phenomena, namely migration among countries and the entrance of women into the labor market in general and into male domains of work in particular. By using countries, territorial borders, and migrants as metaphors of male occupational domains, symbolic gender boundaries, and women crossing them, it is possible to transfer knowledge from a relatively familiar and long standing social problem to a more recent and relatively unknown issue.

Looking at the great increase of women's participation in the labor force in terms of international migration, which includes " . . . uprooting, crossing borders, and resettling in a new country" (Hein, 1994), suggests that the crucial experiences that affect women who enter the world of paid work or traditionally male domains are:

- *Mobility*—moving out of their traditional milieu, whether the home or traditional female work spheres, and crossing over to new unfamiliar surroundings.
- *Contact*—the meeting between genders in the world of work is very similar to that of cross-cultural contact and entails a process of learning and mutual adaptation.
- *Relationships*—building networks and establishing ties with members of the indigenous population or traditional job occupants.

Furthermore, the analogy enabled us to discern more clearly some of the dynamics of sex segregation in the labor market and within occupations, such as labelling, distrust, limiting entrance, erecting barriers, denying "full citizenship," channeling into subordinate positions, and coping with the multi-faceted problem of "acculturation." Underlying these attitudes and activities is the assumption that certain people are strangers; for instance, women in traditionally male-dominated occupations are strangers because *they are not men* (see Simone de Beauvoir's *The Second Sex*) and have not belonged to the group from the beginning (see Simmel, quoted earlier).

The exclusionary stances and practices toward both groups explored here are part of a more general tendency to maintain social divisions and inequality on the basis of ascriptive attributes like race, age, physical appearance, and religion. These features are relatively unchangeable and are "convenient" bases of social distinctions and differential treatment; they surface and become salient particularly in time of confrontation, such as unemployment, and generally when competing for scarce resources.

Gender nevertheless is unique in so far as it is a primary property which cuts across all other categories based on race, ethnicity, national origin, class, age, etc., and shapes social roles and institutions. Gender imagery and expectations tend to spill over to spheres of life in which they are or ought to be *irrelevant*. For instance, gender differentiation is deeply embedded in work roles and organizations; it influences the way work is defined and rewarded, and how people are recruited to jobs (Williams, 1989; Acker, 1990; Ridgeway, 1997). We need to disentangle gender from other characteristics and define more clearly the rules of relevance in various frameworks of social life.

The definitions of what is salient and what is irrelevant in a situation are socially and culturally constructed and transmitted; these definitions are nevertheless "real" if we accept them as such and act upon them. The case of faculty women in the sciences as compared to those in the humanities, mentioned above, can serve as an illustration. There is no apparent logical reason why femaleness should have stronger negative effects in the latter than in the former; moreover, the fact that women have more successful careers in the natural sciences than in the humanities and social sciences is counterintuitive.

Women are limited in their performance of certain tasks by our perceptions and expectations and the structural arrangements built around them. In part, these have been internalized and accepted by women themselves, contributing to the tenacity of sex typing and segregation of occupations. As we have seen in the case of immigrant and ethnic groups, identity and boundary definitions are not static nor can they be accounted for solely by external factors and forces. Changes in the current situation depend in part on women's self-perceptions, agency, and ambition. Stereotypes, images, and distinctions that have been socially constructed can be renegotiated and reconstructed.

Notes

The writing of this article was supported by the Recanati Research Fund in the School of Business Administration.

1. This situation is an improvement over the distribution of faculty women in 1988, which was total 16.2 percent, full professor 4.6 percent, associate professor 7.7 percent, senior lecturer 16.6 percent, lecturer 28.9 percent. The academic tenure-track in Israeli universities is composed of four ranks: lecturer (the entry rank without tenure), senior lecturer (in which tenure is usually granted), associate professor, and full professor.

References

Acker, Joan. 1990. "Hierarchies, Jobs Bodies: A Theory of Gendered Organizations." *Gender & Society* 41:139–158.

Astin, Helen S., and Diane Davis. 1985. "Research Productivity Across the Life and Career Cycles: Facilitators and Barriers for Women." In *Scholarly Writings and Publishing: Issues, Problems, and Solutions*, edited by Mary F. Fox. Westview Press.

Barinaga, M. 1993. "Is There a Female Style in Science?" *Science* 260:384–391.

Baron, James N., and Jeffrey Pfeffer. 1994. "The Social Psychology of Organizations and Inequality." *Social Psychology Quarterly* 57:190–209.

Bar-Yosef, Rivka. 1996. "Exclusion, Closure and Marginalization: Immigrants in Israel." In Poverty and Social Exclusion in the Mediterranean Area, eds. K. Korayem and M. Petmesidou. 1998. Bergen, KROP.

Bem, Sandra. 1993. *The lenses of gender: Transforming the debate on sexual inequality*. New Haven: Yale University Press.

Bielby, Denise D., and William T. Bielby. 1988. "She Works Hard for the Money: Household Responsibilities and the Allocation of Work Effort." *American Journal of Sociology* 93:1031–1059.

Bourdieu, Pierre. 1984. *Distinction: A Social Critique of the Judgment of Taste*. Cambridge, MA: Harvard University Press.

Brekhus, Wayne. 1994. Social Marking and the Mental Coloring of Identity: Sexual Identity Construction and Maintenance in the United States. *Sociological Forum* 11:497–522.

Damian, Natalia and Yehudit Rosenbaum-Tamari. 1996. *The Current Wave of Former Soviet Union Immigrants: Their Absorption Process in Israel*. Ministry of Immigrant Absorption, Planning and Research Division, Jerusalem.

Deaux Kay. 1985. "Sex and Gender." *Annual Review of Psychology* 36:49–81.

England, Paula. 1993. "Introduction." In *Theory on gender/feminism on theory*, ed. Paula England. New York: Aldine De Gruyter.

Epstein, Fuchs Cynthia. 1988. *"Deceptive Distinctions."* New Haven: Yale University Press.

Epstein, Fuchs Cynthia. 1992. "Tinkerbells and Pinups: The Construction and Reconstruction of Gender Boundaries at Work." In *Cultivating Differences: Symbolic Boundaries and the Making of Inequality*, ed. Michele Lamont and Marcel Fournier. Chicago: University of Chicago Press.

Fox, Mary Frank. 1991. "Gender, Environmental Milieu, and Productivity in Science." In *The Outer Circle: Women in the Scientific Community*, ed., Harriet Zuckerman, Jonathan R. Cole, and John T. Bruer. New Haven: Yale University Press.

Gans, Herbert. 1979. "Symbolic Ethnicity: The Future of Ethnic Groups and Cultures in America." *Ethnic Racial Studies* 2:1–20.

Goffman, Erving. 1977. "The Arrangements Between the Sexes." *Theory and Society* 4:299 331.

Gupta, Akhil, and James Ferguson. 1992. "Beyond "Culture": Space, Identity, and the Politics of Difference." *Cultural Anthropology* 7:6–23.

Hein, Jeremy. 1994. "From Migrant to Minority: Among Refugees and the Social Construction of Identity in the United States." *Sociological Inquiry* 64:281–306.

Jacobs, Jerry A. 1989. *Revolving Doors: Sex Segregation and Women's Careers*. Stanford, CA: Stanford University Press.

Kanter, Rosabeth Moss. 1977. *Men and Women of the Corporation*. New York: Basic Books.

Keller, Evelyn F. 1988. "Feminist Perspective on Science Studies." *Science, Technology, and Human Values* 13:235–249.

Kyvic, Svein. 1990. "Motherhood and Scientific Productivity." *Social Studies of Science* 20:149–160.

Lissak, Moshe, and Eli Leshem. 1995. "The Russian intelligentsia in Israel: Between ghettoization and integration." *Israel Affairs* 2:20–36.

Long, Scott J., Paul D. Allison, and Robert McGinnis. 1993. "Rank Advancement in Academic Careers: Sex Differences and the Effects of Productivity. *American Sociological Review* 58:703–722.

Lorber, Judith. 1994. *Paradoxes of gender*. New Haven: Yale University Press.

Malkki, Liisa. 1992. "National Geographic: The Rooting of Peoples and the Territorialization of National Identity Among Scholars and Refugees." *Cultural Anthropology* 7:24–44.

Mannheim, Bilha, and Meira Schiffrin. 1984. "Family Structure, Job Characteristics, Rewards and Strains as Related to Work-Role Centrality of Employed and Self-Employed Professional Women with Children." *Journal of Occupational Behavior* 5:83–101.

Moore, Dahlia, and Nina Toren. 1998. "The Academic 'Hurdle Race': A Case Study." *Higher Education* 35:267–283.

Morgan, Gareth. 1986. *Images of Organization*. Beverley Hills, CA: Sage Publications.

Nagel, Joane. 1994. "Constructing Ethnicity: Creating and Recreating Ethnic Identity and Culture." *Social Problems* 41:152–176.

Reskin, Barbara F. 1987. "Bringing the Men Back in: Sex Differentiation and the Devaluation of Women's Work." *Gender and Society* 2:58–81.

Reskin, Barbara F., and Patricia A. Roos. 1990. *Job Queues, Gender Queues: Explaining Women's Inroads into Male Occupations*. Philadelphia: Temple University Press.

Ridgeway, Cecilia, L. 1997. "Interaction and the Conservation of Gender Inequality: Considering Employment." *American Sociological Review* 62:218–235.

Rosener, Judy B. 1990. "The Retention of Women and People of Color: Are We Asking the Right Questions?" (unpublished manuscript). Prepared for the All-University Conference on Graduate Student and Faculty Affirmative Action.

Rosenfeld, Rachel A. 1991. "Outcome Analysis of Academic Careers." Review prepared for the Office of Scientific and Engineering Personnel, National Research Council.

Rosenfeld, Rachel A., and Arne L. Kalleberg. 1990. "A Cross-National Comparison of Gender Gap in Income." *American Journal of Sociology* 96:69–106.

Schein, Edgar H. 1980. *Organizational Psychology*, 3rd ed., Englewood Cliffs, NJ: Prentice Hall.

Simmel, Georg. 1950. *The Sociology of Georg Simmel*. Edited and translated by Kurt H. Wolff. New York: The Free Press.

Simmel, Georg. 1955. *Conflict and the Web of Group Affiliation*. Ed. and trans. by Reinhard Bendix. The Free Press.

Sonnert, Gerhard, and Gerald Holton. 1995. *Gender Differences in Science Careers: The Project Access Study*. New Brunswick, NJ: Rutgers University Press.

Statistical Report 1997. *Higher Education in Israel*. Council for Higher Education.

Strober, Myra H. 1984. "A Theory of Sex Segregation." In *Sex Segregation in the Workplace: Trends, Explanations, Remedies*, edited by Barbara F. Reskin. Washington D.C.: National Academy of Sciences Press.

Swidler, Ann. 1986. "Culture in Action: Symbols and Strategies." *American Sociological Review* 51:273–286.

Symons, Gladys L. 1986. Coping with the Corporate Tribe: How Women in Different Cultures Experience the Managerial Role. *Journal of Management* 12:379–390.

Toren, Nina. 1988. *Science and cultural context: Soviet scientists in comparative perspective*. New York: Peter Lang.

Toren, Nina. 1991. "The Nexus Between Family and Work Roles of Academic Women in Israel: Reality and Representation. *Sex Roles* 24:651–667.

Toren, Nina. 1994. "Professional Support and Intellectual-Influence Networks of Russian Immigrant Scientists in Israel." *Social Studies of Science* 24:725–743.

Toren, Nina and Vered Kraus. 1987. "The Effect of Minority Size on Women's Position in Academia." *Social Forces* 65:1090–1100.

Wartburg, Michael. 1994. "The Russian-Language Press in Israel: Two Generations." *Jews of the Former Soviet Union. 16*:160–168.
Williams, Christine L. 1989. *Gender Differences at Work: Women and Men in Nontraditional Occupations.* Berkeley: University of California Press.
Williams, Christine L. 1995. *Still a Men's World: Men Who Do Women's Work.* Berkeley: University of California Press.
Yancey, William L., Eugene P. Ericksen, and Richard N. Juliani. 1976. "Emergent Ethnicity: A Review and Formulation." *American Sociological Review 41*:391–402.
Zerubavel, Eviatar. 1991. *The fine line: Making distinctions in everyday life.* New York: The Free Press.
Zerubavel, Eviatar. 1996. "Lumping and Splitting: Notes on Social Classification." *Sociological Forum 11*:421–433.
Zuckerman, Harriet, and Jonathan R. Cole. 1975. "Women in American Science." *Minerva 13*:80–86.
Zuckerman, Harriet, and Jonathan R. Cole. 1987. "Marriage, Motherhood, and Research Performance in Science." *Scientific American 2*:119–125.

About the Contributors

RITA JAMES SIMON is University Professor in the School of Public Affairs and the Washington College of Law at American University. She is the editor of *Gender Issues* and author of *The American Jury, the Insanity Defense: A Critical Assessment of Law and Policy in the Post Hinkley Era* (with David Aaronson), *Adoption, Race and Identity* (with Howard Alstein), *In the Golden Land: A Century of Russian and Soviet Jewish Immigration, Social Science Data and Supreme Court Decisions* (with Rosemary Erickson, and *Abortion: Statutes, Policies, and Public Attitudes the World Over.*

NANCY FONER is a professor of anthropology at the State University of New York, Purchase, and the author of several books on immigration, including *Jamaica Farewell: Jamaican Migrants in London* and *New Immigrants in New York.*

CYNTHIA CRANFORD is a Ph.D. candidate in the Department of Sociology, University of Southern California, Los Angeles, CA.

M.D.R. EVANS's research focuses on comparative, international analyses of stratification, ethnicity, culture, and gender. Her book, *Prejudice or Productivity,* is forthcoming from Westview Press.

TATJANA LUKIC is a graduate student in The Australian National University's International Survey Program.

HARRIET ORCUTT DULEEP is a senior research associate with the Population Studies Center of the Urban Institute.

MONICA BOYD is the Mildred and Claude Pepper Distinguished Professor of Sociology and Research Associate, Center for the Study of Population, Florida State University, Tallahassee, Florida.

SUZANNE M. SINKE is Assistant Professor of History at Clemson University. She is the co-editor with Rudolph Vecoli of *A Century of European Migrations* (1991), and author of a forthcoming book on Dutch immigrant women.

KATHARINE M. DONATO is a demographer and an associate professor in the department of sociology at Rice University. Her major research interests include international migration, health, and social inequality. She has published many articles, including one of the migration patterns and trends of Mexican women in the *International Migration Review*, and a second about the effects of migration on infant mortality in Mexico in *Demography*.

NINA TOREN is a sociologist and professor in the School of Business Administration, The Hebrew University of Jerusalem, Israel. She has published many articles, including "The Nexus Between Family and Work Roles of Academic Women in Israel: Reality and Representation," in *Sex Roles,* and "Professional Support and Intellectual-Influence Networks of Russian Immigrant Scientists in Israel," in *Social Studies of Science.*